Colloquial

Chinese

Mandarin

THE COLLOQUIAL SERIES
Series Adviser: Gary King

The following languages are available in the Colloquial series:

Afrikaans	French	Portuguese
Albanian	German	Portuguese of Brazil
Amharic	Greek	Romanian
Arabic (Levantine)	Gujarati	Russian
Arabic of Egypt	Hausa (forthcoming)	Scottish Gaelic
Arabic of the Gulf	Hebrew	Serbian
and Saudi Arabia	Hindi	Slovak
Basque	Hungarian	Slovene
Bengali	Icelandic	Somali
Breton	Indonesian	Spanish
Bulgarian	Irish	Spanish of Latin America
Cambodian	Italian	Swahili
Cantonese	Japanese	Swedish
Catalan	Korean	Tamil
Chinese	Latvian	Thai
Croatian	Lithuanian	Turkish
Czech	Malay	Ukrainian
Danish	Mongolian	Urdu
Dutch	Norwegian	Vietnamese
English	Panjabi	Welsh
Estonian	Persian	Yoruba
Finnish	Polish	Zulu (forthcoming)

COLLOQUIAL 2s series: *The Next Step in Language Learning*

Chinese	German (forthcoming)	Russian
Dutch	Italian	Spanish
French	Portuguese of Brazil	Spanish of Latin America

All these Colloquials are available in book & CD packs, or separately. You can order them through your bookseller or via our website www.routledge.com.

Colloquial
Chinese
Mandarin

The Complete Course for Beginners

Kan Qian

Routledge
Taylor & Francis Group

LONDON AND NEW YORK

First published 1996
by Routledge

Reprinted 1997, 1998, 2002, 2003 (twice), 2004, 2005, 2006
Revised edition 1999

This edition published 2009 by Routledge
2 Park Square, Milton Park, Abingdon, Oxon OX14 4RN

Simultaneously published in the USA and Canada
by Routledge
270 Madison Ave, New York, NY 10016

*Routledge is an imprint of the Taylor & Francis Group,
an informa business*
© 1996, 2009 Kan Qian

Typeset in 9.5/13pt Helvetica by Graphicraft Limited, Hong Kong
Printed and bound in Great Britain by
TJ International Ltd, Padstow, Cornwall

British Library Cataloguing in Publication Data
A catalogue record for this book is available from the British Library

Library of Congress Cataloging-in-Publication Data
Kan, Qian, 1960–
    Colloquial Chinese: the complete course for beginners / Qian Kan. –
2nd ed.
        p. cm. – (The colloquial series)
    1. Chinese language – Conversation and phrase books – English.
    2. Chinese language – Grammar.   3. Chinese language – Spoken
Chinese.
    I. Title.
    PL1125.E6K36 2009
    495.1′83421 – dc22

                                                        2008030171

ISBN13: 978-0-415-43415-7 (pbk)
ISBN13: 978-0-415-43416-4 (audio CDs)
ISBN13: 978-0-415-43417-1 (pack)
ISBN13: 978-0-415-55159-5 (MP3)

给 爱莎

Contents

Acknowledgements

I am indebted to Dr Andrew Brown, who helped me throughout the writing of the first edition of this book. Not only did he spend many hours polishing my English, but he also put himself in the position of a learner for this book. The criticism and comments he made were extremely helpful in enabling me to search for the most appropriate way of expressing many language points.

Over the last ten years or so, many teachers and learners who used the first and/or the revised edition of this book wrote to me with their extremely useful feedback, to whom I am very grateful. I would particularly like to thank Dr Yip Poching, Chen Guangqin, Wang Xiaoning, Yu Feixia and Guo Zhiyan for taking the time to provide very specific and good suggestions.

My special thanks go to Kan Jia for countless hours of word processing, pinyin annotation and proof-reading the Chinese texts. Finally, I wish to thank the editors and the assistant staff concerned at Routledge for their patience and support throughout the writing of this edition.

Introduction

The Chinese language

Some people in the west believe the Chinese language to be *Cantonese* whereas in fact *Cantonese* is just one of the eight major dialects of the Chinese language. Although different dialects differ immensely in pronunciation, they share the same written form. The Northern dialect (which has many sub-dialects under it) is spoken by 70 per cent of the Chinese population. Therefore, the standard language spoken nationally is based on the pronunciation of the Northern dialect. The name for this standard form is *Putonghua* (common speech) in mainland China, *Guoyu* or *Huayu* (national language) in Taiwan, Hong Kong, and other overseas Chinese communities, and *Mandarin Chinese* in English-speaking countries. Other forms such as *Zhongwen* (Chinese) or *Hanyu* (the *Han* language, *Han* Chinese making up 93 per cent of the Chinese population) are more formal and are often used among Chinese language learners. Native Chinese speakers often use the term *Zhongwen* rather than *Putonghua* when they ask non-native Chinese speakers if they speak Chinese. *Putonghua* is taught in schools and spoken by television and radio presenters in mainland China, and it is the kind of spoken language which is most understood by Chinese speakers. This book deals with *Putonghua*.

Romanization

Various systems have been devised for transcribing Chinese sounds into the Latin script. The system used in this book is called *pinyin*.

Pinyin uses 26 letters in total, 25 of which are English letters. The exception is the letter v, which is replaced by the following symbol: ü. *Pinyin* was adopted as the official system in the People's Republic of China in 1958, and has since become a standard form used by news agencies as well as educational institutions. *Pinyin* has now been adopted almost universally in the west for transliterating Chinese personal names and place names although in older books you may still find earlier romanization systems in use (e.g. Beijing is the *pinyin* transliteration and Peking is the *Wade–Giles* transliteration). In mainland China, *pinyin* is used as a tool to teach the correct pronunciation of *Putonghua* to children starting school. In dictionaries *pinyin* is given next to the character to indicate the pronunciation. Many street signs in big cities in mainland China have *pinyin* directly underneath the Chinese characters.

The speech sounds

Chinese is a vowel-dominated language. A syllable may consist of a single vowel, a compound vowel or a vowel preceded by a consonant. A compound vowel may consist of two vowels or a vowel with a nasal sound, which is treated as one unit. This is probably why consonants are called 'initials' (*shengmu*) and vowels are called 'finals' (*yunmu*) in Chinese.

 1 Initials (CD1; 2)

There are twenty-three initials (some people regard *w* and *y* as semi-vowels) in modern Chinese. Below is a table comparing the twenty-three initials with the English sounds. Some of the Chinese initials are quite similar to English sounds, others less so. Those which differ significantly from the nearest English sounds have explanations next to them. The letter in bold is the Chinese initial:

Initial	*Initial*
b like *b* in *bed*	**zh** like *j* in *jade*, but with the tongue further back
p like *p* in *poor*	**ch** like *ch* in *church*, but with the tongue further back, and the mouth in a round shape

m like *m* in *me*

f like *f* in *foot*

d like *d* in *do*

t like *t* in *tea*

n like *n* in *nose*

l like *l* in *like*

z like *ds* in *beds*

c like *ts* in *bits*

s like *s* in *sale*

sh like *sh* in *sheep*

r like *r* in *road*, but with the tongue loosely rolled in the middle of the mouth

g like *g* in *good*

k like *k* in *kite*

h like *h* in *hat*

w like *w* in *we*

y like *y* in *yes*

j like *j* in *jam*, but with the tongue nearer the teeth and the mouth relaxed

q – raise the front of the tongue to the hard palate, place the tip of the tongue against the back of the lower teeth. It is a bit like the *ch* in *cheese* but with the tongue further forward. The mouth is held more firmly than when pronouncing **j**.

x – place the front of the tongue behind the lower front teeth near the hard palate then let the air pass through the channel between the front of the tongue and the hard palate, rather like whistling through the lower teeth.

2 Finals (CD1; 3)

A final is a single vowel, or compound vowel or a vowel plus a nasal sound, i.e. **n** (like *n* in *in*) and **ng** (like *ng* in *long*). Altogether, there are 35 finals (37 if you count the variant of **i** and **e**). Below is a chart comparing the thirty-five finals with the English sounds. Some of the Chinese final sounds are quite similar to English sounds, others less so. Those that bear no resemblance have explanations next to them. The letters in bold are the Chinese finals:

a like *a* in *father*

ai – between **a** and **ei**

ao like *ow* in *how*

an like *an* in *ban*

ang like *on* in *monster*

e like *ir* in *Sir* (when **e** is preceded by **y/yu**, it is like *e* in *yes*)

ei like *ay* in *lay*

en like *en* in *tender*
eng like *un* in *hunger*
er – combination of *ir* in *Sir* and the retroflex *r* (**er** is never preceded by initials)

i like *ee* in *bee* (when **i** follows initials **z**, **c**, **s**, **zh**, **ch**, **sh** and **r**, it is pronounced very differently from **i** preceded by **b**, **p**, **d**, **t**, **l**, etc. Try to get the initial sound right first and then keep the mouth shape of the initial and say **i**. It simply functions as a helper to make those sounds audible)
ia – combination of **i** and **a**
iao like *eow* in *meow*
ie like *ye* in *yesterday*
iu like *you*
ian – like the Japanese currency word *Yen*
in like *in* in *tin*
iang like *young*
ing like *ing* in *sling*
iong – combination of **i** and **ong** (when no initial precedes **i** and when it is followed by **a**, **e**, **u**, or **o**, **y** replaces **i**, e.g. **ye** instead of **ie**)

o like *our* in *tour*
ou like *oe* in *toe*
ong like *ong* in *ding-dong*

u like *oo* in *too*
ua – combination of **u** and **a**
uo like *war*
uai – combination of **u** and **ai**
ui like *wai* in *wait*
uan like *wan* in *swan*
un like *won* in *wonder*
uang like *wan* in *wanting* (when **u** is not preceded by other initials at the beginning of a syllable, **w** replaces **u**, e.g. **wan** instead of **uan**, **wo** instead of **uo**)

ü like *u* in *tu* (French)
üe – combination of **ü** and a short **ei**
üan – combination of **ü** and a short **an**

ün like *une* in French (when **ü** follows **j**, **q**, **x** and **y**, it is written as **u** without the two dots over it (but still pronounced as **ü**), e.g. **ju**, **qu**, **xu**, **yun**, **yuan**, etc. because **u** cannot occur after **j**, **q**, **x** and **y**)

Although the above two charts should give you some guidance over the pronunciation, access to the audio is essential if you wish to achieve a more accurate pronunciation of these sounds.

Tones

Chinese is a tonal language. In *Putonghua*, there are four tones, five if you include the neutral tone. Since there are only about 400 basic monosyllables which can be combined to make words in Chinese, the use of tones is one way of substantially increasing the number of available monosyllables. Every syllable in isolation has its definite tone. So syllables with different tones may mean different things although they share the same initial and final. For example: **ma** pronounced with the first tone means 'mother' but **ma** pronounced with the third tone means 'horse'.

1 The four tones (CD1; 4)

Name	Pitch-graph (tone mark)
The first tone	‾
The second tone	´
The third tone	ˇ
The fourth tone	`

To illustrate these four tones better, let us first draw a short vertical line to represent the pitch variation within an average person's voice range:

5 ⌐— the high pitch
4 ⊢— the mid-high pitch
3 ⊢— the middle pitch
2 ⊢— the mid-low pitch
1 ⌐— the low pitch

First tone is a high, level tone. Pitch it at 5 and keep it at the same level for a while. It will look something like this in the pitch diagram:

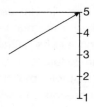

Second tone is a high, rising tone. Pitch it at about 3 and raise it quickly. It will look something like this in the pitch diagram:

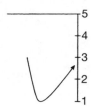

Third tone is a falling and rising tone. Start below 3 and let it drop nearly to the bottom and then rise to somewhere near 2.5. It looks something like this in the pitch diagram:

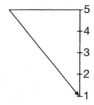

Fourth tone is a falling tone. It falls from 5 right to the bottom, 1. It looks something like this in the pitch diagram:

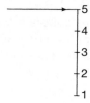

Tones are marked over the vowel (e.g. **tā**) or over the main vowel if it is a compound vowel (e.g. **táo**). The main vowel is the one that comes earliest in this list: **a, o, e, u, i, ü**. Whenever there is no mark over the vowel, the syllable is a neutral tone.

2 Neutral tones

Some syllables in Chinese carry the neutral tone, i.e. they are pronounced weakly, which is like unstressed syllables in English (e.g. *of* in *one of my friends*). If there is no tone mark over the vowel, it means it is a neutral tone. Neutral tones are used in the following cases:

(a) Grammar words such as **le, de** (see 'Words, word order and grammar' below)
(b) The second syllable in some compound words: for example, **wǒmen** (we/us)
(c) A second syllable which is a repetition of the first one: for example, **māma** (mother/mum)
(d) The measure word **ge** when it is not emphasized: for example, sān **ge yuè** (three months) (see 'Words, word order and grammar' for 'measure word' below).

3 Tone change

In connected speech, tones change depending on the adjacent tones and meaning groups. Below are some basic rules of the tone change:

(a) third tone variations

(i) When a third tone is followed by another third tone and they are in one meaning group, the first one changes to the second tone. For example, **nǐ, hǎo**, in actual speech, should be pronounced **Ní hǎo** (Hello).
(ii) When three third tones occur one after another, normally the second one changes to the second tone whilst the other two remain the third tone. For example, **wǒ hěn hǎo**, in actual speech, should be pronounced **wǒ hén hǎo** (I'm very well).

(iii) In some compound words, although the second syllable, which is a third tone when used separately, has become neutral, it still carries enough weight to change the preceding third tone to the second tone. For example, **xiǎo, jiě (jie)**, in actual speech, should be pronounced **Xiáojie** (Miss).

(iv) The first third tone remains unchanged if the second third tone belongs to the next meaning group. For example, **Qǐng gàosu wǒ/nǐde diànhuà hàomǎ** (Please tell me your telephone number).

(b) variation of the negation word **bù**
When the negation word **bù**, which has the fourth tone in isolation, is followed by another fourth tone, **bù** changes to the second tone. For example, **bù** in **Wǒ bú shì Zhōngguórén** (I am not Chinese) should be pronounced with a second tone.

(c) variations of **yī** (one)
When the number word **yī** (one) is used in isolation or at the end of a syllable, it has the first tone (e.g. **yī, shíyī**); but when it precedes first, second and third tones, **yī** usually changes to the fourth tone (e.g. **yìxiē, yìdiǎn**); and when **yī** precedes fourth tones, it can change to the second tone (e.g. **yílù, yíxià**). However, many native speakers do not apply these changes.

Tones can be difficult at first, but remember that in actual communication, the context and facial expressions will all help in conducting a successful conversation. So, do not be put off by the tones. If you listen carefully and mimic, you will be able to pick them up eventually.

In this book, all the dialogues and texts in *pinyin* are marked with tones as if each syllable were in isolation. For example, the phrase **nǐ hǎo** is marked with two third tones, which does not reflect the tone change. The only exception is **bù** (not). It is always marked with the second tone when followed by a fourth tone, e.g. **bú shì** (no).

Words, word order and grammar

1 Words

Chinese characters are called **zì**. A zi is a character which consists of one syllable. It is thus the main building block of the Chinese language. Some zi have meanings on their own (e.g., 我 **wǒ** means 'I; me') and others have to be used with others to form meaningful expressions (e.g. 的 **de** does not mean anything on its own but it can be used to form other words such as 我的 **wǒde**, meaning 'my; mine'). The former are words whilst the latter are called 'particles' or 'grammar words' in this book. A Chinese word, therefore, can consist of one syllable, two or three syllables. For example, the word for Monday consists of three syllables **xīng qī yī**, which is represented by three characters: 星期一. In some books, a space is always inserted between every syllable. For example:

Jīn tiān shì xīng qī yī. Today is Monday.

In this book, for the convenience of English speakers, I have tried to put, wherever possible, those syllables which can be translated into one English word together. The above sentence in this book would be written as follows:

Jīntiān shì xīngqīyī. Today is Monday.

2 Word order

In English, when you ask a question, you have to put the question word first, and reverse the order of the verb and the noun (e.g. *Where are you going?*). In Chinese, you use the normal word order and say 'You are going where?'. In English, one tends to put the most important information at the end of a sentence (e.g. *It is very important to learn Chinese*). In Chinese, the important information or the topic of a sentence usually comes first. Thus you say 'To learn Chinese is very important.' In English, time phrases such as *at 6 o'clock, tomorrow*, occur at the end of a sentence (e.g. *I'll finish my work at 6 o'clock*). In Chinese, time phrases always occur before the verb. Thus you say 'I six o'clock finish work.' These are just a few major differences between English and Chinese in terms of word order. There are many other differences between the two languages which will be dealt with later in the book.

3 Grammar

Chinese grammar is still in the process of being perfected. However, there are a few things you need to know before you start learning Chinese:

(a) Nouns in Chinese are neither singular nor plural. Thus you say 'one book' and 'three book'.

(b) Because of (a) above, verbs (i.e. doing words) have only one form. Thus you say 'I be Chinese' and 'You be British', 'I go China' and 'He go China', etc.

(c) Verbs do not indicate past, present or future. Tenses are indicated by extra grammar words (or 'particles'), time phrases or context. Thus you say 'I go + grammar word + library', 'I yesterday go + grammar word + library', 'I tomorrow go library', etc.

(d) Prepositions such as 'at', 'in', 'on' are not used before time phrases. Thus you say 'My mother Tuesday arrive.'

(e) The largest unit, be it time or place, always comes first. Thus you say 'He January the 11th arrive', 'We from China Beijing come', etc.

(f) There is something called the measure word to be used between a number and a noun. Different measure words are used for different nouns. Thus you say 'two + **běn** + book', but 'two + **ge** + people'.

There is a grammar summary at the end of the book.

Chinese characters

Chinese characters are symbols used to represent the Chinese language. It is widely believed that written Chinese is amongst the world's oldest written languages. Its earliest written records can be traced back 3,500 years. Many of the earliest writings were pictures carved on oracle bones, known as 'pictographs'. Over the years, Chinese characters evolved from pictographs into characters formed of strokes, with their structures becoming systemized and simpler. Below are five different character styles showing the evolution of the characters for the sun and the moon into their present-day form:

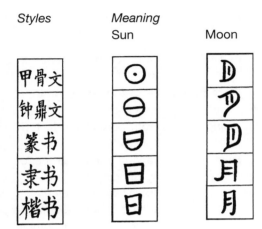

Styles	Meaning	
	Sun	Moon

The total number of Chinese characters is estimated at more than 50,000, of which only 5,000–8,000 are in common use. To read and write competently, one needs about 2,000 of them.

1 Basic strokes

Some characters stand by themselves and are never used to form other characters. But most characters are made of two or more basic structural components. These character components are limited and the basic strokes which form these components are even more limited. A stroke is a single unbroken line drawn by the writer from the time the pen touches the paper until the pen lifts off the paper. Below are the basic strokes:

Stroke	Character Name	Pinyin	English	Explanation
一	横	**Héng**	Horizontal	From left to right ($\rightarrow$)
|	竖	**Shù**	Vertical	From top to bottom ($\downarrow$)
丿	点	**Diǎn**	Left-falling dot and right-falling dot	From right to bottom left ($\swarrow$) From left to bottom right ($\searrow$)

Stroke	Character Name	Pinyin	English	Explanation
ノ	撇	**Piě**	Left-falling	From top right to bottom left (↙)
乀	捺	**Nà**	Right-falling	From top left to bottom right (↘)
╱	提	**Tí**	Rising	From bottom left to top right (↗)
𠃊	钩	**Gōu**	Hook	Various hooks, all made by bringing the pen downward first then adding a hook (some are made quickly and others are made slowly) (亅乚㇂)
㇀丁	折	**Zhé**	Turning	Various turnings, all made with a left to right stroke that turns downward at the end (some are made quickly and others are made slowly) (乙 乛)

Based on the above basic strokes, there are many other combinations such as

𠃌	**héngpiěwāngōu**	(horizontal plus left-falling plus slanting vertical hook),
𠃌	**héngzhégōu**	(horizontal plus turning hook),
𠃊	**shùwwāngōu**	(vertical plus right-turn),
𠃑	**shùzhézhégōu**	(vertical plus horizontal plus vertical hook),
𠄎	**héngzhézhépiě**	(horizontal turning, and another turning plus left-falling), etc.

2 Rules of stroke order

The chart below shows the rules regarding stroke order in writing Chinese characters:

Example	Stroke order	Rule
十	一 十	First horizontal, then vertical
人	丿 人	First left-falling, then right-falling
三	一 二 三	First top, then bottom
儿	丿 儿	First left, then right
问	门 问	First outside, then inside
国	冂 国 国	Finish inside, then close
小	亅 小 小	Middle, then left, then right

3 Head component (radical)

A large number of the modern Chinese characters are formed of two components: one is called the 'head component', also known as 'radical', (部首 **bùshǒu**, 'component heads' in Chinese), indicating the meaning category of the character, and the other is the phonetic, providing a clue to its pronunciation. Remember, there are many characters that consist of several components. Some head components are characters in their own right, whilst other head components only function as a component. There are a great many characters that stand on their own without a head component.

The head component can be on the left, top or bottom and a very few can be on the right.

For example:

马 **mǎ** (horse)

is a character in its own right but it is the phonetic for characters such as

妈 **mā** (mother), 骂 **mà** (to swear)

Let us look at the head component for these two **ma**s:

妈 **mā** (mother) has the woman head component 女 (nǚ) on the left, and 骂 **mà** (to swear) has got two mouth head components on the top (口 口 kǒu).

Below is a table of some of the most commonly used head components:

When in isolation	When in combination	Meaning	Example
人	亻	people	他 **tā**, he
水	氵	water	汤 **tāng**, soup
	冫	ice	冰 **bīng**, ice
火	灬	fire	热 **rè**, hot
	火	fire	灯 **dēng**, light
	宀	roof	家 **jiā**, home
金	钅	metal	钱 **qián**, money
丝	纟	silk	线 **xiàn**, thread
心	忄	heart	懂 **dǒng**, to understand
心	忄	heart	想 **xiǎng**, to think
言	讠	speech	说 **shuō**, to speak
	阝 (right)	abundant	都 **dōu**, all
	阝 (left)	cliff	陡 **dǒu**, steep
	彳	step	行 **xíng**, walk
	犭	dog/animal	狗 **gǒu**, dog
	扌	hand	找 **zhǎo**, to look for
	攵	to tap/knock	收 **shōu**, to receive
爪	爫	hand/claws	采 **cǎi**, to pick up
	艹	grass	茶 **chá**, tea
食	饣	food	饭 **fàn**, food
示	礻	sign/ceremony	礼 **lǐ**, virtue
	辶	advance	远 **yuǎn**, far
	衤	clothes	裙 **qún**, skirt
	疒	illness	疼 **téng**, painful
女	女	woman	妈 **mā**, mother
足	𧾷	foot	跟 **gēn**, to follow
立	立	to stand	站 **zhàn**, to stand
土	土	soil	地 **dì**, floor/earth
王	𤣩	treasure	球 **qiú**, ball
木	木	tree	林 **lín**, forest
目	目	eye/sight	眼 **yǎn**, eye
日	日	sun	明 **míng**, bright
日	曰	sun	星 **xīng**, star
雨	雫	rain	雪 **xuě**, snow
口	口	mouth	吃 **chī**, to eat

When in isolation	When in combination	Meaning	Example
月	月	flesh	脚 **jiǎo**, foot
月	月	moon	明 **míng**, bright
竹	艹	bamboo	笔 **bǐ**, eye

About 2,000 characters have been simplified in mainland China since 1949 so as to improve the literacy of the population. These 2,000 characters are called 'simplified characters' as opposed to 'complex characters' (also known as 'traditional form'). 'Complex characters' are still used in Hong Kong, Taiwan and other overseas Chinese communities. In this book, simplified characters are used throughout.

Structure of this book

There are fifteen lessons in total. The lesson objectives are listed at the beginning of each lesson so that you know exactly what is expected of you. Each of the first fourteen lessons contains two situational dialogues. Lesson 15 has only one text, which takes the form of a personal letter. From Lesson 4 onwards character dialogues appear after the *pinyin* text and characters are also given next to *pinyin* in the vocabulary. It does not mean that you must learn characters at the same time. The choice is yours. The English equivalent given for each word in the vocabulary list is its meaning only in regard to the context of that specific dialogue. Important language points which occur in each dialogue/text are explained with more examples in the 'Notes to dialogue/text' section. At the end of each lesson, there is a reading/listening comprehension section which reinforces what has been introduced earlier. There are plenty of exercises after each dialogue. In the first 5 lessons, there are two Characters sections in each lesson explaining the formation of characters and illustrating how to write some commonly used characters that appear in the dialogue concerned, followed by character exercises. From Lesson 6 onwards, there is only one Characters section just before the Reading/listening comprehension.

Lessons 1–3: These dialogues and vocabulary are in *pinyin*. After each dialogue, there is an idiomatic English translation of the dialogue and the vocabulary. The character versions of the dialogues are provided in Appendix C.

Lessons 4–5: Each dialogue is first in *pinyin*, then in character. After each dialogue, there is an idiomatic English translation of the dialogue. The vocabulary is in *pinyin* and character.

Lessons 6–15: These dialogues and vocabulary are in *pinyin* and character. However, there is no idiomatic English translation of each dialogue. You can find the English translation of those dialogues in Appendix D.

The key to all the exercises and the answers to the questions in the reading/listening comprehension in each lesson are given at the end of the book.

Finally, there are two points about the symbols used in the book: (a) the abbreviation '*Lit.*' or '*lit.*' means 'literal meaning'; and (b) the apostrophe (') is used to separate two syllables whenever there may be a confusion over the syllable boundary (e.g. **qīn'ài** – **n** belongs to the first syllable not the second).

Lesson One
Chūcì jiànmiàn 初次见面
Meeting someone for the first time

> By the end of this lesson, you should be able to:
>
> - say who you are
> - greet people and respond to greetings
> - ask, and respond to, some yes/no questions
> - use some appropriate forms of address
> - write your first Chinese characters

Dialogue 1

Nǐ hǎo!   你好！   How do you do! **(CD1; 6)**

David Smith has just arrived at Beijing Airport. His potential Chinese business partner, Wang Lin, is there to meet him.

WÁNG LÍN	Nín shì Shǐmìsī xiānsheng ma?
DAVID SMITH	Shì de. Nín shì . . . ?
WÁNG LÍN	Nǐ hǎo! Shǐmìsī xiānsheng. Wǒ shì Wáng Lín.
DAVID SMITH	Nǐ hǎo! Wáng xiānsheng. Hěn gāoxìng jiàndào nǐ.
WÁNG LÍN	Wǒ yě hěn gāoxìng jiàndào nǐ. Qǐng jiào wǒ Lǎo Wáng ba.
DAVID SMITH	Hǎo ba, Lǎo Wáng. Jiào wǒ Dàwèi ba.
WÁNG LÍN	Hǎo de, Dàwèi. Huānyíng nǐ lái Zhōngguó.

WANG LIN	*Are you Mr Smith?*
DAVID SMITH	*Yes. You are . . . ?*
WANG LIN	*How do you do, Mr Smith. I'm Wang Lin.*
DAVID SMITH	*How do you do, Mr Wang. I'm very pleased to meet you.*
WANG LIN	*I'm very pleased to meet you too. Please call me Old Wang.*
DAVID SMITH	*Okay, Old Wang. Please call me David.*
WANG LIN	*All right, David. Welcome to China.*

(CD1; 5)

Vocabulary

nín	you [polite form, singular]	**gāoxìng**	be pleased/be happy/be glad
nǐ	you [singular]	**jiàndào**	to meet
shì	be [am, is, are]	**yě**	also/too
Shǐmìsī	Smith	**jiào**	to call/be called
xiānsheng	Mr	**lǎo**	old
ma	[question word, see Note 6]	**Dàwèi**	David
shì de	yes	**ba**	[grammar word, see Note 9]
wǒ	I; me	**hǎo ba /**	Okay/all right
hǎo	good/well	**hǎo de**	
nǐ hǎo	How do you do?/ hello [lit. 'you well/good']	**qǐng**	please
		huānyíng	to welcome
hěn	very	**lái**	to come/to come to
		Zhōngguó	China

Notes on Dialogue 1

■ 1 Greetings

Nǐ hǎo (How do you do?/Hello) is the most common form of greeting in Chinese, which can be used at any time of the day. In response, the person being greeted replies by repeating **nǐ hǎo**. Further greeting expressions will appear throughout the book. Note that when two third tones are together, the first third tone tends to change to a second tone. Thus, in actual speech, **nǐ hǎo** is pronounced **ní hǎo**.

■ 2 Chinese names and forms of address

In Chinese, names always appear in the following order: surname and first name. When titles are used, it is surname and title. Some Chinese people only have one character as their given name, but others have two characters. For example: **Wáng** is the surname, and **Lín** is the given name; in **Dèng Xiǎopíng**, **Dèng** is the surname, and **Xiǎopíng** is the given name. In Chinese, there aren't a set of words that are only reserved for names. So parents can pick and choose whichever character(s) they like to make up names for their children. For example, in the two names given above, **Lín** means 'forest' and **Xiǎopíng** means 'small and ordinary'!

Colleagues and friends usually address each other either by full name (surname + first name) or by putting **lǎo** (old) or **xiǎo** (young/ little) in front of the surname depending on the relative age and seniority of the speaker. For example, a younger person (whose surname is Li) may address a colleague (whose surname is Zhang) who is in his/her fifties as **Lǎo Zhāng** to show respect. Conversely, **Lǎo Zhāng** can call this younger person **Xiǎo Lǐ**. Sometimes, **lǎo** is even used as a friendly term among men in their thirties and forties to address each other. First names are used within families and among close friends.

Titles such as **xiānsheng** (Mr), **nǚshì** (Madam), **xiǎojie** (Miss) are now being used more and more. The term **tóngzhì** (comrade) is on its way out, although it is still used amongst people in their sixties and seventies. Professional titles such as **jīnglǐ** (manager), **jiàoshòu** (professor), **lǎoshī** (teacher) are used as forms of address. For example, if someone is called Lǐ Xīnzi, and he/she is a teacher, this person can be addressed and referred to as **Lǐ Lǎoshī** (*lit*. 'Li teacher').

■ 3 Foreign names

Most foreign names, including personal names and place names, are translated according to their sounds. Some foreign names have standard translations. For example, 'David' is **Dàwèi**, 'Mary' is **Mǎlì**, 'London' is **Lúndūn**, etc.

■ 4 Personal pronouns **wǒ** and **nǐ**

Personal pronouns **wǒ** and **nǐ** ('you' singular) can be used both as the subject and the object. Note their positions in the sentence. The subject comes before the verb; the object comes after the verb. For example:

Wǒ shì Wáng Lín. verb	I am Wang Lin.
Jiào wǒ Dàwèi ba. verb	Call me David.
Hěn gāoxìng jiàndào nǐ. verb	Very pleased to meet you.

This rule applies to all other personal pronouns. Below is a full list of Chinese personal pronouns:

Chinese	English
wǒ	I, me
nǐ	you (singular)
nín	you (polite form, singular)
tā	he/she, him/her
wǒmen	we, us
nǐmen	you (plural)
tāmen	they, them

As you may have noticed, 'he' and 'she' share the same pronunciation (but are represented by different characters). To make plural personal pronouns (e.g. 'we', 'you' and 'they'), simply add **men** to singular personal pronouns **wǒ**, **nǐ** and **tā**. On its own, **mén** has the second tone, but becomes a neutral tone in **wǒmen**, **nǐmen** and **tāmen**.

■ 5 Sentences with **shì**

One of the usages of **shì** (to be) sentences is to say who you are. For example:

Wǒ *shì* Zhāng Píng. | I *am* Zhang Ping.
Tāmen *shì* Zhōngguórén. | They *are* Chinese.

As we can see, the verb **shì** remains the same in the above two sentences, which makes things less complicated. Thus we have:

Wǒ	***shì*** Zhōngguórén.	I *am* Chinese.
Nǐ	***shì*** Zhōngguórén.	You *are* Chinese.
Tā	***shì*** Zhōngguórén.	He/she *is* Chinese.
Wǒmen	***shì*** Zhōngguórén.	We *are* Chinese.
Nǐmen	***shì*** Zhōngguórén.	You *are* Chinese.
Tāmen	***shì*** Zhōngguórén.	They *are* Chinese.

■ 6 Yes/no questions with **ma**

To ask a yes/no question in Chinese (i.e. a question that demands the response 'yes' or 'no'), all you need to do is to add **ma** at the end of a statement and speak with a rising tone as in English. There is no need to change the word order. For example:

Statement | *Yes/no question*

Nǐ shì Shǐmìsī xiānsheng. | **Nǐ shì Shǐmìsī xiānsheng *ma*?** ↗
You are Mr Smith. | Are you Mr Smith?

Tā shì Zhōngguórén. | **Tā shì Zhōngguórén *ma*?** ↗
He/she is Chinese. | Is he/she Chinese?

■ 7 Adjectives

Some adjectives in Chinese are both descriptive and predicative. Descriptive adjectives occur before the noun, for example, **lǎo** (old) in **lǎo rén** (*old* people), whilst predicative adjectives occur after a noun or a pronoun, for example, **lǎo** in **Tā *lǎo*** (He *is* old). Do remember that the verb **shì** (to be) is not used when adjectives function in a predicative position, and these predicative adjectives are usually modified by adverbs such as **hěn** (very), **tǐng** (rather), **tài** (too), etc. For example:

Tā   tǐng   lǎo.
Lit. He/she rather be old.
        She is rather old.

Tāmen hěn *hǎo*.
Lit. They   very good.
        They are very nice.

■ 8 Use of **qǐng**

When the word **qǐng** (please) is used to invite someone politely to do something, as we saw in Dialogue 1, it is always placed at the beginning of a sentence/phrase. For example:

Qǐng lái Zhōngguó.   Please come to China.
Qǐng jiào wǒ Lǎo Wáng ba. Please call me Lao Wang.

■ 9 Use of **ba**

This word does not have any specific meaning on its own; however, if you place it at the end of a sentence/phrase, it makes whatever you say sound friendly and casual. It is often used in conjunction with **qǐng**. It can be broadly translated as 'please' in these contexts. For example:

Qǐng jiào wǒ   Call me Lao Wang, *please*.
Lǎo Wáng *ba*.
Chī *ba*.   Please help yourself (*lit.* 'Eat, please.')

■ 10 Adverb **yě**

The adverb **yě** (also) usually occurs before the phrase it modifies whether it is an adjective phrase or a verbal phrase. For example:

Wǒ *yě* shì Zhōngguórén.
Lit. I   also be Chinese.
        I am also Chinese.

Wǒ *yě* hěn   gāoxìng jiàndào nǐ.
Lit. I   also very be pleased meet   you.
        I'm also very pleased to meet you.

Note that when three third tones are together in **wǒ yě hěn**, the first and the last third tones remain unchanged whilst the second third tone tends to change to the second tone. Thus you say **wǒ yé hěn**.

■ 11 Verb **huānyíng**

If you want to say 'Welcome to China' in Chinese, use the structure 'Welcome you come to China'. Thus, we have **Huānyíng nǐ lái Zhōngguó**. The pronoun **nǐ** can be omitted.

Exercises

Exercise 1

Solve the problems:

(a) How many ways can you think of to address the following:

   (i)   a man named **Zháng Gōngmín**, manager, whom you have just met, and who is older than you;
   (ii) a woman named **Lín Fāng**, single, whom you have known for some time on a strictly business basis, and who is younger than you;
   (iii) a very close friend whose name is **Gǒng Qíbín**, and who is younger than you.

(b) It is late in the evening, you bump into your colleague, **Wáng Lín**, and want to greet him. What do you say?

(c) If you meet a Chinese person for the first time, after the initial how-do-you-do greeting, what else can you say?

Exercise 2

Fill in the blanks:

(a) Wǒ _____ (*be*) Tāng Píng.
(b) Wǒ hěn gāoxìng jiàndào _____ (*her*).
(c) A: Nǐ shì Wáng Lín ma?
    B: _____ (*Yes*).

Exercise 3

Turn the following statements into yes/no questions using **ma**:

(a) Nǐ shì Wáng xiānsheng.
(b) Tā (*He/She*) hěn gāoxìng jiàndào nǐ.
(c) Tāmen (*They*) lái Zhōngguó.

Exercise 4

Re-arrange the word order of the following three groups so that each group becomes a meaningful sentence:

(a) hěn, yě, wǒ, jiàndào, gāoxìng, nǐ
(b) qǐng, jiào, Dàwèi, wǒ
(c) lái, Zhōngguó, nǐ, huānyíng

Characters

Now, let us try writing (or drawing!) some characters. The following four characters in their pinyin form have been used in Dialogue 1:

你好 **nǐ hǎo**   How do you do?/hello (*lit.* 'you well/good')
中国 **Zhōngguó**   China (*lit.* 'central country')

When Chinese children start writing characters, they use square boxes with either shaded or dotted cross lines in the middle:

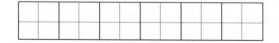

The purpose of the box is to help them get the size and the proportion of the character right.

Writing them in the right stroke order will help in memorizing them.

Character analysis	Head component and its meaning	Stroke order	English
亻(人) + 尔 **ér**	亻(single-person)	你 丿 亻 亻 亻 竹 竹 你 你	you
女 **nǚ** + 子 **zǐ**	女 (female)	好 乚 乄 女 女 奵 奵 好	good, well
中		中 丨 冂 口 中	central
囗 + 玉 **yù**	囗 (enclosure)	国 丨 冂 冂 冃 围 围 国 国	country

You can make up stories for some characters so that it helps you memorize them. Let's take 好 **hǎo** (good/well) as an example. The left side 女 **nǚ** by itself means 'woman' or 'female', and it is the head component. The right side 子 **zǐ** is a formal word for 'son'. Can this possibly reflect a culture where a woman who can give birth to a son is regarded as being capable, and hence good? When these two characters are put together, each component becomes thinner in shape: 好.

Please note that in 你, the single-person head component 亻, when it appears as an independent character, is written as 人 **rén** (person/people).

Now, let us look at 中国. The character 中 **zhōng** means 'central' or 'middle' by itself (it has no head component), and the word 国 **guó** means 'country' by itself. So you now know what **Zhōngguó** really means! This is probably why China is often referred to in books and newspaper articles as 'the Middle Kingdom'. The character inside 国 is 玉 (pronounced **yù**), meaning 'jade'. A country may be interpreted as a place full of treasures such as jade surrounded by walls.

By analysing the initial four characters 你好 and 中国, we have in effect learnt the following four commonly used characters:

| 人 | 女 | 子 | 玉 |

rén   **nǚ**   **zǐ**   **yù**
person woman son   jade

Exercise 5

(1) Draw some square boxes as above and write the above four characters. Try to position the character in the middle of the box, follow the stroke order above and also try to draw each stroke in the right direction (see pages 11 and 12 for details).

(2) Learn all the characters (including the head components) above and turn the following pinyin phrases into characters and then translate them into English:

(a) nǐ hǎo
(b) Zhōngguó
(c) Zhōngguórén

Dialogue 2

Nǐ lèi ma?   你累吗？   Are you tired? **(CD1; 9)**

After their initial greetings, Lao Wang and David move on to talk about the trip.

LǍO WÁNG	Nǐ yīlù shùnlì ma?
DAVID	Hěn shùnlì, xièxie.
LǍO WÁNG	Nǐ lèi ma?
DAVID	Yǒu yīdiǎnr lèi.
LǍO WÁNG	Nǐ xiǎng hē yī bēi kāfēi ma?
DAVID	Tài xiǎng le.

(*later, inside the café . . .*)

LǍO WÁNG	Zhè shì nǐde kāfēi, Dàwèi.
DAVID	Xièxie.
LǍO WÁNG	Bú kèqi.

LAO WANG	*Did you have a nice trip?*
DAVID	*Yes, very nice, thank you.*
LAO WANG	*Are you tired?*
DAVID	*A little bit.*
LAO WANG	*Would you like to have a coffee?*
DAVID	*That would be lovely.*

(later, inside the café)

LAO WANG	*Here's your coffee, David.*
DAVID	*Thank you.*
LAO WANG	*You're welcome.*

(CD1; 8)

Vocabulary

yīlù	journey/trip [*lit.* 'one road' or 'whole way']	**yī**	one
		bēi	cup/glass
shùnlì	to be smooth/nice	**nǐde**	your
xièxie	thank you [*lit.* 'thank thank']	**kāfēi**	coffee
lèi	to be tired	**tài . . . le**	extremely/very much/too
yǒu yīdiǎnr	a little bit [*lit.* 'to have a little']	**zhè**	this
xiǎng	would like/to want	**bù**	no/not
hē	to drink	**bú kèqì**	you are welcome

Notes on Dialogue 2

■ 12 Possessive pronouns (e.g. 'my', 'his', etc.)

Simply add **de** to the personal pronouns **wǒ**, **nǐ**, **tā**, etc. to form possessive pronouns and possessive adjectives. In English, possessive adjectives are different from possessive pronouns (e.g. 'my' in front of nouns, and 'mine' at the end of the sentence). In Chinese, however, they are the same. For example:

Zhè shì *wǒde* kāfēi.	This is *my* coffee.
Zhè bēi kāfēi shì *wǒde*.	This coffee is *mine*.

You must also add **de** to a person's name to indicate the relationship between the person and an object. For example:

Zhè shì Xiǎo Lǐ de kāfēi.   This is Xiao Li's coffee.

Below is a comparison of Chinese and English possessive pronouns and possessive adjectives:

Chinese	English	English
Possessive adjective and pronoun	Possessive adjective (in front of nouns)	Possessive pronoun (at the end of the sentence)
wǒde	my	mine
nǐde	your (singular)	yours (singular)
tāde	his/her	his/hers
wǒmende	our	ours
nǐmende	your (plural)	yours (plural)
tāmende	their	theirs

Often, **de** can be omitted. Thus we can say **Nǐ yīlù shùnlì ma?** instead of **Nǐ(de) yīlù shùnlì ma?** (Was your journey smooth?/Did you have a nice journey?).

■ 13 Two verbs occurring in the same sentence

Whenever there are two or more verbs occurring in the same sentence or phrase, merely put them together. There is no link word 'to' to be used. Also remember that the verbs remain unchanged regardless of the pronoun as we saw earlier in Note 4. For example:

Wǒ *xiǎng jiào* Wáng Lín 'Lǎo Wáng'.
Lit. I   want call Wang Lin 'Lao Wang'.
I *want to call* Wang Lin 'Lao Wang'.

Tā *xiǎng h*ē   yī   bēi kāfēi.
Lit. He want drink one cup coffee.
He'd *like to have* a cup of coffee.

Note that the verb **xiǎng** means 'to want' or 'would like to' only when it precedes another verb.

■ 14 Negation word **bù**

To negate a verb (action verb or static verb such as 'be' and 'be happy') or adverb, simply put **bù** in front of it. For example:

Wǒ *bú* **shì**   **Wáng Lín.**
                verb
Lit. I   not be   Wang Lin.
      I am *not* Wang Lin.

Note that the word **bù** carries the fourth tone. However, when **bù** is followed by another fourth-tone syllable, it should be pronounced with the second tone.

Tā *bù* **xiǎng lái Zhōngguó.**
          verb¹   verb²
Lit. He not want come to China.
      He doesn't want to come to China.

Tāmen hěn *bù* **gāoxìng.**
                verb
Lit. They   very not happy.
      They are very unhappy.

Tāmen *bù* **hěn gāoxìng.**
            adverb
Lit. They   not very be happy.
      They are *not* very happy.

Note that **Tāmen hěn** *bù* **gāoxìng** differs in meaning from **Tāmen** *bù* **hěn gāoxìng**. The former negates the static verb whilst the latter negates the adverb **hěn**.

■ 15 Responding to questions ending with **ma**

In English, yes/no questions are so called because the answers to them almost always involve a *yes* or a *no*. However, in Chinese, **shì de** (yes) and **bú shì** (no) are not often used. They are definitely used if the verb **shì** is in the question. For example:

A: **Nǐ** *shì* **Shǐmìsī xiānsheng ma?**   A: Are you Mr Smith?
B: **Shì de.**   B: Yes.
   or **Bú shì.**   No.

When the verb **shì** is not in the question, usually the main verb which occurs in the question is either repeated in the answer for 'yes' or negated for 'no'. For example:

	A:	**Nǐ** *lèi* **ma?**	A:	Are you tired?
Lit.		You be tired [yes/no question word]?		

	B:	**Hěn** *lèi.* *or* **Bú** *lèi.*	B:	Yes, very tired./No.
Lit.		Very tired. Not tired.		

	A:	**Nǐ xiǎng hē kāfēi ma?**
Lit.		You want drink coffee [yes/no question word]?
		Would you like to have some coffee?

	B:	**Xiǎng, xièxie.** *or* *Bù* **xiǎng, xièxie.**
Lit.		Want, thank thank. Not want, thank thank.
		Yes, thank you. No, thank you.

Note, if you want to say 'Yes, please' in Chinese, add **xièxie** (thank you), not **qǐng** (please), after the verb. The word **qǐng** is used for different purposes (see Note 8 above).

■ 16 Tài . . . le

The word **tài** is often used in conjunction with **le** to mean 'extremely' or 'very much'. The word **le** does not mean anything by itself. Note that you need to put the adjective or the verb (sometimes a verbal phrase) you want to modify in between **tài** and **le**. For example:

Tài hǎo **le.**
adjective

Extremely good.

Tài xiǎng **le.**
verb

I want it *very much*.

Wǒ *tài* xiǎng hē kāfēi **le.**
verbal phrase

I'd *very much* like to have a coffee.

However, the word **le** is omitted when the negation word **bù** is used. For example:

Bú tài lèi.   Not too tired.
Bú tài shùnlì.   Not too smooth.

■ 17 Demonstrative pronouns **zhè** (this) and nà (that)

When the demonstrative pronoun **zhè** is used on its own, it can only appear in the subject position, that is, before the verb **shì**. It is the same for the other demonstrative pronoun **nà**:

Zhè/Nà shì nǐde kāfēi.   This/That is your coffee.
subject

Exercises

Exercise 6

(1) Use the question word **ma** to ask Lao Wang whether:
   (a) he is tired
   (b) he is happy
   (c) he would like to have a coffee

(2) Pretend that you are Lao Wang, and answer the questions first in the positive and then in the negative.

Exercise 7

Complete the following exchanges:

(a) A: Nǐ hǎo.
    B: _____ (*Hello*).
(b) A: Xièxie.
    B: _____ (*You're welcome*).
(c) A: Nǐ shì Wáng Lín ma?
    B: _____ (*Yes*). Wǒ shì Wáng Lín.
(d) A: Zhè shì nǐde kāfēi ma?
    B: _____ (*No*). Zhè shì Lǎo Wáng de.
(e) A: Nǐ xiǎng hē kāfēi ma?
    B: _____ (*Yes, please*).

Exercise 8

Use the word **bù** to negate the following sentences:

(a) Lǎo Wáng xiǎng hē kāfēi. (Lao Wang does not want to have coffee.)
(b) Dàwèi hěn gāoxìng. (David is not very happy.)
(c) Dàwèi hěn gāoxìng. (David is very unhappy.)
(d) Wǒ yīlù hěn shùnlì. (My trip was not very smooth.)
(e) Wǒ yīlù hěn shùnlì. (My trip was very rough.)
(f) Tā shì Shǐmìsī xiānsheng. (He is not Mr Smith.)

Exercise 9

When the question **Nǐ lèi ma?** is asked, how do you respond if
you are:

(a)   very tired
(b)   a little bit tired
(c)   not too tired

Exercise 10

Fill in the blanks:

(a)   Zhè bú shì _____ (*my*) kāfēi. Zhè shì _____ (*his*) kāfēi.
(b)   _____ (*her*) kāfēi bú tài hǎo.
(c)   Zhè bú shì _____ (*mine*). Zhè shì _____ (*David's*).

Characters

The following three characters in their pinyin form have been used
in Dialogue 2:

我	想	喝

我   **wǒ**   I, me
想   **xiǎng**   would like, to want
喝   **hē**   to drink

Character analysis	Head component and its meaning	Stroke order	English
我		我 ㇐ ㇐ 于 手 我 我 我	I, me
木 **mù** + 目 **mù** + 心 **xīn**	心 (heart)	想 ㇐ 十 才 木 机 机 机 相 相 相 想 想 想	want
口 **kǒu** + 日 **rì** + 匂	口 (mouth)	喝 丨 冂 口 吖 吖 吖 吗 吗 唱 唱 喝 喝	drink

(Unexplained components - 日 **rì**: sun/day; 木 **mù**: wood; 目 **mù**: eye)

The character 我 contains no head component. One simply has to write it repeatedly to remember it.

The character 想 is a rather difficult character. The two main parts are the top part and the bottom part. The top part 相 (**xiāng**), which is a character in its own right, is the phonetic, indicating the pronunciation; whilst the bottom part is the head component 心 (meaning 'heart'). Many Chinese characters that involve the working of one's mind have the heart component.

The character 喝 has the mouth head component as drinking has to do with one's mouth.

In fact, by taking the above three characters apart, we have learnt the following characters too:

日	木	目	心	口
rì	mù	mù	xīn	kǒu
sun/day	tree	eye	heart	mouth

Exercise 11

(1) Draw some square boxes and write 我, 想 and 喝 in the right stroke order.

(2) Match the following head components with their meaning categories:

(a)	口	person
(b)	心	mouth
(c)	亻	heart
(d)	女	female

Reading/listening comprehension

I Pronunciation

(1) Tone practice (**CD1; 10**)

When two third tones are together, the first third tone is usually changed to a second tone in actual speech. Practice:

(a) nǐ hǎo → ní hǎo
(b) wǒ xiǎng → wó xiǎng
(c) hěn hǎo → hén hǎo

(2) Underline what you hear **(CD1; 11)**

(a) gǎoxìng   (b) gèqi   (c) huānyíng   (d) xiānsheng
     gāoxìng   kèqi   huāyíng   xiànshēn

(CD1; 12)

II Read the following dialogue, and try to answer the questions below. If you have access to the audio material, listen to it first (try not to look at the script) and then answer the questions in English.

Zhang Ping is at Beijing Airport meeting John Smith from Britain.

ZHANG PING	Nǐ shì Shǐmìsī xiānsheng ma?
JOHN SMITH	Shì de. Nǐ shì . . . ?
ZHANG PING	Nǐ hǎo, Shǐmìsī xiānsheng. Wǒ shì Zhāng Píng.
JOHN SMITH	Nǐ hǎo, Zhāng Píng. Jiào wǒ Yuēhàn ba.
ZHANG PING	Hǎo de, Yuēhàn. Hěn gǎoxìng jiàndào nǐ.
JOHN SMITH	Wǒ yě hěn gǎoxìng jiàndào nǐ.
ZHANG PING	Nǐ lèi ma?
JOHN SMITH	Yǒu yīdiǎnr lèi. Yīlù hěn bú shùnlì.
ZHANG PING	Nǐ xiǎng hē yī bēi kāfēi ma?
JOHN SMITH	Tài xiǎng le.

QUESTIONS

(1) What does John Smith prefer to be called?
(2) Did John Smith have a pleasant trip?
(3) What suggestion does Zhang Ping make?
(4) What is John Smith's response to Zhang Ping's suggestion?

Lesson Two
Xìngmíng, guójí hé niánlíng
姓名，国籍和年龄
Name, nationality and age

By the end of this lesson, you should be able to:

- say what your name is
- say what your nationality is and where you come from
- say how old you are
- ask other people questions regarding the above three subjects
- use some appropriate expressions to respond to compliments
- count from 0 to 99
- say goodbye
- write more characters

Dialogue 1

Nǐ jiào shénme? 你叫什么？ What's your name?
(CD1; 14)

Amy, an American, is travelling in China. She sits opposite Fang Chun, a young Chinese man, on a train. They soon strike up a conversation.

FĀNG CHŪN Nǐ huì shuō Zhōngwén ma?
AMY Huì shuō yīdiǎnr.
FĀNG CHŪN Tài hǎo le. Wǒ jiào Fāng Chūn. Jiào wǒ Xiǎo Fāng ba. Nǐ jiào shénme?

AMY	Wǒ jiào Àimǐ.
FĀNG CHŪN	Nǐ shì Yīngguórén ma?
AMY	Bú shì.
FĀNG CHŪN	Nǐ shì nǎ guó rén?
AMY	Nǐ cāi.
FĀNG CHŪN	Wǒ bù zhīdào.
AMY	Wǒ shì Měiguórén. Nǐ shì nǎlǐ rén, Xiǎo Fāng?
FĀNG CHŪN	Wǒ shì Běijīngrén. Nǐde Zhōngwén hěn hǎo.
AMY	Nǎli, nǎli.

FANG CHUN	*Can you speak Chinese?*
AMY	*Just a little.*
FANG CHUN	*Wonderful. My name is Fang Chun. Please call me Xiao Fang. What's your name?*
AMY	*My name is Amy.*
FANG CHUN	*Are you British?*
AMY	*No.*
FANG CHUN	*Which country do you come from?*

AMY	*Have a guess.*
FANG CHUN	*I don't know.*
AMY	*I'm American. Whereabouts do you come from?*
FANG CHUN	*I'm from Beijing. Your Chinese is very good.*
AMY	*Not really.*

(CD1; 13)

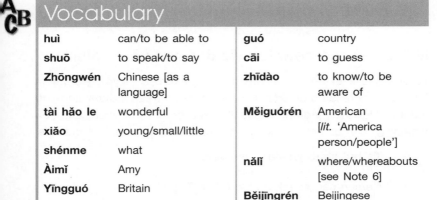

Vocabulary

huì	can/to be able to	**guó**	country
shuō	to speak/to say	**cāi**	to guess
Zhōngwén	Chinese [as a language]	**zhīdào**	to know/to be aware of
tài hǎo le	wonderful	**Měiguórén**	American [*lit.* 'America person/people']
xiǎo	young/small/little		
shénme	what	**nǎlǐ**	where/whereabouts [see Note 6]
Àimǐ	Amy		
Yīngguó	Britain	**Běijīngrén**	Beijingese [*lit.* 'Beijing person/people']
rén	person/people		
Yīngguórén	British [*lit.* 'Britain person/people']	**nǎli**	not really/not at all [*lit.* 'whereabouts']
nǎ	which		

Notes on Dialogue 1

■ 1 Use of **huì**

The word **huì**, known as an 'auxiliary verb' in grammatical terms, precedes other verbs to indicate whether a person has the ability to do something. To ask questions such as 'Can you speak Chinese?', simply add **ma** at the end of the statement. For example:

Statement	*Yes/no question*
Dàwèi *huì* **shuō Zhōngwén**.	Dàwèi **huì shuō Zhōngwén** *ma*?
David can speak Chinese.	Can David speak Chinese?

To answer a yes/no question which involves the word **huì**, you say **huì** for 'yes' and **bú huì** for 'no'. For example:

> A: **Àimǐ huì shuō Zhōngwén ma?**
> Can Amy speak Chinese?
> B: *Huì.*
> *Yes. She can.*

> A: **Xiǎo Fāng huì shuō Yíngwén ma?**
> Can Xiao Fang speak English?
> B: *Bú huì.*
> *No. He can't.*

■ 2 Difference between **yīdiǎnr** and **yǒu yīdiǎnr**

In Dialogue 2 of Lesson 1, we had the expression **yǒu yīdiǎnr** (a little bit). There is no difference in meaning between **yīdiǎnr** and **yǒu yīdiǎnr**. However, **yīdiǎnr** is usually used before the noun, and **yǒu yīdiǎnr** (**yī** can be omitted here) is used before the verb. For example:

> **Tā huì shuō *yīdiǎnr* Yīngwén.**
> noun
> He/she can speak *a little bit* of English.

> **Wǒ *yǒu yīdiǎnr* (or *yǒu diǎnr*) lèi.**
> verb
> *Lit.* I   a   little bit   be tired.
> I'm *a bit* tired.

■ 3 Question word **shénme**

When **shénme** (what) is used in a question, it occurs in the same place as where the information required should appear in the reply. For example:

> A: **Nǐ jiào   shénme?**
> *Lit.*   You be called what?
> *What's your name?*

> B: **Wǒ jiào   Lín Hóng.**
> *Lit.*   I   be called Lin Hong.
> My name is *Lin Hong*.

This rule applies to the positioning of all question words.

■ 4 Nǐ jiào shénme?

When you ask a Chinese person **Nǐ jiào shénme?** (What is your name?), you are usually given the full name (i.e. surname + first name). If you simply want to find out someone's surname, you ask **Nǐ *xìng* shénme?** (*lit.* 'You are *surnamed* what?'). If you want to be really formal, you ask **Nín guì xìng?** (*lit.* 'You honourable surname?'). The personal pronoun **nín** is a polite form of **nǐ** (you).

■ 5 Question word nǎ

Whenever the question word **nǎ** (also pronounced **něi** by some people) precedes nouns, such as **guó** (country) in Dialogue 1, it means 'which'. For example:

> **Nǐ shì *nǎ* guó rén?**
>   noun
> *Lit.* You be which country person?
>   *Which* country do you come from?

■ 6 Question word nǎlǐ

The question word **nǎlǐ** (where/whereabouts) is used if you want to find out whereabouts someone originally comes from. For example:

> A: **Nǐ shì Zhōngguó *nǎlǐ* rén?**
> *Lit.*   You be China whereabouts person?
>   *Whereabouts* in China do you come from?

> B: **Shànghǎirén.**
> *Lit.*   Shanghai person.
>   Shanghai.

■ 7 Names of countries

Names of countries are translated into Chinese arbitrarily. Some of them are based on the pronunciation, but others are not. Some of them have the word **guó** (country) in them, but others do not. By adding **rén** (person/people) to country/place names, we refer to the people who live in that country/place. For example:

Country/city		Its people	
Fǎguó	France	**Fǎguórén**	French
Déguó	Germany	**Déguórén**	German
Àodàlìyà	Australia	**Àodàlìyàrén**	Australian
Xīnxīlán	New Zealand	**Xīnxīlánrén**	New Zealander
Rìběn	Japan	**Rìběnrén**	Japanese
Xīnjiāpō	Singapore	**Xīnjiāpōrén**	Singaporean
Táiwān	Taiwan	**Táiwānrén**	Taiwanese
Xiāng Gǎng	Hong Kong	**Xiāng Gǎngrén**	Hong Kongese
Yìdàlì	Italy	**Yìdàlìrén**	Italian
Lúndūn	London	**Lúndūnrén**	Londoner
Yīnggēlán	England	**Yīnggēlánrén**	English
Sūgēlán	Scotland	**Sūgēlánrén**	Scottish
Wēi'ěrshì	Wales	**Wei'ěrshìrén**	Welsh

■ 8 Ways of referring to different languages

To refer to the language spoken in a particular country, in most cases you can add either **wén** or **yǔ** (language) to the first syllable of a country's name or add **huà** (speech/talk) to the whole name of a country. For example:

Country		Its language	
Yīngguó	Britain	**Yīngwén/ Yīngyǔ/ Yīngguóhuà**	English
Fǎguó	France	**Fǎwén/Fáyǔ/Fǎguóhuà**	French
Déguó	Germany	**Déwén/Déyǔ/Déguóhuà**	German
Rìběn	Japan	**Rìwén/Rìyǔ/Rìběnhuà**	Japanese

However, this rule does not apply to some countries. For countries such as Italy and Spain, you must add **wén**, **yǔ** or **huà** to the whole name of the country. For example:

Country		Its language	
Yìdàlì	Italy	**Yìdàlìwén/ Yìdàlìyǔ/ Yìdàlìhuà**	Italian
Xībānyá	Spain	**Xībānyáwén/Xībānyáyǔ/Xībānyáhuà**	Spanish

There are many ways of referring to the Chinese language. These include: **Hànyǔ** (literally '**hàn** language' since the **hàn** Chinese race comprises the vast majority of the population); **Zhōngwén** (a more formal term); **Zhōngguóhuà** (a less formal term); **Pǔtōnghuà** (lit.

'common speech', which is the Modern Standard Chinese); **Guóyǔ** (used in Taiwan, *lit.* 'national language' as opposed to regional dialects); and **Huáyǔ** (used among Chinese communities abroad, **huá** is another adjective for 'Chinese'). However, Chinese people realize that the terms most commonly used by Chinese-language learners are **Zhōngwén**, **Hànyǔ** and **Pǔtōnghuà**.

■ 9 Use of **zhīdào**

The verb **zhīdào** (to know/to be aware of) is mostly used to talk about things you know or people you know of but not personally. It can be followed by a noun phrase or a sentence. For example:

> **Wǒ bù** *zhīdào* **nǐ   shì nǎ   guó   rén.**
> *Lit.* I   not know   you be which country person.
>   I don't know which country you come from.

Compare the word order of **nǐ shì nǎ guó rén** after the verb **zhīdào** to that of the question **Nǐ shì nǎ guó rén?** (Which country are you from?) in Note 5 above. You will notice that the word order is exactly the same.

■ 10 Polite talk **nǎli, nǎli**

It is part of Chinese culture to be over-modest. When a person is complimented, he/she is supposed to deny the compliment. One of the expressions used on such occasions is **nǎli**, meaning 'not at all' or 'not really' and it is usually repeated. Another way of responding to a compliment is simply to deny what has been said. For example:

A: **Nǐde Zhōngwén hěn hǎo.**
    Your Chinese is very good.

B: **Bù hǎo, bù hǎo.**
    Not good, not good.

Exercises

Exercise 1

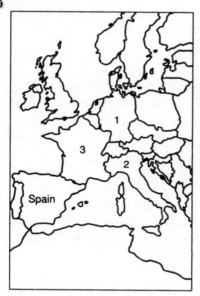 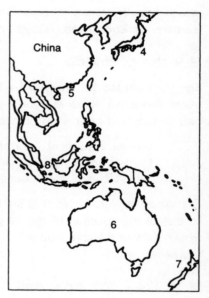

Look at the maps and match the number of each country/region with the corresponding Chinese name listed below. Then translate each name into English:

(a) Rìběn   (e) Xiāng Gǎng
(b) Fǎguó   (f) Xīnxīlán
(c) Déguó   (g) Xīnjiāpō
(d) Àodàlìyà   (h) Yìdàlì

Exercise 2

Give the Chinese terms for the people who live in the following countries/places:

(a) Britain   (e) Taiwan
(b) America   (f) Hong Kong
(c) China   (g) Australia
(d) Italy   (h) Japan

Exercise 3

Give the Chinese terms for the language(s) spoken in the following countries/places:

(a) Britain
(b) America
(c) China
(d) Italy

(e) Taiwan
(f) France
(g) Hong Kong
(h) Japan

Exercise 4

You meet a Chinese person for the first time. What do you say to her if you want to find out the following?

(a) her name
(b) whereabouts she comes from
(c) whether she speaks English

Exercise 5

Fill in the gaps using **yīdiǎnr** or **yǒu yīdiǎnr**:

(a) Àimǐ huì shuō _____ Zhōngwén.
(b) Dàwèi _____ lèi.
(c) Wáng Lín _____ bù gāoxìng.
(d) Xiǎo Lǐ xiǎng hē _____ kāfēi.

Exercise 6

Complete the other half of the exchange:

(a) A: _____?
    B: Wǒ shì Měiguórén.
(b) A: _____?
    B: Tā shì Běijīngrén.
(c) A: Nǐde Zhōngwén hěn hǎo.
    B: _____ (*Not really.*)
(d) A: Nǐ huì shuō Rìwén ma?
    B: _____ (*No, I can't.*)

Exercise 7

Translate into Chinese:

(a) Which country does Amy come from?
(b) I cannot speak English.
(c) She is not Japanese.
(d) I don't know what he is called.

Characters

The following characters in their pinyin form have been used in Dialogue 1:

说 **shuō**   to speak
中文 **Zhōngwén**   Chinese (language)
北京 **Běijīng**   Beijing
人 **rén**   person

Let us first recognize the two characters for **Běijīng** (*lit.* 'north capital'):

北 | 京

běi   jīng

Now let us see the stroke order of three new characters:

Character analysis	Head component and its meaning	Stroke order	English
讠 + 兑 **duì**	讠 (言) (speech)	说 ` 讠 讠 讠 讠 讠 讠 讠 说	speak
亠 + 乂	亠 (cover)	文 ` 亠 亠 文	language, culture
人		人 丿 人	person

(Unexplained component - 兑 **duì**: exchange)

中 in 中文 is the same as 中 in 中国 **Zhōngguó**. See page 25 for its stroke order.

Exercise 8

(1) Draw some square boxes and write 说中文 in the right stroke order.

(2) Make up a story about the character 说.

(3) Give the English meaning to the following two phrases after 人 is added to each of them:

(a) 北京
(b) 中国

Dialogue 2

Nǐ duō dà le? 你多大了？ How old are you?
(CD1; 16)

Amy and Xiao Fang get on very well with each other. The conversation becomes more personal.

AMY	Xiǎo Fāng, nǐ jīn nián duō dà le?
XIǍO FĀNG	Wǒ sānshí'èr suì le.
AMY	Zhēnde? Nǐ kànshangqu èrshíwǔ suì zuǒyòu.
XIǍO FĀNG	Guòjiǎng. Nǐ duō dà le?
AMY	Wǒ èrshíyī.
XIǍO FĀNG	Nǐ zhēn niánqīng. Zhème shuō, wǒ yīnggāi shì Lǎo Fāng.
AMY	Duìbuqǐ, qǐng màn yīdianr shuō.
XIǍO FĀNG	Wǒ yīnggǎi shì Lǎo Fāng.
AMY	Bú dùi, bú dùi. Nǐ shì 'Xiǎo Fāng'.

(five minutes before the train arrives at Beijing, they say goodbye)

XIǍO FĀNG	Rènshi nǐ, wǒ hěn gāoxìng, Àimǐ.
AMY	Wǒ yě shì, Xiǎo Fāng.
XIǍO FĀNG	Zàijiàn, Àimǐ.
AMY	Zàijiàn, Xiǎo Fāng.

AMY	*Xiao Fang, how old are you this year?*
XIAO FANG	*I'm thirty-two years old.*
AMY	*Really? You look about twenty-five.*
XIAO FANG	*I'm flattered. How old are you?*
AMY	*I'm twenty-one years old.*
XIAO FANG	*You are really young. In that case, I should be 'old Fang'.*
AMY	*Excuse me. Please say it slowly.*
XIAO FANG	*I should be 'old Fang'.*
AMY	*No, no. You are 'young Fang'.*

(five minutes before the train arrives at Beijing, they say goodbye)

XIAO FANG	*I'm so pleased that I've got to know you, Amy.*
AMY	*Me too, Xiao Fang.*
XIAO FANG	*Goodbye, Amy.*
AMY	*Bye, Xiao Fang.*

(CD1; 15)

Vocabulary

jīn nián	this year	**niánqīng**	to be young/young
duō	how	**zhème shuō**	in that case [*lit.* 'so speak']
dà	to be old/to be large/to be big/large/big	**yīnggāi**	should/ought to
le	[grammar word, see Note 13]	**duìbuqǐ**	excuse me/pardon
		màn	slowly/slow
sānshí'èr	thirty-two	**duì**	to be correct/correct
suì	years old		
zhēn de?	really?	**bú duì**	to be incorrect/incorrect
kànshangqu	to appear/to seem/to look	**rènshi**	to know (somebody)/to get to know (somebody)
zuǒyòu	about/approximate [*lit.* 'left right']		
guòjiǎng	to be flattered [*lit.* 'over-praising']	**wǒ yě shì**	me too/same here [*lit.* 'I also am']
èrshíyī	twenty-one	**zàijiàn**	goodbye [*lit.* 'again meet']
zhēn	really		

Notes on Dialogue 2

■ 11 Nǐ duō dà le?

This question is used to ask about an adult's age. Generally, Chinese people (including women!) are not offended by the question **Nǐ duō dà le?** (How old are you?). When the predicative adjective **dà** (to be big/old) is used in this context, it refers to someone's age, not their size. The word **lǎo** (to be old) we learnt in Lesson 1 is not appropriate here because **Nǐ duō *lǎo* le?** implies that the person being asked does look very very old.

■ 12 Numbers (CD1; 17)

0–9		10–19		20–29	
líng	zero	**shí**	ten	**èrshí**	twenty
yī	one	**shíyī**	eleven	**èrshíyī**	twenty-one
èr (liǎng)	two	**shí'èr**	twelve	**èrshí'èr**	twenty-two
sān	three	**shísān**	thirteen	**èrshísàn**	twenty-three
sì	four	**shísì**	fourteen	**èrshísì**	twenty-four
wǔ	five	**shíwǔ**	fifteen	**èrshíwǔ**	twenty-five
liù	six	**shíliù**	sixteen	**èrshíliù**	twenty-six
qī	seven	**shíqī**	seventeen	**èrshíqī**	twenty-seven
bā	eight	**shíbā**	eighteen	**èrshíbā**	twenty-eight
jiǔ	nine	**shíjiǔ**	nineteen	**èrshíjiǔ**	twenty-nine

Numbers 30, 40, etc. . . . 90 are formed by adding **shí** (ten) to **sān** (three), **sì** (four), etc. . . . **jiǔ** (nine). Thus we have: **sānshí** (thirty), **sìshí** (forty), **wǔshí** (fifty), etc. The numbers 31–9, 41–9, etc., use the same principle as 21–9 above. An apostrophe (') is used to mark the break between two syllables whenever there is ambiguity in pronunciation. Thus we have **shí'èr** (twelve) instead of **shíèr**.

■ 13 Grammar word le

This grammar word **le** (also called 'past particle') in this context suggests a change of state. For instance, when someone says **Wǒ èrshíyī suì le** (I'm twenty-one years old), the speaker means that he/she has already become twenty-one (both **suì** and **le** can be omitted, but **suì** must be used if the age is less than ten). For example:

Mǎlì sānshíbā. *or* **Mǎlì sānshíbā** *suì.*   Mary is thirty-eight.
Línlin wǔ *suì.*   Linlin is five.

Note that (a) **le** must be used in the question **Nǐ duō dà le?** (How old are you?); and (b) in saying one's age, the verb **shì** (to be) is not used.

■ 14 Use of **kànshangqu**

The use of the verb **kànshangqu** is very similar to the English verbs 'to look', 'to appear' or 'to seem' when they are used in affirmative sentences. For example:

> **Xiǎo Fāng** *kànshangqu* **hěn niánqīng.**
> Xiao Fang *looks* very young.

> **Nǐ** *kànshangqu* **yǒu yīdiǎnr lèi.**
> You *look* a little tired.

To negate sentences containing **kànshangqu**, put the negation word **bù** after **kànshangqu** and before the adverb or adjective. For example:

>   **Xiǎo Fāng kànshangqu** *bú* **tài gāoxìng.**
> *Lit.* Xiao Fang look   not too happy.
>   Xiao Fang doesn't look very happy.

■ 15 Use of **zuǒyòu**

When this phrase is used after numbers, it means 'about' or 'approximately'. For example:

>   **Zhāng jīnglǐ**   **sìshí** *zuǒyòu.*
> *Lit.* Zhang Manager forty about.
>   Manager Zhang is *about* forty.

■ 16 Polite talk **guòjiǎng**

The expression **guòjiǎng** (to be flattered), which is often repeated (e.g. **guòjiǎng, guòjiǎng**), is used on similar occasions to the phrase **nǎli, nǎli** (not really/not at all) we saw in Dialogue 1. It is another way of responding to a compliment. For example:

> A: **Nǐ kànshangqu hěn jīngshen.**   You look very smart.
> B: *Guòjiǎng, guòjiǎng.*   *I'm flattered.*

■ 17 Use of màn **yīdiǎnr**

This adverbial phrase, meaning 'a little bit slowly', can be placed either before the verb or after the verb (if the verb takes no object). For example:

> **Qǐng màn yīdiǎnr shuō.**
> *Lit.* Please slowly a bit speak.
> Please speak a little slowly.

> **Qǐng shuō màn yīdiǎnr.**
> *Lit.* Please speak slowly a little.
> Please speak a little slowly.

■ 18 Topic structure

It is very common, but not essential, in the Chinese language to put the topic of the sentence first. For example:

> **_Rènshi nǐ_, wǒ hěn gāoxìng.**
> topic
> *Lit.* To know you, I very be pleased.
> I'm very pleased *to have met you.*

> **_Lái Zhōngguó_, wǒ hěn gāoxìng.**
> topic
> *Lit.* To come to China, I very be happy.
> I'm so happy *that I've come to China.*

■ 19 Use of **rènshi**

As in Note 18 above, the sentence **_Rènshi nǐ_, wǒ hěn gāoxìng** can be translated as 'I'm very pleased to have met you'. It can also be translated as 'I'm very pleased that I've got to know you'.

In Note 9 of this lesson, we saw the verb **zhīdào** (to know). **Rènshi** is another verb meaning 'to know', except that in this case it means 'to know somebody personally'. Let us compare these two verbs:

Wǒ bù _zhīdào_ tā _rènshi_ Àimǐ. I didn't know that she knew Amy.

You can say **Wǒ _zhīdào_ Àimǐ**, but it means simply that you either have heard about Amy or just know who she is.

Exercises

Exercise 9

Describe Amy and Fang Chun – the two characters in this lesson (e.g. their nationality, age, etc.).

Exercise 10

Complete the other half of the conversation:

(a) A: Nǐde Zhōngwén hěn hǎo.
    B: _____ (*Not really*).
(b) A: Dàwèi duō dà le?
    B: _____ (*about 30*).
(c) A: Mǎlì shì Měiguórén.
    B: _____ (*Incorrect*). Tā shì Yīngguórén.

Exercise 11

Fill in the blanks using **rènshi** (to know somebody) or **zhīdào** (to know something):

(a) Wǒ bù _____ tā huì shuō Zhōngwén.
(b) Xiǎo Fāng _____ Àimǐ.
(c) Tā bù _____ Àimǐ shì nǎ guó rén.
(d) Wǒ hěn xiǎng _____ Xiǎo Fāng.

Exercise 12

Turn the following sentences into questions regarding the underlined parts (the underlined part is the information you wish to obtain):

   Example: Àimǐ shì <u>Měiguórén</u>. → Àimǐ shì nǎ guó rén?

(a) Tā jiào <u>Fāng Chūn</u>.
(b) Xiǎo Fāng shì <u>Běijīngrén</u>.
(c) Àimǐ jīn nián <u>èrshíyī suì</u>.

Exercise 13

Translate into Chinese:

(a) She doesn't look very happy.
(b) Lǎo Wáng looks very young.
(c) You look a little tired.

Characters

The following are the Chinese characters for the numbers 1–10:

Pinyin	Character	Stroke order	English
yī	一	一	one
èr	二	一 二	two
sān	三	一 二 三	three
sì	四	丨 冂 冂 四 四	four
wǔ	五	一 亐 五 五	five
liù	六	、 亠 宀 六	six
qī	七	一 七	seven
bā	八	丿 八	eight
jiǔ	九	丿 九	nine
shí	十	一 十	ten

Now let us learn how to write **zàijiàn** (goodbye):

Character analysis	Head component and its meaning	Stroke order	English
一 + 冉 rán	一 (one)	再　一　厂　冂　冉　冉　再	again
见		见　丨　冂　见　见	to see

(Unexplained component - 冉 **rán**: slowly)

Exercise 14

(1) Write the following numbers in characters:

(a) 6
(b) 18
(c) 23
(d) 45

(2) Draw some square boxes and write 再见 in the right stroke order.

Reading/listening comprehension

(CD1; 18)

I Read the following dialogue, and try to answer the questions below. If you have access to the audio material, listen to it first (try not to look at the script) and then answer the questions in English.

Two Chinese people, Meixin and Liu Li, are talking about David.

MĚIXĪN	Nǐ rènshi Dàwèi ma?
LIÚ LÌ	Rènshi.
MĚIXĪN	Tā shì nǎ guó rén?
LIÚ LÌ	Yīngguórén.
MĚIXĪN	Tā huì shuō Zhōngwén ma?
LIÚ LÌ	Huì shuō yīdiǎnr.
MĚIXĪN	Nǐ zhīdào tā duō dà le ma?
LIÚ LÌ	Wǒ bù zhīdào. Nǐ xiǎng rènshi tā ma?
MĚIXĪN	Hěn xiǎng.

QUESTIONS

(1) Does Liu Li know David?
(2) Which country is David from?
(3) Does David speak Chinese?
(4) Does Liu Li know how old David is?
(5) Does Meixin want to meet David?

(CD1; 19)

II Read aloud the following phrases or words and add on the correct tone marks to reflect the change of tones in actual speech. If you have access to the audio, listen to it first, and then add on the correct tone marks. Just to remind you: (‾) first tone; (´) second tone; (ˇ) third tone; (`) fourth tone.

(1) **xiexie** (thank you)
(2) **Yingguoren** (British)
(3) **shuo Zhongwen** (speak Chinese)
(4) **tai hao le** (wonderful)
(5) **zaijian** (goodbye)
(6) **wo ye shi** (me too)
(7) **bu keqi** (you're welcome)
(8) **bu dui** (incorrect)

Lesson Three
Zài gōngsī de jùhuì shang
在公司的聚会上
At a company party

By the end of this lesson, you should be able to:

- exchange greetings in a more sophisticated way
- use some time-related phrases
- use question words **nǎr** (where) and **shéi** (who)
- use **le** to indicate a past action or an action which has taken place
- use some measure words
- negate some verbs with **méiyǒu** or **méi**
- write more characters and recognize two useful signs

Dialogue 1

Zěnme yàng? 怎么样? How are you? **(CD1; 21)**

Amy and Xiaolan are very good friends as well as working for the same company. Amy also knows Xiaolan's husband, Yanzhong. They haven't seen each other for a long time and have just met at a party.

AMY	Xiǎolán, hǎo jiǔ bú jiàn. Nǐ zěnme yàng?
XIĂOLÁN	Wǒ hěn hǎo. Nǐ hǎo ma? Nǐ kànshangqu yǒu diǎnr lèi.
AMY	Wǒ SHÌ hěn lèi. Zuìjìn wǒ hěn máng. Yánzhōng zěnme yàng?
XIĂOLÁN	Hái hǎo, xièxie. Tā zuótiān chūmén le.

AMY   Qù nǎr le?

XIǍOLÁN   Měiguó. Xià ge xīngqī huílai. Nǐde nán péngyou lái le ma?

AMY   Lái le . . .

(*at this very moment, David, Amy's boy-friend, passes by*)

AMY   Dàwèi, ràng wǒ jièshào yīxià. Zhè shì wǒde hǎo péngyou Xiǎolán. Xiǎolán, zhè shì wǒde nán péngyou Dàwèi.

DAVID   Nǐ hǎo, Xiǎolán. Jiàndào nǐ, wǒ hěn gāoxìng.

XIǍOLÁN   Wǒ yě shì, Dàwèi. Wǒmen zhōngyú jiànmiàn le.

AMY   *Xiaolan, I haven't seen you for ages. How are you?*

XIAOLAN   *I'm very well. Are you well? You look a little tired.*

AMY   *I **am** tired. I've been very busy recently. How is Yanzhong?*

XIAOLAN   *Fine, thanks. He went away yesterday.*

AMY   *Where has he gone?*

XIAOLAN   *America. He's coming back next week. Has your boy-friend come with you?*

AMY   *Yes . . .*

(at this very moment, David, Amy's boy-friend, passes by)

AMY	David, let me introduce you to my good friend, Xiaolan. Xiaolan, this is my boy-friend, David.
DAVID	Hello, Xiaolan. I'm very pleased to meet you.
XIAOLAN	Me too, David. We meet at last.

 (CD1; 20)

Vocabulary

hǎo	very	**qù**	to go/to go to
jiǔ	long [as of time]	**nǎr**	where
bú jiàn	not see	**xià ge**	next
zěnme	how	**xīngqī**	week
Zěnme yàng?	How are you?/ How are things?	**huílai**	to return/come back
		nán	male
shì	[emphatic word]	**péngyou**	friend
zuìjìn	recently	**ràng**	to let/to allow
máng	to be busy	**jièshào**	to introduce
hái hǎo	to be all right/to be fine	**yīxià**	[see Note 9]
		wǒmen	we
zuótiān	yesterday	**zhōngyú**	finally/at last
tā	he	**jiànmiàn**	to meet
chūmén	to be away/to go away		

Notes on Dialogue 1

■ 1 Hǎo jiǔ bú jiàn

This is a very common expression to be used if you have not seen someone for a long time. Literally, the phrase means 'very long no see'. The word **hǎo**, although the same **hǎo** as in **nǐ hǎo** (hello), in this instance means 'very' and is used as an adverb. There is an element of informality as well as exaggeration when **hǎo** is used to mean 'very' or 'so'. For example:

Wǒ hǎo lèi.	I'm so tired.
Tā hǎo gāoxìng jiàndào nǐ.	He is so happy to see you.

■ 2 **Zěnme yàng?**

The greeting expression **Nǐ zěnme yàng?** (How are you?/How are things?) is used very often among colleagues and friends – basically people who know each other. It is one of those phrases which is difficult to analyse grammatically. Let us concentrate on its usage. If the question is aimed at the person you are speaking to, **nǐ** (you) is usually omitted. If you enquire about someone or something, you must place that person or thing at the beginning of the question. For example:

Nǐde nán péngyou zěnme yàng? How is *your boy-friend*?
Zhōngguó zěnme yàng? How is *China*?

In response to the question **Nǐ zěnme yàng?**, you may use some of the following expressions:

Hěn hǎo.	Very well.	**Bú tài hǎo.**	Not very well.
Hái hǎo.	Fine.	**Bù hǎo.**	Not well.
Hái bú cuò.	Not bad.	**Hěn zāo.**	Terrible.
Mǎma hūhu.	Just so-so.		

■ 3 Emphatic **shì**

In order to emphasize certain phrases, the word **shì** (*lit.* 'to be') can be used before these phrases. Whenever **shì** is used for emphatic purposes in this book, it will be capitalized to distinguish it from ordinary **shì** (be). For example:

Měixīn *SHÌ* **hěn máng.** Meixin *IS* very busy.
subject

Wǒ *SHÌ* **bù xiǎng hē kāfēi.** I *DON'T* want to have coffee.
subject

When emphatic **shì** is used in sentences with the verb **kànshangqu** (to look/to seem), which we saw in Lesson 2, **shì** appears after the verb. For example:

Jiājia **kànshangqu** *SHÌ* **hěn niánqīng.**
     verb
Jiajia does look very young.

Note that this rule does not apply to sentences where the word **shì** (to be) is used in the first place. Thus you *cannot say* **Wǒ** *SHÌ* **shì**

Yīngguórén (another emphatic word has to be used in this case, see Note 20 below).

■ 4 Use of **máng**

When the English sentence 'She is busy with work' is translated into Chinese, it becomes 'Her work is busy'. For example:

> **Shūlán de gōngzuò hěn máng.**
> *Lit.*   Shulan's   work   very be busy.

In such cases, the word **de** can be omitted. If you are asked to specify what you are busy with, you can put such information after **máng**. For example:

> A: **Nǐ   zuìjìn   *máng*   shénme?**
> *Lit.*   You recently be busy what?
> A: What have you been *busy* with recently?
>
> B: **Máng *gōngzuò*.**
> *Lit.*   Busy   work.
> B: Busy with *work*.

■ 5 Time-related phrases

In Chinese, time-related phrases (e.g. 'next week', 'today') are placed either at the beginning of a sentence or before the verb. For example:

> **Yuēhàn *xià ge xīngqī* lái   Táiwān.**
> *Lit.*   John   next   week come Taiwan.
> John is coming to Taiwan *next week*.
>
> ***Xià ge xīngqī*, Yánzhōng qù Yīngguó.**
> *Lit.*   Next   week, Yanzhong go Britain.
> Yanzhong is going to Britain *next week*.

Note that when a time-related phrase such as **xià ge xīngqī** (next week) is used, the context itself makes it very clear that it is a future event we are talking about. This sentence order applies to questions as well (see Note 6 below).

■ 6 Question word **nǎr**

In Note 5 of Lesson 2, we saw the question word **nǎ** (which). The same word also means 'where'. When **nǎ** means 'where', it is spelt with an **r** at the end, i.e. **năr**, and hence pronounced with the tongue rolled up a little. As with **shénme** (what) and **năli** (whereabouts) which we saw earlier, **năr** is also placed where the information required should appear in the reply. For example:

> A: **Nĭ   xià ge xīngqī qù *năr*?**
> *Lit.* You next   week go where?
> A: *Where* are you going next week?

> B: **Wŏ xià ge xīngqī qù *Făguó*.**
> *Lit.* I   next   week go France.
> B: I'm going to *France* next week.

■ 7 More on **le**

In Note 13 of Lesson 2, we saw one usage of the particle **le** (in **Nĭ duō dà *le*?**). Here, in Dialogue 1, **le** is added after some verbs to indicate that an event happened in the past (especially when a time-related phrase such as 'yesterday' is used). For example:

> **Ruìqiū zuótiān chūmén *le*.**   Rachel *went away* yesterday.
> **Tā qù năr *le*?**   Where *did* she go?
>   [she may be back already]

Depending on the context, especially when no time-related phrases are used, **le** can either indicate a past event or an event which has happened and is still happening:

> **Ruìqiū chūmén *le*.**   Rachel *has been away*. [she is still away]
> **Tā qù năr *le*?**   Where *has* she *gone*? [she is still away]

If there are other words/phrases (i.e. objects) after the verb, and they are not very long, **le** can be placed either after the verb or after the object. For example:

> **Mĕixīn qù Táiwān *le*.**   *or*   **Mĕixīn qù *le* Táiwān.**

Depending on the context, these two sentences can either mean 'Meixin went to Taiwan' or 'Meixin has gone to Taiwan'. Note that **le** cannot be added to every verb.

■ 8 Omission of the personal pronoun

The personal pronoun **Tā** (he) is omitted from the following two sentences in Dialogue 1: **Qù năr le?** and **Xià ge xīngqī huílai.** The complete sentences should be **Tā qù nǎr le?** and **Tā xià ge xīngqī huílai.** The omission of personal pronouns (e.g. 'I', 'you', 'he/she') is very common in the spoken language if they can be easily inferred from the context.

■ 9 Use of **yīxià**

The word **yīxià** does not have any specific meaning in this context except that it softens the abruptness of **Ràng wǒ jièshào** . . . (Let me introduce . . .). Without the use of **yīxià**, it sounds rather bossy and tactless.

■ 10 Difference between **jiànmiàn** and **jiàndào**

We saw earlier in Lesson 1 the verb **jiàndào** in **Hěn gāoxìng** *jiàndào* **nǐ** (Very pleased to meet you). Here, we have the sentence **Wǒmen zhōngyú** *jiànmiàn* **le** (We meet at last). The main difference between the two verbs lies in their usage:

X + ***jiàndào*** + Y
two or more people + ***jiànmiàn*** OR X and Y + ***jiànmiàn***

For example:

<u>**Xiǎolán**</u> **zuótiān** *jiàndào* **le** <u>**Dàwèi**</u>.
Xiaolan *met* David yesterday.

<u>**Wǒmen**</u> **xià ge xīngqī** *jiànmiàn*.
We are going *to meet* next week.

Exercises

Exercise 1

Solve the problems:

(a)   You have not seen a Chinese friend of yours for a long time, and you have just bumped into him. What do you say?
(b)   You want to introduce your good friend Amy and your Chinese friend Xiao Lin to each other. What do you say?

Exercise 2

Use emphatic sнì to rewrite the following sentences, and then translate them into English:

(a) Yuēhàn bú tài máng.
(b) Xiǎolán de gōngzuò hěn máng.
(c) Wáng Lín kànshangqu hěn lǎo.

Exercise 3

Translate into Chinese:

(a) A: Where did you go yesterday?
     B: I went to London.
(b) A: Where are you going next week?
     B: China.
(c) A: Where has Yanzhong gone?
     B: He's gone to America.

Exercise 4

Place **le** in an appropriate place in the following sentences, and then
translate them into English:

(a) Ānnà qù Měiguó.
(b) Xiǎolán hē yī bēi kāfēi.
(c) Yánzhōng zuótiān chūmén.

Exercise 5

Fill in the blanks using **jiàndào** or **jiànmiàn**:

(a) Xiǎolán zhōngyú _____ le Dàwèi.
(b) Tāmen xià ge xīngqī _____.
(c) Xiǎolán hé (*and*) Yánzhōng zuótiān _____ le.
(d) Wǒ bù xiǎng _____ Zhāng Píng.

Characters

The following characters in their pinyin form have been used in
Dialogue 1:

忙	**máng**	busy/be busy
男	**nán**	male/man
朋友	**péngyǒu**	friend
我们	**wǒmen**	we; us

我 (**wǒmen**, I/me) in 我们 (**wǒmen**, we/us) has been introduced in Lesson 1. Here are the analysis and the stroke orders for the rest of the above characters:

Character analysis	Head component and its meaning	Stroke order	English
忄 + 亡 **wáng**	忄 (standing heart)	忙 丨 忄 忄 忄 忙 忙	busy
田 **tián** + 力 **lì**	田 (field)	男 丨 冂 日 田 田 男 男	male, man
月 **yuè** + 月	月 (moon, flesh)	朋 丿 刀 月 月 刖 朋 朋 朋	friend
𠂇 + 又 **yòu**	又 (also, a hand)	友 一 𠂇 方 友	friend, friendly
亻 + 门 **mén**	亻 (person)	们 丿 亻 亻 亻 们 们	[plural particle]

(Unexplained components - 亡 **wáng**: death; 力 **lì**: labour; 门 **mén**: door, acting as phonetic)

Exercise 6

(1) Draw some square boxes and write 忙 and 男朋友 in the right stroke order.

(2) Make up a story about the characters 忙 and 男 to help you remember them.

(3) Write down the components in the above table that function as phonetics (i.e. indicating the pronunciation).

(4) If you see the following two characters as signs, what would they mean (女 has been introduced in Lesson 1)?

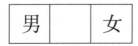

Dialogue 2

Tā jiéhūn le ma?   他结婚了吗？   Is he married?
(CD1; 23)

Later at the party, a colleague of Xiaolan's, Lin Fang (female), chats with Xiaolan.

LÍN FĀNG	Xiǎolán, nà liǎng ge rén shì shéi?
XIǍOLÁN	Nánde jiào Dàwèi. Shì wǒmen gōngsī de fù jīnglǐ.
LÍN FĀNG	Tā zhēn shuài. Nǐ zhīdào tā jiéhūn le ma?
XIǍOLÁN	Méiyǒu jiéhūn. Búguò, tā yóu nǔ péngyou le.
LÍN FĀNG	Ài! Zhēn kěxī.
XIǍOLÁN	Wèishénme?
LÍN FĀNG	Méi shénme. Nà ge nǔde shì shéi?
XIǍOLÁN	Tā jiù shì Dàwèi de nǔ péngyou. Tā jiào Àimǐ.

LIN FANG	*Xiaolan, who are those two people?*
XIAOLAN	*The man is called David. He is the deputy manager of our company.*
LIN FANG	*He is really smart. Do you know if he is married?*
XIAOLAN	*No, he isn't. But he's got a girl-friend.*
LIN FANG	*What a shame!*
XIAOLAN	*Why?*
LIN FANG	*Nothing. Who is that woman?*
XIAOLAN	*She is David's girl-friend. She's called Amy.*

Vocabulary

nà	that [see Note 12]		**búguò**	however/but
liǎng	two		**yǒu**	to have/have got
gè	[measure word, see Note 11]		**nǚ**	female
			ài	[exclamation word]
shéi	who		**zhēn kěxī**	what a shame/pity! [*lit.* 'really pity']
gōngsī	company			
fù	deputy/vice		**wèishénme**	why
jīnglǐ	manager		**méi shénme**	nothing [*lit.* 'not anything']
shuài	to be smart			
jiéhūn	to be married		**nà ge nǚde**	that woman
méiyǒu	not		**jiù**	[emphatic word]

Notes on Dialogue 2

◼ 11 Measure word

Discussing quantities of things in Chinese can be a little complicated in that something called a 'measure word' must be used between a number and its noun. In Lesson 1, we came across one of these measure words: **bēi** in **yī bēi kāfēi**. Different categories of nouns require different measure words. For instance, **gè** (often pronounced with neutral tone) is used for human beings, whereas **tóu** is used for animals and **tiáo** is used for things such as a scarf, a tie, trousers, etc. For example:

Wǒ rènshi sān *ge* Yīngguórén.
I know three British people.

Tā yǒu wǔ *tiáo* lǐngdài.
He has five ties.

See page 290 for the most commonly used measure words. At this stage, if you cannot remember which measure word goes with which category of nouns, use **gè** instead.

■ 12 Demonstrative adjectives **nà** and **zhè**

Measure words are also used between demonstrative adjectives **nà** and **zhè** and nouns. In Note 17 of Lesson 1, we saw **nà** and **zhè** as demonstrative pronouns on their own and they can only occur in the subject position. When **nà** and **zhè** are used with a measure word, they can be used in other positions too. For example:

> **<u>*Zhè ge rén*</u> shì wǒde jīnglǐ.**
> subject
> This person is my manager.

> **Nǐ rènshi <u>nà ge rén</u> ma?**
>   object
> Do you know that person?

A number can be inserted between **nà/zhè** and a measure word. Whenever the number is one (**yī**), it is almost always omitted. So **nà yī ge rén** becomes **nà ge rén** (that person). When numbers other than one plus measure words are used, **nà** means 'those' and **zhè** means 'these':

> **nà *liǎng* ge rén**   those two people
> **zhè *sān* bēi kāfēi**   these three cups of coffee

Note that when **nà** and **zhè** precede a measure word, they can also be pronounced '**zhèi**' and '**nèi**' respectively.

■ 13 **Nǐ zhīdào . . . ma?** (Do you know if . . . ?)

The object after the verb **zhīdào** can be a sentence. In English, this objective clause needs to be linked by a word such as 'if', 'that' or 'whether'. In Chinese, there is no link word used in this case. For example:

> **Nǐ zhīdào ( ) tā jiéūn le ma?**
> *Lit.* You know   he married + [ma].
> *Do you know if he is married?*

> **Wǒ bù zhīdào ( ) tā shì Běijīngrén.**
> *Lit.* I   not know   he is Beijing person.
> *I didn't know that he was from Beijing.*

■ 14 Use of **liǎng**

When you count, the number to use for two is **èr**. However, if you want to say 'two somethings', you should almost always use **liǎng** instead. For example:

liǎng bēi kāfēi   *two* cups of coffee
liǎng ge Běijīngrén   *two* Beijing people

■ 15 Changing adjectives to nouns by adding **de**

Adjectives such as **nán** (male) and **nǚ** (female) can be changed into nouns by adding **de** after them. Thus we have:

Adjective		Noun	
nán	male	**nán*de***	man
nǚ	female	**nǚ*de***	woman
lǎo	old	**lǎo*de***	the old one
xiǎo	young/small	**xiǎo*de***	the young/small/little one

Note that we can also add the word **rén** (person/people) after **nán** and **nǚ** to form nouns **nán rén** (*lit.* 'male *person*') for 'man' and **nǚ rén** (*lit.* 'female *person*') for 'woman', which are more formal than **nánde** and **nǚde**. On public signs, 男 (**nán**) means 'men's toilet', and 女 (**nǚ**) means 'women's toilet'.

■ 16 Linking two nouns with **de**

Another use of **de** is to link two nouns, the second being subordinate to the first. It is equivalent to the English word 'of' or apostrophe plus 's'. For example:

gōngsī *de* jīnglǐ
company's manager/the manager *of* the company

Àimǐ *de* nán péngyou
Amy's boy-friend

■ 17 Question word **shéi**

The question word **shéi** ('who'), also pronounced **shuí** can appear at the beginning or at the end of the question depending on how you want your question to be structured. For example:

    Shéi **shì nǐmen gōngsī de jīnglǐ?**
Lit. Who be your   company's manager?
    Who is the manager of your company?

    Nǐmen gōngsī de jīnglǐ   **shì** *shéi***?**
Lit. Your   company's manager be who?
    Who is the manager of your company?

■ 18 Negation word **méiyǒu**

So far, we have been using **bù** to negate adverbs, adjectives and verbs for present and future events. Another important negation word is **méiyǒu** (**yǒu** is often omitted). It is mainly used to: (a) indicate that an action *has not* taken place; (b) indicate that an action *did not* happen; and (c) negate the verb **yǒu** (to have). You must never use **méi** to negate an adverb or an adjective. It is only verbs (i.e. 'doing words') which can be negated by **méi** or **méiyǒu**. Simply add **méi** or **méiyǒu** before the verb. With the verb **yǒu** (to have), just add **méi** in front of it. For example:

    Zuótiān wǒ *méiyǒu* **qù Lúndūn.** I did*n't* go to London yesterday.
    Dàwèi *méiyǒu* **lái.** David has*n't* arrived.
    Wú Hái *méi* **yǒu nán péngyou.** Wu Hai has*n't* got a boy-friend.

Remember: whenever **méi** or **méiyǒu** is used, **le** is not usually used. **Le** can only be used together with **méi yǒu** (not have) when you want to indicate that you had something before but now it is running out. For example:

    Wǒ *méi yǒu* **kāfēi** *le***.** I've run out of coffee.
    Kāfēi *méi yǒu le***.** Coffee is running out.

■ 19 Pronoun **shénme**

Earlier, in Lesson 2, we saw **shénme** (what) used as a question word. **Shénme** can also be used as a pronoun meaning 'anything' and it is usually used with the negation word **méi** to form negative sentences. For example:

    Wǒ *méi* **shuō** *shénme***.**
    I did*n't* say *anything.*/I said *nothing.*

Tā *méi* hē *shénme*.
He did*n't* drink *anything*./He drank *nothing*.

■ 20 Emphatic word **jiù**

In Note 3 of Dialogue 1 above, we mentioned that sentences with the verb **shì** (to be) cannot be emphasized by the emphatic word sʜɪ̀. The correct word to use in such cases is **jiù**. Simply add **jiù** in front of **shì**. For example:

Wǒ *jiù* shì Zhāng Bīn.
I ᴀᴍ Zhang Bin. [often used on the telephone]

Tā *jiù shì* gōngsī de jīnglǐ.
She ɪs the manager of the company.

Exercises

Exercise 7

Referring to the two dialogues in this lesson, answer the following questions in Chinese:

(a) Xiǎolán rènshi Àimǐ ma?
(b) Àimǐ rènshi Lín Fāng ma?
(c) Àimǐ jiéhūn le ma?
(d) Shéi shì Dàwèi?

Exercise 8

Translate into Chinese using appropriate measure words:

(a) fifteen American people   (b) two Chinese people
(c) three men   (d) eight cups of coffee
(e) four good friends

Exercise 9

Complete the other half of the conversation:

(a) A: Nǐ yǒu kāfēi ma?
     B: _____ (*Yes, I have.*)

(b) A: Dàwèi yǒu nǚ péngyou ma?

B: _____ (*No, he hasn't.*)

(c) A: Wǒ bú huì shuō Yīngwén.

B: _____ (*What a shame!*)

Exercise 10

Turn the following sentences into questions regarding the underlined parts, which is the information you wish to obtain:

Example: Tā jiào <u>Wáng Xiǎolán</u>. → Tā jiào *shénme?*

(a) Yánzhōng qù <u>Měiguó</u> le.

(b) <u>Dàwèi</u> shì wǒmen gōngsī de fù jīnglǐ.

(c) Xiǎolán shì <u>Zhōngguórén</u>.

(d) Wǒ xià ge xīngqī qù <u>Táiwān</u>.

Exercise 11

Use **méi(yǒu)** or **bù** to negate the following sentences, then translate them into English:

(a) Wǒ xià ge xīngqī qù Zhōngguó.

(b) Zhēnní jiéhūn le.

(c) Xiǎo Fāng yǒu Yìdàlì kāfēi.

(d) Wáng Píng rènshi Měixīn.

(e) Zuótiān wǒmen qù le Lúndūn.

(f) Wǒ xiǎng hē kāfēi.

(g) Wǒ zhīdào tā yǒu nǚ péngyou le.

Exercise 12

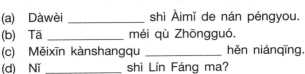

Fill in the blanks using emphatic words **jiù** or sHì:

(a) Dàwèi _____ shì Àimǐ de nán péngyou.

(b) Tā _____ méi qù Zhōngguó.

(c) Měixīn kànshangqu _____ hěn niánqīng.

(d) Nǐ _____ shì Lín Fáng ma?

Characters

The following characters in their pinyin form have been used in Dialogue 2:

他	**tā**	he; him
她	**tā**	she; her
没(有)	**méi(yǒu)**	not; no
有	**yǒu**	to have

他	她	没	有

Character analysis	Head component and its meaning	Stroke order	English
亻 + 也 **yě**	亻 (person)	他 ノ 亻 仁 仲 他	he; him
女 + 也	女 (woman)	她 乚 ㄑ 女 如 妁 她	she; her
氵 + 殳 **shū**	氵 (water)	没 丶 丶 氵 氵 沪 沙 没	no/not
𠂇 + 月	月 (moon, flesh)	有 一 ナ 𠂇 有 有 有	have

(Unexplained components - 也 **yě**: also; 殳 **shū**: an ancient weapon)

Exercise 13

(1) Match the character with its pinyin and the English meaning:

(a)

i) 她	**tā** (she; her)
ii) 好	
iii) 女	

(b)

i) 你	**tā** (he; him)
ii) 他	
iii) 也	

(c)

i) 女朋友	**nán péngyou** (boy-friend)
ii) 男朋友	
iii) 小朋友	

(d)

i) 友	**yǒu** (to have)
ii) 月	
iii) 有	

(2) Use each of the following components to form a character or two (you can add things to the right or the left; and you can go back to Lessons 1 and 2 for other components introduced):

(a) 亻 (b) 忄 (c) 氵 (d) 女

Reading/listening comprehension

I Pronunciation

(1) Neutral tone practice: listen and repeat **(CD1; 25)**

zěnme	xià ge
huílai	péngyou
wǒmen	wèishénme

(2) Underline what you hear **(CD1; 26)**

(a)	gōngsī	(c)	kěxī
	gōngzī		kèqi
(b)	búguò	(d)	jiéhūn
	bǔguò		jiěhèn

(CD1; 27)

II Listen to/read the following passage carefully, and then write 'true' or 'false' next to the sentences on the following page.

Vocabulary

zhàngfu	husband
hé	and

Wǒ jiào Zhū Mǐn. Wǒ shì Zhōngguórén. Wǒ yǒu yī ge Yīngguó péngyǒu. Tā jiào Mǎlì. Mǎlì yǐjīng jiéhūn le. Tāde zhàngfu jiào Yuēhàn. Mǎlì kànshangqu hěn niánqīng. Tā jīn nián sìshí suì zuǒyòu. Yuēhàn wǔshí suì zuǒyòu. Xià ge xīngqī tāmen qù Zhōngguó.

TRUE OR FALSE?

(1) Zhū Mǐn shì Zhōngguórén. _____

(2) Zhū Mǐn yǒu sān ge Yīngguó péngyou. _____

(3) Zhū Mǐn de Yīngguó péngyou jiào Àimǐ. _____

(4) Mǎlì kànshangqu bù lǎo. _____

(5) Mǎlì méi jiéhūn. _____

(6) Yuēhàn shì Mǎlì de zhàngfu. _____

(7) Mǎlì hé Yuēhàn zuótiān qù le Zhōngguó. _____

Lesson Four
Wèn shíjiān 问时间
Asking the time

By the end of this lesson, you should be able to:

- tell the time
- obtain information regarding time
- use the verb **yǒu** (to have) appropriately
- ask yes/no questions in another way
- make an appointment
- apologize
- attract someone's attention
- recognize and write more characters

Dialogue 1

Jǐ diǎn le? 几点了？ What's the time? (CD1; 29)

Linlin and her mother are British Chinese and are visiting Shanghai for the first time. They are staying in a hotel. They arrived late last night, and forgot to adjust their watches to the local time. It is now morning. They ask one of the receptionists . . .

LÍNLIN	Zǎoshang hǎo!
RECEPTIONIST	Zǎoshang hǎo!
LÍNLIN	Qǐng wèn, xiànzài jǐ diǎn le?
RECEPTIONIST	Jiǔ diǎn shí fēn.
LÍNLIN	Xièxie.

RECEPTIONIST	Bú xiè.
LÍNLIN	Cāntīng jǐ diǎn kāimén?
RECEPTIONIST	Yǐjing kāimén le. Zǎocān shì cóng qī diǎn dào jiǔ diǎn bàn.
LÍNLIN	Xièxie. Huí jiàn!
RECEPTIONIST	Huí jiàn!
LÍNLIN	Māma, hái yǒu èrshí fēnzhōng. Wǒmen kuài qù chī zǎofàn ba.
MĀMA	Hǎode.

LÍNLIN	早上好！
RECEPTIONIST	早上好！
LÍNLIN	请问，现在几点了？
RECEPTIONIST	九点十分。
LÍNLIN	谢谢。
RECEPTIONIST	不谢。
LÍNLIN	餐厅几点开门？
RECEPTIONIST	已经开门了。早餐是从七点到九点半。
LÍNLIN	谢谢。回见！
RECEPTIONIST	回见！
LÍNLIN	妈妈，还有二十分钟。
	我们快去吃早饭吧。
MĀMA	好的。

LINLIN	*Good morning.*
RECEPTIONIST	*Good morning.*
LINLIN	*What's the time now please?*
RECEPTIONIST	*It's ten past nine.*
LINLIN	*Thank you.*
RECEPTIONIST	*You are welcome.*
LINLIN	*What time does the restaurant open?*
RECEPTIONIST	*It's already open. Breakfast is from seven to half past nine.*
LINLIN	*Thank you. See you later.*
RECEPTIONIST	*See you later.*
LINLIN	*Mum, we've got twenty minutes left. Let's hurry up and go and have breakfast.*
MOTHER	*OK.*

(CD1; 28)

Vocabulary

zǎoshang	早上	morning
wèn	问	to ask
xiànzài	现在	now
jǐ	几	how many
jiǔ	九	nine
diǎn	点	o'clock
shí	十	ten
fēn	分	minute
cāntīng	餐厅	restaurant/dining-room [*lit.* 'meal hall']
kāimén	开门	to be open/to open
yǐjing	已经	already
qī	七	seven
zǎocān	早餐	breakfast [formal]
cóng . . . dào	从 . . . 到 . . .	from . . . to
bàn	半	half
huí jiàn	回见	see you later
māma	妈妈	mum/mother
hái	还	still/also
èrshí	二十	twenty
fēnzhōng	分钟	minute
kuài	快	soon/quickly/hurry up
zǎofàn	早饭	breakfast

Notes on Dialogue 1

■ 1 Polite way of asking for information **Qǐng wèn . . .**

Early in Lesson 1 (Note 8), we had the word **qǐng** (please) used to invite
someone politely to do something. The same word is used in **qǐng wèn**,
which literally means 'please ask . . .'. This is a polite phrase which is
used when asking for information or help. It can be broadly translated
as 'May I ask . . . ?' or 'Could you tell me . . . please?' For example:

Qĭng wèn, nĭ jiào shénme?
May I ask what your name is?

Qĭng wèn, nĭ shì Sīfāng ma?
Could you tell me please if you are Sifang?

■ 2 Telling the time

To tell the time, the key words are **diăn** (o'clock), **fēn** (minute), **bàn** (half), **kè** (quarter) and **chà** (lacking/minus). The hour comes first, then the minute. For example:

A   7:10   qī *diăn* shí *fēn*
B   8:05   bā *diăn* wŭ *fēn* or bā diăn líng wŭ
C   9:15   jiŭ *diăn* yī *kè* or jiŭ *diăn* shí wŭ *fēn*
D   10:30   shí *diăn* sānshí fēn or shí *diăn* bàn
E   2:45   liăng diăn sìshíwŭ *fēn* or liăng diăn sān kè or sān
            diăn *chà* yī kè or sān diăn *chà shí* wŭ

Note that (a) the minute word **fēn** can be omitted once the minute is over ten; (b) if you want to omit the word **fēn** when the minute is less than ten, put the word **líng** (zero) after **diăn** (see B above); (c) do not use the word **fēn** when **kè** or **bàn** is used; (d) use the number **liăng** (two) not **èr** in telling the time; (e) to say '2:45', use any of the four expressions in (E) above. Because there are no terms equivalent to the English abbreviations *a.m.* and *p.m.* in Chinese, it is either the context or the adding of words such as **zăoshang bā diăn** (*lit.* 'morning eight o'clock'), **xiàwŭ liăng diăn** (*lit.* 'afternoon two o'clock') or **wănshang bā diăn** (*lit.* 'evening eight o'clock') which enables people to make such a distinction.

■ 3 **Jĭ diăn le?**

The question word **jĭ** (how many) is used to ask number-related questions and the person who asks the question expects a small number. The literal translation for **Jĭ diăn le?** is very awkward. It is something like 'How many o'clock already?' (as **le** indicates that something has already happened). The best thing to do is simply to remember that **Jĭ diăn le?** is the equivalent of the English 'What time is it?' or 'What's the time?' In answering the question, you can say the time with or without **le**. For example:

A: **Qǐng wèn, jǐ diǎn le?**   A: What time is it, please?
B: **Sān diǎn sānshí wǔ.**   B: It's three thirty-five.

Note that there is no Chinese equivalent of 'It is . . .' to be used before the time.

Similar to other question words, **jǐ** occurs in the place where the information required in the reply should appear. For example:

A: **Cāntīng   jǐ diǎn   kāimén?**
Lit.   Restaurant what time open?
     What time does the restaurant open?

B: **Cāntīng   qī diǎn   kāimén.**
Lit.   Restaurant seven o'clock open.
     The restaurant opens at seven.

Note that (a) the phrase indicating the time always occurs before the verb; and (b) no extra word like *at* in English is needed before the time.

■ 4 Use of **yǐjing . . . le**

If you use **yǐjing** (already) before some verbs or predicative adjectives, you *must* use **le** in the same phrase/sentence. Put **le** at the very end of the phrase/sentence. For example:

Tā *yǐjing* lèi *le*.
He is tired *already*.

Zhēnní *yǐjing* qù Zhōngguó *le*.
Jane has *already* gone to China.

However, the word **le** can be used without **yǐjing** to indicate that an event has already happened. For example:

Zhēnní qù Zhōngguó *le*.
Jane went to China./Jane has gone to China.

■ 5 Difference between **fēn** and **fēnzhōng**

The word **fēn** is only used when telling the time, whereas **fēnzhōng** is used as a unit of time when referring to the length of time. For example:

> **Xiànzài shì liǎng diǎn shí fēn.**
> Now it's ten past two.

> **Wǒ yǒu sānshí fēnzhōng chī wǔfàn.**
> I have got thirty minutes to eat lunch.

■ 6 Use of **kāimén**

The verb **kāimén** (*lit.* 'open door'), meaning 'to be open' or 'to open', is used to refer to the opening time of various shops and organizations. You cannot use this verb to say 'open the coffee jar', for example. That is to say, the verb **kāimén** cannot take an object. For example:

> **Cāntīng qī diǎn kāimén.**
> The restaurant *opens* at seven.

> **Xià ge xīngqī cāntīng bù kāimén.**
> Next week, the restaurant is not *open*.

■ 7 Position of **kuài**

When **kuài** (quickly/soon) is used as an adverb, it is placed before verbs in those sentences that ask for help, or that give orders. For example:

A child begs his/her mother:

> **Nǐ   kuài huílai ba.**
> *Lit.*   You soon return please.
>   Please come back *soon*.

A mother says to a child:

> **Kuài   yīdiǎnr chī.**
> *Lit.*   Quickly a little   eat.
>   Eat a bit *quickly*.

Exercises

Exercise 1

Use the clock faces to tell the time:

(a)

(b)

(c)

(d)

(e)

(f)

Exercise 2

Match the times to the clocks:

(a)

(b)

(c)

(d)

(e)    (f)

(1) bā diǎn líng wǔ
(2) shíyī diǎn èrshí fēn
(3) shí'èr diǎn bàn
(4) jiǔ diǎn yī kè
(5) liǎng diǎn sìshíwǔ
(6) sì diǎn chà wǔ fēn

Exercise 3

Solve the problem:

(a) You see a Chinese person early in the morning. What do you say to greet him/her?
(b) You want to find out what time it is. What do you say?
(c) You want to ask a Chinese person's name in a polite way. How do you phrase your question?
(d) How many ways can you think of to respond to **Xièxie** (Thank you)?

Exercise 4

Fill in the blanks and then translate the sentences into English:

(a) Zǎofàn shì _____ (from) qī diǎn _____ (to) bā diǎn bàn.
(b) Wǒmen yǒu wǔ _____ (minutes) hē kāfēi.
(c) _____ (Now) shì liù diǎn bàn.
(d) Tā _____ (already) jiéhūn le.

Exercise 5

Translate into Chinese:

(a) What time does the restaurant open?
(b) Do you know what time the restaurant opens?
(c) David is already thirty years old.
(d) Please come to Britain soon.

Characters

Let us first recognize the sign for 'Restaurant' inside a hotel:

cān   tīng

餐 (**cān**) is a formal word for 'meal/food'. It is a rather complex character that consists of 3 parts: 歺 + 又 (**yòu**, again) at the top and 食 (**shí**, food) at the bottom. 厅 (**tīng**) by itself means 'hall'. This term is only used to refer to a restaurant attached to a hotel or some other organization.

As all the new words from this lesson onwards are given in both the pinyin and character forms, you can decide which characters you wish to learn. Therefore, there will be less and less analysis of characters but more complex character exercises. For this lesson, let us analyse the following three words (but five characters) that have appeared in Dialogue 1:

现在	**xiànzài**	now
早上	**zǎoshang**	morning
还	**hái**	still

Character analysis	Head component and its meaning	Stroke order	English
王 + 见 jiàn	王 (jade)	现 一 二 干 王 刃 玑 珂 现	appear
		在 一 ナ 冇 扗 午 在	at
日 + 十	日 (sun)	早 ㅣ 冂 曱 日 旦 早	early
上 **shàng**		上 ㅣ ㅏ 上	up
辶 + 不 **bù**	辶 (walking)	还 一 ㄱ 不 不 不 还 还	still

(Unexplained component - 不 **bù**: no)

Some of the above components are characters in their own right. These three are the most commonly used ones:

wáng   jiàn   bù

王 (**wáng**), when used as head component, the meaning association is 'jade'; but when it is used on its own, it means 'king'; and it is also a common surname which we have seen in 老王 (**Lǎo Wáng**) in Lesson 1. 见 (**jiàn**, to meet) is the same characters as in 再见 (**zàijiàn**, goodbye) in Lesson 2. Finally, 不 (**bù**) is the negation word.

Exercise 6

(1) Draw some square boxes and write 现在, 早上 and 还 in the right stroke order.

(2) Give pinyin to the following phrase or short sentence and then translate them into English:

(a)   不好
(b)   我想见你。
(c)   她现在忙。
(d)   早上好!

Dialogue 2

Qù yóuyǒng   去游泳   Going swimming (CD1; 31)

Linlin wants to find out if there is a swimming pool in the hotel. She asks a receptionist in the hotel . . .

LÍNLIN	Zhè ge fàndiàn yǒu yóuyǒng chí ma?
RECEPTIONIST	Duìbuqǐ, méi yǒu.
LÍNLIN	Méi guānxì.

(*She then rings a fitness centre . . .*)

LÍNLIN	Duìbuqǐ, nǐmen zhōngxīn yǒu yóuyǒng chí ma?
CENTRE STAFF	Yǒu liǎng ge. Yī ge dàde, yī ge xiǎode.

LÍNLIN	Tài hǎo le. Nǐ kěyǐ gàosu wǒ kāimén shíjiān ma?
CENTRE STAFF	Dāng rán kěyǐ. Dàde cóng zǎoshang qī diǎn kāi dào xiàwǔ liǎng diǎn.
	Xiǎode cóng xiàwǔ sān diǎn kāi dào wǎnshang jiǔ diǎn.
LÍNLIN	Xièxie. (*She puts the phone down and asks her mother.*) Māma, nǐ xiǎng yóuyǒng ma?
MĀMA	Xiǎng, búguò, wǒ yǒu diǎnr è. Zánmen xiān chī wǔfàn, hǎo bù hǎo?
LÍNLIN	Hǎo ba. Jǐ diǎn chī?
MĀMA	Yī diǎn, zěnme yàng?
LÍNLIN	Hǎo de. Nǎme, zánmen sì diǎn qù yóuyǒng, xíng ma?
MĀMA	Xíng.

LÍNLIN	这个饭店有游泳池吗？
RECEPTIONIST	对不起，没有。
LÍNLIN	没关系。
. . .	
LÍNLIN	对不起，你们中心有游泳池吗？
CENTRE STAFF	有两个。一个大的，一个小的。
LÍNLIN	太好了。你可以告诉我开门时间吗？
CENTRE STAFF	当然可以。大的从早上七点开到下午两点。小的从下午三点开到晚上九点。
LÍNLIN	谢谢。(. . .) 妈妈，你想游泳吗？
MĀMA	想，不过，我有点儿饿。咱们先吃午饭，好不好？
LÍNLIN	好吧。几点吃？
MĀMA	一点，怎么样？
LÍNLIN	好的。那么，咱们四点去游泳，行吗？
MĀMA	行。

LINLIN	*Is there a swimming pool in this hotel?*
RECEPTIONIST	*I'm sorry. There isn't.*
LINLIN	*It doesn't matter.*
(She then rings a fitness centre . . .)	
LINLIN	*Excuse me. Are there any swimming pools in your centre?*
CENTRE STAFF	*Yes, there are two. A large one and a small one.*
LINLIN	*Great. Can you tell me the opening times?*

CENTRE STAFF	*Of course I can. The big one is open from seven in the morning to two in the afternoon, and the small one is open from three in the afternoon to nine in the evening.*
LINLIN	*Thank you. (She puts the phone down and asks her mother.) Mum, would you like to swim?*
MOTHER	*Yes, I would. But I'm a little hungry. Shall we have lunch first?*
LINLIN	*Fine. What time?*
MOTHER	*How about one o'clock?*
LINLIN	*That's fine. In that case, shall we go swimming at four o'clock?*
MOTHER	*OK.*

(CD1; 30)

Vocabulary

fàndiàn	饭店	hotel
yóuyǒng chí	游泳池	swimming pool
duìbuqǐ	对不起	I'm sorry/excuse me
méi guānxì	没关系	it doesn't matter/it's all right/it's ok
nǐmende	你们的	your
zhōngxīn	中心	centre
dàde	大的	the large one/the big one
xiǎode	小的	the small one
kěyǐ	可以	could/can
gàosu	告诉	to tell
shíjiān	时间	time
dāng rán	当然	of course
kāi	开	to be open
xiàwǔ	下午	afternoon
wǎnshang	晚上	evening
yóuyǒng	游泳	to swim
è	饿	to be hungry
zánmen	咱们	we
xiān	先	first of all

chī	吃	to eat
wǔfàn	午饭	lunch
nǎme	那么	in that case
hǎo bu hǎo?	好不好？	is it all right/is it ok?
xíng ma?	行吗？	is it ok?
xíng	行	all right/can do/will do/fine

Notes on Dialogue 2

■ 8 Use of **yǒu**

Yǒu means 'to have'. In English, you say *There is a library at the university*; but in Chinese, this sentence becomes 'The university has a library' because there is no 'there is/are' construction in the Chinese language. For example:

> **Zhè ge fàndiàn *yǒu* sān ge cāntīng.**
> *Lit.* This hotel have three restaurants.
> There are three restaurants in this hotel.

> **Wǒmende gōngsī *yǒu* liù ge Zhōngguórén.**
> *Lit.* Our company have six Chinese people.
> There are six Chinese people in our company.

■ 9 Use of **duìbuqǐ**

When the phrase **duìbuqǐ** is used to apologize, it means 'I'm sorry'; and when it is used to attract someone's (usually a stranger's) attention, it means 'Excuse me'. If someone says **duìbuqǐ** as an apology, one of the appropriate things to say in response is **Méi guānxi** (It doesn't matter). For example:

A: *Duìbuqǐ*. **Wǒ méi yǒu kāfēi.**
   I'm sorry. I haven't got coffee.
B: **Méi guānxi. Chá yě xíng.**
   It doesn't matter. Tea will do.

A: *Duìbuqǐ*. **Qǐng wèn, jǐ diǎn le?**
   Excuse me. What's the time, please?
B: **Sān diǎn shí fēn.**
   Ten past three.

■ 10 Use of **kěyǐ**

Another way of making your request more polite when asking for information, or permission to do something, from other people is to use **kěyǐ** (could/can/may) before the verb. For example:

Nǐ _kěyǐ_ gàosu wǒ nǐ jiào shénme ma?
Could you tell me what your name is?

Wǒ _kěyǐ_ qù Zhōngguó ma?
May I go to China?

■ 11 Verbs used as adjectives

Some verbs (mostly verbs consisting of two syllables), without changing their forms, can be used in front of nouns as adjectives to modify nouns. For example:

Verb		Adjective	
kāimén	to be open	**_kāimén_ shíjiān**	_opening_ hour/s
yóuyǒng	to swim	**_yóuyǒng_ chí**	_swimming_ pool
jièshào	to introduce	**_jièshào_ xìn**	letter of _introduction_

■ 12 Use of **fàn**

The word **fàn** means 'food' or 'meal'. One of the common greetings among neighbours is **Nǐ chī _fàn_ le ma?** (Have you eaten?). If you have had your meal, you say **Chī le** (_lit._ 'Eat already'); and if you have not had your meal, you say **Méi chī** (_lit._ 'Not eat'). The word **fàn** is used to form the following expressions we have come across so far:

zǎofàn (breakfast) _comes from_ **zǎoshang** (morning) and **fàn**
wǎnfàn (supper/dinner) _comes from_ **wǎnshang** (evening) and **fàn**
zhōngfàn or **wǔfàn** (lunch) _comes from_ **zhōngwǔ** (noon) and **fàn**

■ 13 Yes/no question **Hǎo bù hǎo?**

The question **Hǎo bù hǎo?** (_lit._ 'Good not good?'), is identical in meaning to **Hǎo ma?** (Is it all right?). All questions ending with **ma** can be rephrased according to the pattern below:

(Subject) + verb or predicative adjective + **bù** + repetition of the previous verb

For example:

Nǐ shì Zhōngguórén ma? *becomes* **Nǐ** *shì bú shì* **Zhōngguórén?**
Are you Chinese?
(Nǐ) è ma? *becomes* **(Nǐ)** *è bú è?* Hungry?

The reply for the first question above is still **Shì de** for 'Yes' and **Bú shì** for 'No'. The reply for the second question is **È** for 'Yes' and **Bú è** for 'No'. Note that (a) the subject can sometimes be omitted; and (b) the verb or predicative adjective after **bù** must be the same as the one before **bù**. If there are two verbs in one question such as

Nǐ <u>xiǎng</u> <u>hē</u> kāfēi ma?   Would you like to have a coffee?
    verb¹ verb²

the pattern becomes '(Subject) + verb¹ + **bù** + verb¹ + verb² + object'. The above question thus becomes:

Nǐ *<u>xiǎng</u> bù <u>xiǎng</u>* <u>hē</u> kāfēi?
    verb¹   verb¹   verb²

If the verb requires **méi** as its negation word, **méi** is used instead of **bù**. For example:

Nǐ yǒu kāfēi ma? *becomes* **Nǐ yǒu** *méi* **yǒu kāfēi?** Do you have some coffee?

■ 14 Affirmative sentences + **. . . xíng ma?**, **. . . hǎo ma?** or **. . . zěnme yàng?**

One way of making a suggestion and then seeking agreement or asking for permission is to add one of the following phrases – **xíng ma?/xíng bù xíng?**, **hǎo ma?/hǎo bù hǎo?** (Is it OK/Is it fine?) and **Zěnme yàng?** (How about . . . ?) – to affirmative sentences. Most of the time, the above phrases are interchangeable. Just remember that . . . **xíng ma/xíng bù xíng** can be used for asking for permission as well as making a suggestion whereas . . . **hǎo ma?/hǎo bù hǎo?** and . . . **zěnme yàng?** are only used for making a suggestion. For example:

Wǒ wǎnshang liù diǎn bàn lái, *xíng ma?*
I'm coming at half past six in the evening. *Is that OK?*

Wǒmen shí'èr diǎn chī wǔfàn, hǎo ma?
Let's have lunch at twelve, shall we?

Bā diǎn, zěnme yàng?
How about eight o'clock?

■ 15 Omission of the second syllable in a two-syllable verb

Verbs such as **yóuyǒng** (to swim) and **kāimén** (to be open) are two-syllable verbs. The second syllable, i.e. **yǒng** in **yóuyǒng**, **mén** in **kāimén**, is often omitted (a) in a reply to the question where the verb in its full form has already been mentioned; and (b) when the phrase **cóng . . . dào . . .** (from . . . to . . .) is used. For example:

A: **Nǐ** *yóuyǒng* **le ma?**
   Did you *swim*?

B: *Yóu* **le. Wǒ cóng liǎng diǎn** *yóu* **dào sì diǎn.**
   Yes, I *did*. I *swam* from two o'clock to four o'clock.

A: **Cāntīng** *kāimén* **ma?**
   Is the dining-room *open*?

B: *Kāi*. **Cóng liù diǎn** *kāi* **dào jiǔ diǎn bàn.**
   Yes. It *opens* from six to half past nine.

Note that the one-syllable verb always occurs before **dào** in the phrase **cóng . . . dào** (from . . . to . . .), with the exception of **shì** (to be) which is placed before **cóng**. For example:

Wǎnfàn *shì* **cóng liù diǎn dào shí diǎn.**
Dinner *is* from six to ten.

Yóuyǒng chī cóng liǎng diǎn *kāi* **dào wǔ diǎn bàn.**
The swimming pool *opens* from two to half past five.

■ 16 Tone of **nǐmende**

The word **mén** carries the second tone in isolation. When it is added to **nǐ** to form **nǐmen** ('you' plural), **mén** becomes toneless. When the toneless **de** is added to **nǐmen**, we get two neutral tones together.

Exercises

Exercise 7

Solve the problems:

(a) You want to ask the receptionist in your hotel some questions but the receptionist is not aware of your presence. To attract his/her attention, what do you say?

(b) What do you say if you want to find out what time the swimming pool opens?

(c) You are late for your appointment. What do you say if you want to apologize?

Exercise 8

Use complete sentences to state the times at which you usually do the following:

(a) chī zǎofàn   (b) chī wǔfàn
(c) chī wǎnfàn   (d) yóuyǒng
(e) qǐ chuáng   (f) shàng bān
(g) shàng kè   (h) xià bān
(i) xià kè   (j) shuìjiào

New words:

qǐ chuáng	to get up
shàng bān	to go to work
shàng kè	to go to class
xià bān	to finish work
xià kè	to finish class
shuìjiào	to go to bed

Exercise 9

Translate the following into Chinese using **yǒu** (to have):

(a) There are twenty large hotels in Dàlián.
(b) There are two restaurants in our hotel.
(c) Are there any Chinese people in this company?
(d) There isn't a swimming pool in this hotel.

Exercise 10

Rewrite the following questions without changing their meanings, and then translate them into English:

Example: Nǐ lèi ma? → Nǐ lèi bú lèi?

(a) Tā shì Yīngguórén ma?
(b) Nǐ zuìjìn máng ma?
(c) Zhāng Bīn yǒu nǚ péngyou ma?
(d) Nǐ xiǎng qù Zhōngguó ma?

Exercise 11

The following are replies to questions or comments. Make up an appropriate question or comment which could precede the reply:

(a) Méi guānxi.
(b) Xiànzài qī diǎn èrshíwǔ.
(c) Cāntīng liù diǎn kāimén.
(d) Huí jiàn.

 Exercise 12

You want to ask your Chinese friend if it is OK:

(a) to have lunch at 12:30
(b) to go swimming at 4:00pm
(c) to call her 'Xiao Li'

Characters

Let us first recognize the sign for the swimming pool. All three characters have the water head component 氵:

yóu   yǒng   chí

Now, let us analyse the following three characters:

饭店   **fàndiàn**   hotel; restaurant
饿   **è**   be hungry

Character analysis	Head component and its meaning	Stroke order	English
饣 + 反 **fǎn**	饣 (food)	饭 丿 饣 饣 饣 饣 饭 饭	food
广 **guǎng** + 占 **zhàn**	广 (broad)	店 丶 广 广 广 庐 庐 店 店	shop
饣 + 我	饣 (food)	饿 丿 饣 饣 饣 饣 饣 饣 饣 饿 饿 饿	hungry

(Unexplained components - 反 **fǎn**: acting as phonetic; 占 **zhàn**: to occupy)

Exercise 13

(1) Draw some square boxes and write 饭店 and 饿 in the right stroke order.

(2) As we have learnt that the 早 in 早上 (**zǎoshang**) means 'early'; and 饭 in 饭店 (**fàndiàn**) means 'food', what would 早饭 mean in English?

(3) If 中 in 中国 (**Zhōngguó**) means 'central', what would 中饭 mean in English?

(4) Match the following signs with their English translation:

(a)	(b)	(c)
北京饭店	餐厅	游泳池

(i) swimming pool　(ii) Beijing Hotel　(iii) restaurant (inside a hotel)

Reading/listening comprehension

(CD1; 33)

I Read the following dialogue carefully. If you have access to the audio material, listen to the dialogue first (try not to look at the script) and then answer the multiple-choice questions by ticking the most appropriate phrase.

Vowcabulary

jīntiān	today
hǎo zhǔyi	good idea

Guangmeng and Fang Chun share the same office at work. They are planning to do something together.

GUĀNGMÈNG	Fāng Chūn, nǐ jīntiān máng ma?
FĀNG CHŪN	Bú tài máng.
GUĀNGMÈNG	Zánmen qù yóuyǒng, hǎo ma?

FĀNG CHŪN   Hǎo zhǔyi. Búguò, wǒ xiànzài hěn è.
GUĀNGMÈNG   Nàme, zánmen xiān qù chī wǔfàn. Cāntīng jǐ diǎn
              kāimén?
FĀNG CHŪN   Shí'èr diǎn bàn.
GUĀNGMÈNG   Hái yǒu shíwǔ fēnzhōng kāimén.
FĀNG CHŪN   Shí'èr diǎn sìshí qù chī wǔfàn, xíng ma?
GUĀNGMÈNG   Xíng. Sān diǎn qù yóuyǒng, zěnme yàng?
FĀNG CHŪN   Hǎo de.

QUESTIONS
(1) Fāng Chūn jīntiān máng ma?
     (a) hěn máng   (b) bù hěn máng   (c) bù máng
(2) Guāngmèng xiǎng gàn ('do') shénme?
     (a) yóuyǒng   (b) chī wǔfàn   (c) hē kāfēi
(3) Fāng Chūn xiǎng xiān gàn ('do') shénme?
     (a) hē kāfēi   (b) yóuyǒng   (c) chī wǔfàn
(4) Cāntīng jǐ diǎn kāimén?
     (a) shíyī diǎn bàn   (b) shí'èr diǎn sānshí   (c) shí'ēr diǎn
(5) Xiànzài jǐ diǎn le? (*at the time when they talk*)
     (a) shí'èr diǎn yī kè (b) shíyī diǎn èrshíwǔ   (c) shí'èr diǎn bàn
(6) Tāmen jǐ diǎn qù yóuyǒng?
     (a) liáng diǎn bàn   (b) sān diǎn   (c) sān diǎn shí fēn

 (CD1; 34)

II Listen and add on the correct tone marks to the following words.

(1) **hui jian** (see you later)
(2) **canting** (dining-room)
(3) **duibuqi** (I'm sorry/Excuse me)
(4) **dade** (the large one)
(5) **bu mang** (not busy)
(6) **bu lei** (not tired)

Lesson Five
Jiārén hé péngyou 家人和朋友
Family and friends

By the end of this lesson, you should be able to:

- describe your family and ask about someone else's family
- ask and respond to questions regarding one's occupation
- use the present continuous tense
- ask after someone
- recognize and write more characters

Dialogue 1

Jiǎngjiang nǐ jiā de qíngkuàng 讲讲你家的情况
Tell me about your family (CD1; 36)

John has just met a Chinese lady, Yingli, when cycling on the city wall in Xi'an. They soon start to chat. Yingli has told John about her family and now she is asking John about his family . . .

YĪNGLÌ	Yuēhàn, gāi nǐ jiǎngjiang nǐ jiā de qíngkuàng le.
JOHN	Hǎo ba. (*He gets a photo out of his wallet*) Zhè shì wǒ tàitài, Xiùwén. Tā shì Zhōngguórén.
YĪNGLÌ	Zhēn de? Tā hěn piāoliang. Tā hái zài gōngzuò ma?
JOHN	Tā bù gōngzuò le. Wǒmen dōu tuìxiū le.
YĪNGLÌ	Zhè liǎng ge shì bú shì nǐmende háizi?
JOHN	Shì de. Tāmen yǒu Zhōngwén míngzì. Zhè shì wǒmende érzi, jiào Dàyǒng. Zhè shì wǒmende nǚ'ér, Měifāng.
YĪNGLÌ	Dàyǒng zài shàng zhōng xué ma?

JOHN	Bù, tā yǐjīng shì dà xuéshēng le!
YĪNGLÌ	Shì ma? Tā xué shénme zhuānyè?
JOHN	Xīnlǐ xué.
YĪNGLÌ	Hěn yǒu yìsi.
JOHN	Měifāng yǐjing jiéhūn le. Zhè shì tā zhàngfu, Zhāng Jīng . . .

YĪNGLÌ	约翰，该你讲讲你家的情况了。
JOHN	好吧。（...）这是我太太，秀文。她是中国人。
YĪNGLÌ	真的？她很漂亮。她还在工作吗？
JOHN	她不工作了。我们都退休了。
YĪNGLÌ	这两个是不是你们的孩子？
JOHN	是的。他们有中文名字。这是我们的儿子，叫大勇。这是我们的女儿，美芳。
YĪNGLÌ	大勇在上中学吗？
JOHN	不，他已经是大学生了！
YĪNGLÌ	是吗？他学什么专业？
JOHN	心理学。
YĪNGLÌ	很有意思。
JOHN	美芳已经结婚了。这是她丈夫，张京...

YINGLI	*It's your turn to tell me about your family, John.*
JOHN	*OK. (. . .) This is my wife, Xiuwen. She is Chinese.*

YINGLI	*Really? She is very beautiful. Is she still working?*
JOHN	*No, she no longer works. Both of us have retired.*
YINGLI	*Are these two your children?*
JOHN	*Yes. They have Chinese names. This is our son, Dayong, and this is our daughter, Meifang.*
YINGLI	*Is Dayong at secondary school?*
JOHN	*No. He is already a university student.*
YINGLI	*Is that so? What subject does he study?*
JOHN	*Psychology.*
YINGLI	*That's very interesting.*
JOHN	*Meifang is already married. This is her husband, Zhang Jing . . .*

(CD1; 35)

Vocabulary

Yuēhàn	约翰	John
gāi . . . le	该 . . . 了	it is . . . turn to/it is time to . . .
jiǎngjiang	讲讲	to tell/talk about
jiā	家	family
qíngkuàng	情况	situation
tàitai	太太	wife/Mrs
piāoliang	漂亮	to be beautiful/beautiful
dōu	都	both; all
tuìxiū	退休	to retire; to be retired
háizi	孩子	children
míngzì	名字	name
wǒmende	我们的	our; ours
érzi	儿子	son
nǚ'ér	女儿	daughter
zài	在	[grammar word, see Note 9]
shàng	上	to go to; to attend
zhōng xué	中学	secondary/school
dà xuéshēng	大学生	university student [*lit.* 'big school student']

xué	学	to learn/to study
zhuānyè	专业	subject/major
xīnlǐxué	心理学	psychology
yǒuyìsi	有意思	interesting
zhàngfu	丈夫	husband
Xiùwén/Dàyǒng/	秀文/大勇/	[personal names]
Měifāng/Zhāng Jīng	美芳/张京	

Notes on Dialogue 1

■ 1 Kinship terms

Kinship terms in the Chinese language are more complicated than in English. In addition to those terms in the dialogue, below are some other frequently used kinship terms:

Chinese	*English*
bàba	dad/father
gēge	elder brother
jiějie	elder sister
dìdi	younger brother
mèimei	younger sister
nǎinai	grandmother (on father's side)
yéye	grandfather (on father's side)
shūshu	uncle (on father's side)
gūgu	aunt (on father's side)
wàipó/lǎolao	grandmother (on mother's side)
wàigōng/lǎoye	grandfather (on mother's side)
jiùjiu	uncle (on mother's side)
ā'yí	aunt (on mother's side)

Note that the repeated words do not carry any tones. The above terms can be used both to refer to someone and to address someone. For example:

<u>Wǒde *māma*</u> shì zhōng xué lǎoshī.
term of reference
My mother is a secondary-school teacher.

Xièxie nǐ, *gēge*.

term of address

Thank you, elder brother.

If you have more than one elder brother, say three, they are called and referred to as:

dà gē (*lit.* 'big brother')   the eldest brother
èr gē   the second eldest brother
sān gē   the third eldest brother

The third elder brother, if you have only three, can also be called and referred to as **xiǎo gē** (little elder brother). The same principle applies to other kinship terms such as **jiějie** (elder sister). However, one usually calls one's younger sister(s) or brother(s) by their first names instead of **mèimei** or **dìdi**.

■ 2 Use of **gāi . . . le**

Colloquially, if you wish to say 'It's somebody's turn', use the construction **gāi** + personal pronoun + **le**. For example:

Gāi wǒ le.   *It's my turn.*

A sentence can be inserted between **gāi** and **le** to indicate that it is already somebody's turn to do something. For example:

Gāi **wǒ zuòfàn** *le.*   *It's my turn* to cook.
Gāi **tā yóuyǒng** *le.*   *It's her turn* to swim.

■ 3 Use of **qíngkuàng**

Words like **qíngkuàng** (situation/present condition), which are very vague in meaning, are often used in Chinese to express the English equivalents of 'yourself', 'about', 'things', etc. For example:

Qǐng gàosu wǒ nǐ tàitai de *qíngkuàng*.
Please tell me *about* your wife.

Qíngkuàng **bù hǎo.**
Things are not good.

■ 4 Omission of de from **wǒde, nǐde** and **tāde**

The word **de** is most likely to be omitted from **wǒde** (my), **nǐde** (your), **tāde** (his/her), etc. if the noun that follows it is a kinship term. However, if one-syllable adjectives such as **xiǎo**, **lǎo** are used before the noun, **de** cannot be omitted. For example:

> **Wǒ tàitai bú huì shuō Yīngwén.**
> My wife can't speak English.

> **Wǒde xiǎo dìdi hěn cōngming.**
> My little brother is very clever.

■ 5 Titles used to refer to one's spouse

In mainland China, the term **àiren** (lit. 'love person') is used both in spoken and written Chinese to refer to both 'husband' and 'wife'. The formal term for 'husband' is **zhàngfu** and 'wife' is **qīzi**. The terms **tàitai** and **xiānsheng** can mean 'Mrs' and 'Mr' in one context and 'wife' and 'husband' in another context (**xiānsheng** can also be used to refer to one's teacher). In Hong Kong, Taiwan and other international Chinese communities, the terms **tàitai** and **xiānsheng** are widely used to mean 'wife' and 'husband'. Since most married Chinese women keep their maiden names, it is thus inappropriate to use **tàitai** (Mrs) to address a married woman (see Note 2 of Lesson 1 for other titles).

■ 6 Construction . . . **bù** . . . **le**

The construction . . . **bù** + verb + **le** conveys the meanings of '. . . no longer/not . . . any more'. Often, the verbs being negated are verbs indicating habitual behaviour. For example:

> **Tā tàitai bù gōngzuò le.**
> His wife no longer works.

> **Wǒ bù xiǎng qù Zhōngguó le.**
> I don't want to go to China any more.

■ 7 Use of **dōu**

This word, always placed after the pronoun, can convey the meanings of 'both' or 'all' depending on the context. For example:

Tāmen *dōu* xiǎng xiān chī wǔfàn.
They *all* want to have lunch first.

Wǒ hé wǒ zhàngfu *dōu* tuìxiū le.
Lit. I and my husband both have been retired.
Both my husband and I are retired.

To say 'none of us . . .', or 'neither . . .', simply add the negation word before the verb:

Tāmen *dōu bù* xiǎng xiān chī wǔfàn.
None of them wants to have lunch first.

Wǒ hé wǒ zhàngfu *dōu bù* gōngzuò le.
Neither I *nor* my husband works any more.

■ 8 Construction **shì bú shì**

An alternative to the . . . **shì** . . . **ma?** question is . . . **shì bú shì** . . . ?
(see Note 13 of Lesson 4). For example:

Nǐ *shì* Wáng Lín *ma?* *becomes* **Nǐ *shì bú shì* Wáng Lín?** (Are you Wang Lin?)

■ 9 Continuous tense particle **zài**

In Chinese, the continuous tense, i.e. 'somebody *is/was doing* something', is indicated by the grammar word **zài** (or **zhèngzài**), which is placed before the verb. Depending on the context, sentences with **zài** or **zhèngzài** can refer either to something which is happening at present (habitual activity) or to something which is happening at the very moment when the sentence is uttered. For example:

Nǐ bàba hái *zài* gōngzuò ma?   Is your father still working?

HABITUAL

Wǒ *zhèngzài* chī wǔfàn.   I am having my lunch.

MOMENTARY

However, you must use **zài**, not **zhèngzài**, in the following two cases:

(a)   when the negating word **bù** is used;
(b)   when an adverb such as **hái** (still) is used.

For example:

Tā *bú* zài chī wǎnfàn.
He is *not* having his supper.

Xiǎo Wáng *hái* zài yóuyǒng ma?
Is Xiao Wang *still* there swimming?

■ 10 Use of the verb **shàng**

The verb **shàng** (to go to) is interchangeable with **qù** (to go to) in most cases. The main difference is that **shàng** is more colloquial and informal. For example:

A: **Nǐ *shàng/qù* nǎr?**   Where are you *going*?
B: ***Shàng/Qù* cāntīng.**   Dining-room.

However, **shàng** must be used in the following:

shàng xué   to *go to* school (any school)
shàng jiē   to *go to* the town
              (*lit.* 'go to the street')

When **le** is used after **shàng xué** or **shàng xiǎoxué**, it means 'to have started school':

A: **Nǐde érzi *shàng (xiǎo)xué* le ma?**   B: **Méi shàng.**
     Has your son *started school* yet?   Not yet.

Let us see the difference between **shàng** and **qù** in the following sentences:

Zhēnní yǐjing *shàng* xiǎoxué *le*.
Jane *has started* primary school.

Zhēnní yǐjing *qù* xiǎoxué *le*.
Jane *has gone to* the primary school. [She may be a pupil, a teacher there or she may have gone there for a visit.]

You may have noticed that when the words **xiǎo** (small), **zhōng** (middle/medium) and **dà** (big/large) precede **xué** (to study), we get:

xiǎo xué   primary school
zhōng xué   secondary school/middle school
dàxué   university

If we add the word **shēng** (i.e. one who studies) to **xué**, we have the noun **xuéshēng** (student). If we add **xiǎo**, **zhōng** and **dà** to **xuéshēng**, we have: **xiǎo xuéshēng** (primary school pupil), **zhōng xuéshēng** (secondary school student) and **dà xuéshēng** (university student). Note that **shēng** can be pronounced with a neutral tone.

■ 11 To negate **yǒu yìsi**

To negate **yǒu yìsi**, the negation word **méi** must be used. You can say either **méi yǒu yìsi** or **méi yìsi** (with **yǒu** omitted) to mean 'to be not interesting' or 'to be boring'. If adverbs such as **hěn** (very) are used, (a) they must be placed before the negation word; and (b) **yǒu** is always omitted. For example:

> **Zhè běn shū *méi yǒu yìsi.***   This book *is not interesting.*
> **Zhè ge rén *hěn méi yìsi.***   This person *is very boring.*

Exercises

Exercise 1

Match the Chinese kinship terms on the left with their English equivalents on the right:

(1) **jiějie**	(5) **mèimei**	(a) elder brother		(e) grandfather
(2) **dìdi**	(6) **ā'yí**	(b) elder sister		(f) grandmother
(3) **gēge**	(7) **nǎinai**	(c) younger sister		(g) uncle
(4) **yéye**	(8) **shūshu**	(d) younger brother		(h) aunt

Exercise 2

Change the following sentences into the present continuous tense using **zài** and then translate them into English:

(a) Wǒ māma hē kāfēi.
(b) Yīngméi chī zǎofàn ma?
(c) Tā bù yóuyǒng.
(d) Nǐ bàba gōngzuò ma?

Exercise 3

Fill in the blanks using **qù** or **shàng**:

(a) Nǐ àirén (*spouse*) _____ nǎr le?
(b) Wǒmende érzi zài _____ dàxué.
(c) Tāmen xià ge xīngqī _____ Zhōngguó.
(d) Nǐde nǚ'ér _____ xiǎo xué le ma?

Exercise 4

Answer the following questions in Chinese regarding Dialogue 1:

(a) Yuēhàn jiéhūn le ma?
(b) Shéi shì Yuēhàn de tàitai?
(c) Yuēhàn de tàitai shì nǎ guó rén?
(d) Yuēhàn hé ('*and*') tāde tàitai yǒu háizi ma?
(e) Tāmende háizi jiào shénme?
(f) Dàyǒng shì bú shì zhōng xuésheng?
(g) Zhāng Jīng shì shéi?

Exercise 5

Translate the following sentences into Chinese:

(a) They have two children – a daughter and a son.
(b) Both children have Chinese names.
(c) We have all retired.
(d) They no longer work.
(e) My younger brother hasn't started school yet.
(f) Going to school is very interesting.
(g) What subject do you study?
(h) Please say something about your husband.
(i) It is my turn to speak Chinese.

Characters

Let us look at the following two characters that appeared in Dialogue 1:

家   **jiā**   family, home
都   **dōu**   both, all

Character analysis	Head component and its meaning	Stroke order	English
宀 + 豕 **shì**	宀 (roof)	家 丶 丶 宀 宁 宁 宁 豕 豕 家 家	home, family
者 **zhě** + 阝	阝 (city)	都 一 十 土 耂 耂 者 者 者 者 都都	both, all; capital

(Unexplained components - 豕 shì: pig; 者 zhě: person)

These are two quite interesting characters. It is only a home (家) if there are pigs under your roof (a sign of wealth in the old days)! The character 都 was originally pronounced 'dū', meaning 'capital'. Hence the head component of city makes sense.

Exercise 6

(1) Draw square boxes and write the above two characters in the right stroke order.

(2) Check the Vocabulary on pages 95–6 and list the characters that share the following components. Then learn to write these characters.

(a) 忄   (b) 讠   (c) 氵   (d) 辶

(e) 心   (f) 王   (g) 亻

Dialogue 2

Nǐ gàn shénme gōngzuò? 你干什么工作？
What do you do? (CD1; 38)

Miao Lan and Wu Xiaohong are good friends. When Miao Lan is on a business trip in Shenzhen, Wu Xiaohong, who lives in Guangzhou, makes a special trip to Shenzhen to meet Miao Lan.

MIÁO LÁN	Xiǎo Wú, tīngshuō nǐ huàn gōngzuò le.
	Nǐ xiànzài gàn shénme gōngzuò?
WÚ XIǍOHÓNG	Dāng dǎoyóu. Wǒ hěn xǐhuān zhè ge gōngzuò.

MIÁO LÁN	Zài nǎ jiā gōngsī?
WÚ XIǍOHÓNG	Guǎngzhōu Lǚyóu Jú.
MIÁO LÁN	Tài hǎo le.
WÚ XIǍOHÓNG	Nǐ fùmǔ de shēntǐ hǎo ma?
MIÁO LÁNn	Hěn hǎo, xièxie.
WÚ XIǍOHÓNG	Tāmen xiànzài zhù zài nǎr?
MIÁO LÁN	Zài Shànghǎi. Nǐ bàba, māma hái zhù zài Guǎngzhōu ma?
WÚ XIǍOHÓNG	Shì de. Tāmen cháng shuōqǐ nǐ. Nǐ zài Shēnzhèn dāi jǐ tiān?
MIÁO LÁN	Kěxī zhǐ dāi sì tiān. Kǒngpà wǒ zhè cì méi yǒu shíjiān qù kàn tāmen. Qǐng wèn tāmen hǎo.
WÚ XIǍOHÓNG	Wǒ huì de.

MIÁO LÁN	小吴，听说你换工作了。你现在干什么工作？
WÚ XIǍOHÓNG	当导游。我很喜欢这个工作。
MIÁO LÁN	在哪家公司？
WÚ XIǍOHÓNG	广州旅游局。
MIÁO LÁN	太好了。
WÚ XIǍOHÓNG	你父母的身体好吗？
MIÁO LÁN	很好，谢谢。
WÚ XIǍOHÓNG	他们现在住在哪儿？
MIÁO LÁN	在上海。你爸爸、妈妈还住在广州吗？
WÚ XIǍOHÓNG	是的。他们常说起你。你在深圳待几天？
MIÁO LÁN	可惜只待四天。恐怕我这次没有时间去看他们。请问他们好。
WÚ XIǍOHÓNG	我会的。

MIAO LAN	*Xiao Wu, I've heard that you've changed jobs. What job are you doing now?*
WU XIAOHONG	*(I've) become a tourist guide. I like this job very much.*
MIAO LAN	*In which company?*
WU XIAOHONG	*Guangzhou Tourist Bureau.*
MIAO LAN	*Wonderful.*
WU XIAOHONG	*Are your parents in good health?*
MIAO LAN	*Quite well, thank you.*
WU XIAOHONG	*Where do they live now?*

MIAO LAN	*In Shanghai. Are your mother and father still living in Guangzhou?*
WU XIAOHONG	*Yes, they are. They always talk about you. How many days are you staying in Shenzhen for?*
MIAO LAN	*It's a pity that I'm only staying for four days. I'm afraid I don't have time to go to see them this time. Please send them my regards.*
WU XIAOHONG	*I will.*

(CD1; 37)

Vocabulary

Wú	吴	[a common surname]
tīngshuō	听说	to have heard [*lit.* 'hearsay']
huàn	换	to change
gàn	干	to do
dāng	当	to become
dǎoyóu	导游	tourist guide
xǐhuān	喜欢	to like
zài	在	at/in/to be at/to be in
jiā	家	[measure word]
lǚyóu	旅游	tourism, to travel
jú	局	bureau/office
fùmǔ	父母	parents
shēntǐ	身体	health
zhù	住	to live
Shànghǎi	上海	Shanghai
bàba	爸爸	father/dad
Guǎngzhōu	广州	[place name]
cháng	常	often/frequent
shuōqǐ	说起	to mention/talk about
Shēnzhèn	深圳	[place name]
dāi	待	to stay

tiān	天	day
kǒngpà	恐怕	I'm afraid . . .
kěxī	可惜	pity that . . .
zhǐ	只	only
zhè cì	这次	this time
kàn	看	to see/to visit
huì de	会 . . . 的	will

Notes on Dialogue 2

■ 12 Nǐ gàn shénme gōngzuò?

If you want to ask someone what job he/she is doing, you say: **Nǐ gàn shénme gōngzuò?** (*lit.* 'You do what job?'). In a context where the conversation centres around jobs, the above sentence can be translated as 'What do you do?' However, if you want to know literally what someone is doing at the very moment of your speech, you say **Nǐ zài gàn shénme?** (What are you doing?). Look at the different answers to these questions:

A: **Nǐ gàn shénme gōngzuò?**   What do you do?
B: **Wǒ shì xiǎo xué lǎoshī.**   I'm a primary school teacher.

A: **Línlin, nǐ zài gàn shénme?**   What are you doing, Linlin?
B: **Wǒ zài chī wǎnfàn.**   I'm having my dinner.

Here are some useful terms when describing jobs:

yīshēng	doctor	jìzhě	journalist
hùshi	nurse	mìshu	secretary
gōngchéngshī	engineer	kuàiji	accountant
yīnyuèjiā	musician	chúshī	chef
zuòjiā	writer	jǐngchá	police officer
yǎnyuán	actor/actress		

■ 13 Use of zài

In terms of character representation, this **zài** is the same as the continuous tense indicator **zài**, which must be placed before the verb (see Note 9 above). However, this **zài** can mean 'to be at/in' or simply 'at/in' and is always placed before the noun in affirmative sentences or before the question words in questions. For example:

Wǒ fùmǔ zài Zhōngguó. My parents *are in* China.
noun

Nǐ zhù zài nǎr? Where do you live?
question word

Most verbs follow prepositional phrases. Exceptions to this rule are the verbs **zhù** (to live) and **dāi** (to stay), which can be followed by or preceded by prepositional phrases:

Tā jiějie zhù zài Xī'ān.
verb prepositional phrase
Her elder sister lives *in Xi'an*.

Tā jiějie zài Xī'ān zhù.
prepositional phrase verb
Her elder sister lives *in Xi'an*.

To negate the first sentence above, put the negation word **bù** in front of the verb **zhù**, and to negate the second sentence above, put **bù** in front of **zài**:

Tā jiějie bú zhù zài Xī'ān.
Her elder sister *does not* live in Xi'an.

Tā jiějie bú zài Xī'ān zhù.
Her elder sister *does not* live in Xi'an.

In English, you say *I work for ICI*, and in Chinese, you can say:

Wǒ zài ICI gōngzuò.
Lit. I at ICI work.

■ 14 More on measure words

So far, we have learnt two measure words: **gè** before people, swimming pools, restaurants, etc.; and **bēi** before drinks. In Dialogue 2, we have a new measure word, **jiā**, which is often used before companies, organizations, shops, restaurants, etc. For example:

Zhè jiā fàndiàn hěn hǎo.
This hotel is very good.

Wǒ bú zài zhè _jiā_ gōngsī gōngzuò.
I'm not working for this company.

The noun **tiān** (day) is one of the few exceptions to the rule of using measure words between numbers and nouns. No measure word is needed between a number and **tiān**. Thus we say, for example, **sān tiān** (three days) _not_ **sān gè tiān**. When **sān tiān** is used in sentences, it can mean '_for_ three days'. For example:

Wǒ zài Běijīng dāi le _sān tiān_.
I stayed in Beijing _for three days_.

■ 15 Showing concern over someone else's parents

It is very common among Chinese people to enquire about each other's parents, especially their health. The commonly used expression is **Nǐ fùmǔ de shēntǐ hǎo ma?** (_lit._ 'Your parents' health is good?'). Sometimes, **de** is omitted.

■ 16 More on question word **jǐ**

We saw this question word previously in Lesson 4 when it was used to ask about the time. This question word can also be used to ask other number-related questions. However, you must remember that whenever this question word is used, the questioner expects a small number (less than twenty) in the reply. For example:

A: **Nǐ zài Běijīng dāi _jǐ_ tiān?**
How many days are you staying in Beijing for?

B: **Liǎng tiān.**
Two days.

If A expects B to stay in Beijing for two years, for instance, he/she has to ask the question in a different way. Let us look at another example:

A: **Nǐmende gōngsī yǒu _jǐ_ gè Měiguórén?**
How many Americans are there in your company?

B: **Jiǔ ge.**
Nine.

■ 17 Use of **cháng**

This adverb, meaning 'often' or 'frequently', is always placed before the verb, and it is often repeated like some other one-syllable words. For example:

Nǐ *cháng* yóuyǒng ma?	Do you *often* swim?
Lǐ Fāng *chángcháng* chūmén.	Li Fang is *frequently* away.
Wǒ bù *cháng* hē kāfēi.	I don't *often* drink coffee.

■ 18 Use of **yǒu shíjiān** and **méi yǒu shíjiān**

The Chinese equivalent of *I have time to swim* is **Wǒ *yǒu shíjiān* yóuyǒng**. And the Chinese equivalent of *I don't have time to swim* is **Wǒ *méi yǒu shíjiān* yóuyǒng** or **Wǒ *méi shíjiān* yóuyǒng**. Let us look at some more examples:

A: **Nǐ jīntiān wǎnshang *yǒu shíjiān* ma?**
 Do you *have time* tonight?

B: **Yǒu (shíjiān).**
 Yes, I do.

Xiǎo Wáng *méi shíjiān* lái kàn nǐ.
Xiao Wang *doesn't have time* to come to see you.

■ 19 Verb **kàn**

In Chinese, for anything that is seen, we use the verb **kàn**. Thus you can say **kàn péngyou** (to visit/see friends), **kàn shū** (to read a book), **kàn zhàopiān** (to look at the photos), **kàn diànyǐng** (to see a film), **kàn diànshì** (to watch television) and **kàn zúqiú** (to watch the football).

■ 20 Construction **Qǐng wèn . . . hǎo**

The phrase **Qǐng wèn** + somebody + **hǎo** literally means 'Please ask somebody good', which can be broadly translated as 'Please say hello to somebody' or 'Please give somebody my regards'. For example:

Qǐng *wèn* nǐ tàitai *hǎo*.	*Please say hello* to your wife.
Qǐng *wèn* nǐ fùmǔ *hǎo*.	*Please give* your parents *my regards*.

■ 21 Another use of **huì**

The **huì** which we saw earlier in Lesson 2 means 'to be able to' or 'can'. Another meaning of **huì** is to express one's willingness to do something or to predict that something is likely to happen. When **huì** means 'will', **de** follows it in short replies or occurs at the end of affirmative sentences. For example:

A: **Nǐ *huì* jiàndào Liú Xiǎoméi ma?**
Will you see Liu Xiaomei?

B: ***Huì de.***
Yes, I *will*.

Tā *huì* lái chī wǎnfàn *de*.
He *will* come for dinner.

Exercises

Exercise 7

Translate the following sentences into English, differentiating between **zài** ('to be at/in', or 'at/in') and **zài** (continuous tense indicator):

(a) Tā bú zhù zài Běijīng.
(b) Nǐ fùmǔ hái zài gōngzuò ma?
(c) Mǎ Lān zài chī zǎofàn.
(d) Wáng Lín zài Běijīng Fàndiàn gōngzuò.

Exercise 8

Change the following statements into questions using **jǐ** and paying particular attention to the underlined words:

Example: **Běijīng Fàndiàn yǒu <u>sān</u> ge cāntīng.** → **Běijīng Fàndiàn yǒu *jǐ* ge cāntīng?**

(a) Lǎo Wáng yǒu <u>sān</u> ge háizi.
(b) Wǒ zài Běijīng Fàndiàn zhù le <u>wǔ</u> tiān.
(c) Tā hē le <u>liǎng</u> bēi kāfēi.
(d) Lǐ Píng yǒu <u>sì</u> ge gēge.

Exercise 9

Based on what we have learnt in this lesson, what do you say on the following occasions in Chinese:

(a) You want to ask your Chinese friend if she has time to go swimming.
(b) Your Chinese friend wants to invite you to a party but unfortunately you don't have time, so you apologize, saying . . .
(c) You want to ask a Chinese person what job he does.
(d) You want to ask your Chinese friend to pass on your regards to her parents.

Exercise 10

Fill in the blanks with appropriate measure words if necessary:

(a) Wǒ zài Shànghǎi dāi le shí _____ tiān.
(b) Zhè liǎng _____ rén hěn méi yìsi.
(c) Nǐ zài nǎ _____ gōngsī gōngzuò?
(d) Wǒmende dàxué yǒu yī _____ yóuyǒng chí.
(e) Tā hē le sān _____ kāfēi.

Exercise 11

Translate the following into Chinese:

(a) I like my work very much.
(b) I want to go to visit my parents.
(c) Will he come to visit me?
(d) Fang Shu works for the Beijing Tourist Bureau.
(e) Where do you live?

Characters

Let us first recognize the following 3 important city names:

上	海		广	州		深	圳

shàng hǎi **guǎng zhōu** **shēn zhèn**

Literally, 上海 means 'above sea'; 广州 means 'extensive region' as the character 州 (**zhōu**) is an old name for an administrative region and 深圳 means 'deep ditch in the field' as it used to be a large paddy field.

Let us now look at the following two characters that appeared in Dialogue 2:

换 **huàn** to change
看 **kàn** to see

Character analysis	**Head component and its meaning**	**Stroke order**	**English**
扌+ 奂 **huàn**	扌(hand)	换 一 十 扌 扌 扩 扚 扚 扚 换 换	to change
𠂒 + 目	目 (eye)	看 一 二 三 手 手 看 看 看 看	to see

(Unexplained components - 奂 **huàn** acts as a phonetic here; 𠂒 comes from 手 **shǒu**: hand)

To change things, you need your hand, hence the hand head component (扌); and to see things, you put your hand over your eyes (imagine you are trying to see something in the distance under the bright sun!).

Exercise 12

(1) Draw some square boxes and write the above two characters in the right stroke order.
(2) Re-arrange the following 8 characters so that you get the following 4 city names: Beijing, Guangzhou, Shenzhen, Shanghai.

(a) 海 (b) 北 (c) 上 (d) 州
(e) 京 (f) 圳 (g) 广 (h) 深

Reading/listening comprehension

(CD1; 40)

I Read the following dialogue first, and then answer the questions in English. If you have access to the audio material, listen first, and then answer the questions.

Vocabulary

fānyì	translator/interpreter	**àiren**	spouse [*lit.* 'love person']
míngtiān	tomorrow	**lǎoshī**	teacher [*lit.* 'old master']

Yang Ning and Gu Liang, who are very good friends, have not seen each other for a long time. They run into each other, and . . .

YÁNG NÍNG	Hǎo jiǔ bú jiàn, Gù Liáng. Tīngshuō nǐ huàn gōngzuò le.
GÙ LIÁNG	Shì de.
YÁNG NÍNG	Shénme gōngzuò?
GÙ LIÁNG	Zài Běijīng Lǚyóu jú dāng fānyì.
YÁNG NÍNG	Yǒu yìsi ma?
GÙ LIÁNG	Tǐng yǒu yìsi. Nǐ zěnme yàng, Yáng Níng?
YÁNG NÍNG	Wǒ jiéhūn le.
GÙ LIÁNG	Zhēnde? Nǐ àiren gàn shénme gōngzuò?
YÁNG NÍNG	Tā shì xiǎo xué lǎoshī. Nǐ xiǎng rènshi tā ma?
GÙ LIÁNG	Dāngrán xiǎng.
YÁNG NÍNG	Jīntiān wǎnshang nǐ yǒu shíjiān ma?
GÙ LIÁNG	Kǒngpà méi yǒu.
YÁNG NÍNG	Míngtiān wǎnshang ne?
GÙ LIÁNG	Míngtiān wǎnshang yǒu shíjiān.
YÁNG NÍNG	Nàme, nǐ lái wǒmen jiā chī wǎnfàn.
GÙ LIÁNG	Tài hǎo le. Xièxie.

QUESTIONS

(1) What is Gu Liang's current occupation?
(2) Does Gu Liang like his new job?
(3) What is the surprise news from Yang Ning?
(4) What does Yang Ning's wife do as a job?
(5) When and where is Gu Liang going to meet Yang Ning's wife?

 (CD1; 41)

II Underline the words/phrase you hear

(1) jiéhūn   (2) lǚyóu   (3) shíjiàn
     jīnhūn   lǜyè   shíjiān
(4) gānliàn   (5) dàxuě
     guǎnlǐ   dàxué

Lesson Six
Rìqī hé tiānqì 日期和天气
The date and the weather

> By the end of this lesson, you should be able to:
>
> - say the days of the week, dates, months and years
> - use time expressions appropriately
> - find out information regarding dates and days
> - use the question words **shénme shíhou**, **duō jiǔ** and **háishì**
> - make simple comments on the weather
> - recognize and write more characters

Dialogue 1

Jīntiān shì xīngqī jǐ? 今天是星期几?
What day is it today? (CD1; 43)

Below is a dialogue in a classroom between a teacher and her pupils in a primary school in China.

TEACHER	Tóngxuémen hǎo!
ALL PUPILS	Lǎoshī hǎo!
TEACHER	Jīntiān shì xīngqī jǐ?
PUPIL A	Jīntiān shì xīngqī'èr.
TEACHER	Yī ge xīngqī yǒu jǐ tiān?
PUPIL B	Yī ge xīngqī yǒu qī tiān.
TEACHER	Yī nián yǒu jǐ ge yuè?
PUPIL C	Yī nián yǒu shí'èr ge yuè.
TEACHER	Míngtiān shì jǐ hào?

PUPIL D   Míngtiān shì èrlínglíngbā nián yīyuè shíbā hào.
TEACHER   Yī nián yǒu jǐ ge jìjié? Tāmen shì shénme?
PUPIL E   Sì ge jìjié. Tāmen shì chūntiān, xiàtiān, qiūtiān hé
            dōngtiān.

TEACHER   同学们好！
ALL PUPILS 老师好！
TEACHER   今天是星期几？
PUPIL A   今天是星期二。
TEACHER   一个星期有几天？
PUPIL B   一个星期有七天。
TEACHER   一年有几个月？
PUPIL C   一年有十二个月。
TEACHER   明天是几号？
PUPIL D   明天是二零零八年一月十八号。
TEACHER   一年有几个季节？它们是什么？
PUPIL E   四个季节。它们是春天、夏天、秋天和冬天。

  (CD1; 42)

Vocabulary

tóngxuémen	同学们	pupils, students
lǎoshī	老师	teacher
jīntiān	今天	today
xīngqī'èr	星期二	Tuesday

nián	年	year
yuè	月	month
míngtiān	明天	tomorrow
hào	号	date
èrlínglíngbā	二零零八	2008
yīyuè	一月	January
jìjié	季节	season
tāmen	它们	they [when referring to non-human things]
chūntiān	春天	spring
xiàtiān	夏天	summer
qiūtiān	秋天	autumn
hé	和	and
dōngtiān	冬天	winter

Notes on Dialogue 1

■ 1 Classroom greetings

In Chinese schools, whether primary schools or universities, pupils and students all call their teachers **lǎoshī** rather than Mr or Miss (see Note 2 of Lesson 1). The teacher may address the whole class using the term **tóngxuémen** (pupils, students). The suffix **men** is to make this plural. Note this can only be added to a few nouns.

■ 2 Days of the week (CD1; 44)

To form the words for the first six days of the week, put **xīngqī** in front of the numbers from 'one' to 'six'. The word **xīngqī** literally means 'week' when used by itself but for our purposes here we can think of it as meaning 'weekday':

Chinese	*English*
xīngqī*yī*	Monday
xīngqī*'èr*	Tuesday
xīngqī*sān*	Wednesday
xīngqī*sì*	Thursday
xīngqī*wǔ*	Friday
xīngqī*liù*	Saturday

'Sunday' is **xīngqīrì** or **xīngqītiān**, **rì** being a formal term for 'the sun' and **tiān** meaning 'day' or 'sky'.

■ 3 Months of the year

The word for 'month' is **yuè**. Simply place numbers from 'one' to 'twelve' in front of **yuè**:

Chinese	English	Chinese	English
yīyuè	January	**qīyuè**	July
èryuè	February	**bāyuè**	August
sānyuè	March	**jiǔyuè**	September
sìyuè	April	**shíyuè**	October
wǔyuè	May	**shíyīyuè**	November
liùyuè	June	**shí'èryuè**	December

■ 4 Year and date

If you want to express a particular year, simply say the numbers individually. However, remember to use the word **nián** (year) at the end to differentiate the year from other numbers. For example:

1994   **yījiǔjiǔsì** *nián*   2010   **èrlíngyīlíng** *nian*

The order for a date including month and year is the reverse of that used in English. The date is thus spoken in the following order: year, month and then day. Also the term **hào** or **rì** (the former is the spoken form and the latter the written form for 'date') must be used. For example:

27 December 2001   **èrlínglíngyī nián shí'èryuè èrshíqī** *hào/rì*
10 February 1994   **yījiǔjiǔsì nián èryuè shí** *hào/rì*

■ 5 Absence of prepositions in front of time phrases

In English, prepositions such as *at*, *in*, *on* or *for* must be put in front of the time, the month, the day, the date and expressions of duration. In Chinese, it is all very simple because such words are not needed in front of time phrases. For example:

Wǒ māma *xīngqīsān* **lái kàn wǒmen.**
My mother is coming to see us *on Wednesday*.

Xīnháng *liùyuè qī hào* kāishǐ gōngzuò.
Xinhang starts working *on 7 June*.

Note that in the above two sentences, both time phrases refer to a particular day or date, so they are put in front of the verb. If the time phrase refers to a period of time, it is usually put after the verb. For example:

Wǒ zài Lúndūn <u>zhù le</u> *liǎng nián*.
verb
I lived in London *for two years*.

Tā zài Běijīng <u>xué le</u> *bā ge yuè* Zhōngwén.
verb
He learnt Chinese in Beijing *for eight months*.

■ 6 Use of measure word **gè** before years, months and weeks

In Note 14 of Lesson 5, we saw the omission of the measure word **gè** in between the number and the noun **tiān** (day). The same principle applies to **nián** (year), i.e. there is no need to use measure words between the number and the noun **nián**. For example:

Wǒ xué le *sān nián* Yīngwén.　　I learnt English for *three years*.

However, you *must* use the measure word **gè** in between the number and the noun **yuè** (month). For example: **sān *ge* yuè** (three months) as opposed to **sān yuè** (March). As for **xīngqī** (week), you can either use **gè** or drop it. Both usages are correct:

<blockquote>

Tā zài Běijīng dāi le *sān ge xīngqī*.
or　**Tā zài Běijīng dāi le *sān xīngqī*.**
He/she stayed in Beijing for *three weeks*.
</blockquote>

■ 7 More on the question word **jǐ**

When **jǐ** is used to ask the current day (or day in the near future) and the date, it means 'which' rather than 'how many'. For example:

<blockquote>

Jīntiān shì xīngqī　*jǐ*?
Lit.　Today　is　weekday which?
　　What day is it today?
</blockquote>

>   **Jīntiān shì jǐ   hào?**
> *Lit.* Today   is   which date?
>   *What*'s the date today?

The question **Jīntiān shì jǐ hào?** can be replied to with a full answer specifying the year, the month and the date, or by just giving the date, depending on the context:

>   A: **Xià ge xīngqī'èr shì jǐ   hào?**
> *Lit.*   Next   Tuesday   is   which date?
>   What's next Tuesday's date?
>
>   B: **Èrshíwǔ hào.**
>   *25th.*

To ask questions such as 'How many days/weeks/months/seasons . . . ?', the measure word **gè** must be used between the question word **jǐ** and **yué** (month) and **xīngqī** (week), but not **nián** (year) or **tiān** (day). For example:

>   **Yī nián yǒu jǐ *ge*   yuè?**
> *Lit.* A year have how many months?
>   How many months are there in a year?
>
>   **Nǐ xué le *jǐ*   nián Zhōngwén?**
> *Lit.* You learnt how many years Chinese?
>   For *how many years* did you learn Chinese?

■ 8 Use of **hé**

The conjunction word **hé** (and) is never used to link two sentences. When two sentences share the same subject (e.g. 'you', 'I'), the subject is omitted in the second sentence and a comma is used. For example:

Tā jīnnián èrshí suì, shì dà xuésheng.
He is twenty this year *and* he is a university student.

The word **hé** is only used to link two or more than two nouns, pronouns or noun phrases. Even then, it can be omitted. And, if you want to say 'somebody and I', 'I' is usually mentioned first in Chinese. For example:

Wǒ yǒu liǎng ge gēge, yī ge dìdi.
I have two elder brothers and one younger brother.

Wǒ hé Xiǎo Lǐ xǐhuān yóuyǒng, *(hé)* dǎ pīngpāng qiú.
Xiao Li and I like swimming and playing table-tennis.

Exercises

Exercise 1

Look at the following calendars and answer the questions:

(a) Jīntiān shì xīngqī jǐ?

MARCH 2009
29
SUNDAY

(b) Jīntiān shì jǐ yuè jǐ hào?

MAY 2008
1
THURSDAY

(c) Nǐ jǐ hào qù Zhōngguó?

OCTOBER 2008
2
TUESDAY

(d) Nǐ māma xīngqī jǐ lái Táiwān?

JUNE 2009
12
FRIDAY

Exercise 2

Fill in the blanks with the measure word **gè** (or with neutral tone **ge**) when necessary, and then translate the sentences into English:

(a) Xiǎo Fāng zài Shēnzhèn dāi le sān _____ tiān (*three days*).
(b) Wǒ yǒu sān _____ yuè (*three months*).

(c)   Wǒ zhàngfu xiǎng zài Zhōngguó lǚyóu liǎng _____ xīngqī
      (*two weeks*).
(d)   Wǒ dìdi zài Xī'ān gōngzuò le sì _____ nián (*four years*).
(e)   Wáng Dōngpíng yǒu wǔ _____ gēge (*five elder brothers*).
(f)   Bǎoluó xiǎng bā _____ yuè (*August*) qù Táiwān.

Exercise 3

Translate the following sentences from English to Chinese:

(a)   For how many years did Liu Hong live in Guangzhou?
(b)   Tomorrow is Thursday.
(c)   For how many months did David learn Chinese?
(d)   I want to go to China this March.
(e)   What is next Friday's date?
(f)   My husband has two younger brothers and one elder sister.

Dialogue 2

Shénme shíhou . . . ?   什么时候 . . . ?   When . . . ?
(CD1; 46)

Mick is planning to go to Beijing and he wants to find out what
the weather is like. So he is chatting with Li Fang, a Chinese
student who comes from Beijing.

MICK	Lǐ Fāng, Běijīng de dōngtiān lěng ma?
LǏ FĀNG	Fēicháng lěng. Cháng xiàxuě.
MICK	Xiàtiān zěnme yàng?
LǏ FĀNG	Qīyuè hé bāyuè tèbié rè.
MICK	Shénme jìjié zuì hǎo?
LǏ FĀNG	Qiūtiān, shíyuè zuǒyòu. Zěnme? Nǐ dǎsuàn qù Běijīng ma?
MICK	Shì'a.
LǏ FĀNG	Shénme shíhou?
MICK	Jìrán nǐ shuō shíyuè zuì hǎo, wǒ jiù míng nián shíyuè qù.
LǏ FĀNG	Nǐ qù lǚyóu háishì gōngzuò?
MICK	Lǚyóu jiā gōngzuò.
LǏ FĀNG	Nǐ qù duō jiǔ, Mǐkè?
MICK	Lǚyóu liǎng ge xīngqī, gōngzuò sān tiān, yīgòng dàyuē sān ge xīngqī.

MICK	李芳，北京的冬天冷吗？
LǏ FĀNG	非常冷。常下雪。
MICK	夏天怎么样？
LǏ FĀNG	七月和八月特别热。
MICK	什么季节最好?
LǏ FĀNG	秋天，十月左右。怎么？你打算去北京吗？
MICK	是啊。
LǏ FĀNG	什么时候？
MICK	既然你说十月最好，我就明年十月去。
LǏ FĀNG	你去旅游还是工作？
MICK	旅游加工作。
LǏ FĀNG	你去多久，米克？
MICK	旅游两个星期，工作三天，一共大约三个星期。

(CD1; 45)

Vocabulary

Lǐ Fāng	李芳	[personal name]
lěng	冷	to be cold
fēicháng/tèbié	非常/特别	extremely/very
xiàxuě	下雪	to snow
qīyuè	七月	July
bāyuè	八月	August
rè	热	to be hot
zuì	最	most
zuì hǎo	最好	best; you'd better
shíyuè	十月	October
zěnme	怎么	why [see Note 11]
dǎsuàn	打算	to plan
shì'a	是啊	yes
shénme shíhou	什么时候	when
lǚyóu	旅游	to travel/travelling
jìrán . . . jiù . . .	既然... 就 . . .	as . . . then . . .
shuō	说	to say
míng nián	明年	next year

háishì	还是	or [see Note 16]
jiā	加	plus
duō jiǔ	多久	how long
Mǐkè	米克	Mick
yīgòng	一共	altogether
dàyuē	大约	approximately/about

Notes on Dialogue 2

■ 9 Use of **zuì**

In English, the word *most* cannot be put in front of every adjective or adverb (e.g. 'the most difficult' but 'the easiest'). However, in Chinese, the word **zuì**, meaning 'most', can be placed in front of every word or verbal phrase to describe its degree. For example:

Xiǎo Wáng zuì niánqīng.	Xiao Wang is the young*est*.
Zhè běn shū zuì yǒu yìsi.	This book is *most* interesting.
Tā zuì bù xǐhuan zuòfàn.	He dislikes cooking *most*.

■ 10 More on **de** after adjectives

One-syllable adjectives such as **hǎo** (good), **lǎo** (old), **dà** (big), etc. can be put before nouns without using **de**. For example:

hǎo **péngyou**	*good* friend
lǎo **dà xuésheng**	*old* university student
dà **fàndiàn**	*big* hotel

Most two-syllable adjectives such as **piàoliang** (beautiful), **gāoxìng** (happy), etc., when used to modify nouns, require the use of **de** before the noun. For example:

| **gāoxìng** *de* **yī tiān** | happy day |
| **piàoliang** *de* **fàndiàn** | beautiful hotel |

However, once these adjectives (both one-syllable and two-syllable) are modified by adverbs such as **tèbié** (extremely), **hěn** (very), **zuì** (most), etc., **de** must be used in between the adjective and the noun. For example:

zuì **hǎo** *de* **péngyou**	*best* friend
tèbié **dà** *de* **fàndiàn**	*extremely* big hotel
hěn *lǎo* *de* **dà xuésheng**	*very* old university student
fēicháng **piàoliang** *de* **dàyī**	*very* beautiful coat

■ 11 Use of **zěnme**

Although **zěnme** is translated as 'why?' in this context, it is not actually seeking an answer but is used to express surprise. For example:

A: **Māma, zánmen jǐ diǎn chī fàn?**
Mum, what time are we going to eat?

B: *Zěnme*, **nǐ è le ma?**
Why? Are you already hungry?

However, **zěnme** can mean 'how come?', which is weaker than **wèishénme** (why?), which we learnt in Lesson 3. For example:

A: **Nǐ jīntiān zěnme bù gāoxìng?**
How come you aren't happy?

B: **Wǒ yě bù zhīdào.**
I don't know either.

A: **Nǐ *wèishénme* jīntiān bù shàng xué?**
Why are you not going to school today?

B: **Yīnwèi jīntiān shì xīngqītiān.**
Because it's Sunday.

■ 12 Addition of **a**

In spoken Chinese, especially in southern China, **a** is frequently attached to some short expressions. It does not carry any specific meaning but merely adds a touch of informality and friendliness. For example, if someone is knocking on your door, you can say **Shéi'a?** (Who is it?). Also, when you see something beautiful, you can say **Zhēn piàoliang'a!** (Really beautiful!).

■ 13 Position of the question words **shénme shíhou**

These question words mean 'when'. They are normally used to ask about dates and days rather than the actual time. They are usually placed before the verb. For example:

Nǐ érzi *shénme shíhou* **qù Xiāng Gǎng gōngzuò?**
When is your son going to Hong Kong to work?

Nǐ māma *shénme shíhou* **lái Yīngguó?**
When is your mother coming to England?

■ 14 Construction **Jìrán . . . jiù . . .**

Jiù usually goes with the expression **jìrán** to mean 'as . . . (then
. . .)'. It is the same word as the emphatic **jiù** in Lesson 3 but here
it is used differently. The first half of the construction gives a
reason, and the second half is either a suggestion or a decision. For
example:

Jìrán nǐ tàitai shēntǐ bù hǎo, nǐ *jiù* **huí jiā ba.**
As your wife is not feeling well, please go home.

Jìrán shíyuè shì zuì hǎo de jìjié, wǒ *jiù* **shíyuè qù Běijīng.**
As October is the best season, I shall go to Beijing in October.

■ 15 Different terms for 'last', 'next' and 'this'

You can use **shàng ge** (last), **xià ge** (next) and **zhè ge** (this) together
with **xīngqī** (week) and **yuè** (month), but not with **tiān** (day) and **nián**
(year). Below is a chart illustrating the differences:

Chinese	English	Chinese	English
zuótiān	yesterday	**shàng ge yuè**	last month
jīntiān	today	**zhè ge yuè**	this month
míngtiān	tomorrow	**xià ge yuè**	next month
shàng ge xīngqi	last week	**qù nián**	last year
zhè ge xīngqī	this week	**jīn nián**	this year
xià ge xīngqī	next week	**míng nián**	next year

■ 16 Question word **háishì**

Whenever you want to ask a question which gives two or more
options, and you want the respondant to specify one or the other,
put **háishì** in between the last two choices. Thus, **háishì** can only
be used to raise questions. For example:

Nǐ shì Yīngguórén *háishì* **Měiguórén?**
Are you British *or* American?

Nǐ xiǎng hē kāfēi, chá háishì shuǐ?
Would you like to have coffee, tea or water?

■ 17 Question words **duō jiǔ**

The question words **duō jiǔ** (how long?) are used if you have no idea at all of duration – for how long the other person is staying in Beijing, for example:

Nǐ dǎsuàn zài Běijīng dāi *duō jiǔ*?
How long are you staying in Beijing for?

But if you know that he/she is only staying for a couple of days, weeks, etc. you use the question word **jǐ tiān** (how many days?), **jǐ ge xīngqī** (how many weeks).

■ 18 Difference between **dàyuē** and **zuǒyòu**

The word **zuǒyòu** (about/around) was introduced earlier, in Lesson 2. The difference between **zuǒyòu** and **dàyuē** is that they occur in different positions in the sentence. **Dàyuē** is always put in front of the phrase it modifies, whilst **zuǒyòu** always follows the phrase it modifies. For example:

A: **Nǐ dǎsuàn zài Měiguó dāi duō jiǔ?**
How long do you plan to stay in America?
B: ***Dàyuē* liǎng ge yuè.**
About two months.

Jiājia sānshí suì *zuǒyòu*.
Jiajia is *about* thirty years old.

Exercises

Exercise 4

Translate the following expressions into Chinese, paying attention to the use of **de**: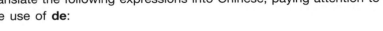

(a) my best friend
(b) extremely big swimming pool
(c) small restaurant

(d)   that young and beautiful university student
(e)   the oldest man

Exercise 5

Convert the following statements into questions using **shénme shíhou** (when?) or **duō jiǔ** (how long?), paying special attention to the underlined words, and then translate the sentences into English:

(a)   Mǐkè dǎsuàn <u>míng nián</u> qù Zhōngguó.
(b)   Zhāng Jūn zài Táiwān gōngzuò le <u>wǔ nián</u>.
(c)   Lǎo Lǐ de nǚ'ér <u>xià ge yuè</u> shàng xué.
(d)   Wǒ xiǎng zài Shànghǎi dāi <u>sān tiān</u>.

Exercise 6

Fill in the blanks using **dàyuē** or **zuǒyòu**:

(a)   Wǒmen dǎsuàn liù diǎn _____ chī wǎnfàn.
(b)   A: Nǐ zài Shēnzhèn gōngzuò le duō jiǔ?
       B: _____ sān nián bàn.
(c)   Wáng jīnglǐ sìshíwǔ suì _____.
(d)   Wǒde Yīngguó péngyou _____ liùyuè lái kàn wǒ.

Exercise 7

Translate the following sentences into Chinese:

(a)   Do you want to have lunch at twelve or one o'clock?
(b)   Do you often swim?
(c)   Why are you unhappy?
(d)   Since you are not hungry, I'll eat first.
(e)   How many days are you going to stay in Beijing?
(f)   How long have you been learning Chinese for?

Characters

So far in this book, we have come across a few very common Chinese surnames. They are:

| 王 | 张 | 李 | 吴 |

Wáng   Zhāng   Lǐ   Wú

In English, when clarifying a word, you can spell it out. So what do people do in Chinese? Let us first analyse their components, and then it becomes easier to explain.

Surname	Character analysis	Head component and its meaning	Pinyin
王	王 **wáng**	王 (king)	**Wáng**
张	弓 **gōng** + 长 **cháng**	弓 (arrow)	**Zhāng**
李	木 **mù** + 子 **zǐ**	木 (wood)	**Lǐ**
吴	口 **kǒu** + 天 **tiān**	口 (mouth)	**Wú**

(Unexplained components - 长 **cháng**: length; 天 **tiān**: sky, day)

In order to distinguish the above surnames from similar sounding characters that also serve as surnames, people take their surname apart. For example, for 张, people would say '弓 **gōng** 长 **cháng** 张 **zhāng**', meaning 'the **zhāng** with the arrow and the length'. For the surname 吴, you'll hear people say '口 **kǒu** 天 **tiān** 吴 **wú**', meaning 'the **wú** with the mouth and sky'. As 王 cannot be taken further apart, you'll hear people simply say '三横王' (**sān héng wáng**), meaning 'the **wáng** with three horizontal strokes'.

As for Chinese given names, there is not a set of words that are devoted to names only. One can choose whichever character or characters one likes to form a name. So many children's names reflect their parents' hopes and expectations.

Exercise 8

(1) Convert the following Chinese names into pinyin:

(a) 张朋
(b) 王京
(c) 李海
(d) 吴月

(2) Check the Vocabulary for both Dialogue 1 (pp. 116–17) and Dialogue 2 (pp. 123–4) and list the characters that share the following components. Then learn to write those characters.

(a) 月　　(b) 口　　(c) 扌　　(d) 亻　　(e) 心

(3) Read the postcard in characters on page 131, and circle the characters that you recognize.

Reading/listening comprehension

 (CD1; 47)

I Below is a postcard in both pinyin and characters from Feng Ying, who lives in the United States, to her parents, who live in China. Read it carefully and then answer the questions in Chinese. If you have access to the audio material, listen first, and then answer the questions in Chinese.

 Vocabulary

亲爱的	**qīn'àide**	dear
写信	**xiě xìn**	to write a letter
旧金山	**Jiùjīnshān**	San Francisco
告诉	**gàosu**	to tell
想你们的	**xiǎng nǐmende**	missing you

Qīn'àide Bàba, Māma:

Nǐmen hǎo! Nǐmen zuìjìn shēntǐ hǎo ma?

Wǒ zuìjìn cháng chūmén. Xià ge xīngqīsān, wǒ qù Jiùjīnshān gōngzuò jiā kàn péngyou, dasuàn dāi liǎng ge xīngqī zuǒyòu. Jiùjīnshān de xiàtiān hěn rè, búguò fēicháng yǒu yìsi.

Gēge hǎo ma? Gàosu tā gěi wǒ xiě xìn. Qǐng wèn tā hǎo.

　　　　　　　　　　　　　　　　　Xiǎng nǐmende,
　　　　　　　　　　　　　　　　　Yǐng
　　　　　　　　　　　　　　　　　2008. 7. 8

亲爱的爸爸，妈妈：

你们好！你们最近身体好吗？

我最近常出门。下个星期三，我去旧金山工作加看朋友，打算待两个星期左右。旧金山的夏天很热，不过非常有意思。

哥哥好吗？告诉他给我写信。请问他好。

想你们的，
颖
2008, 7, 8

QUESTIONS

(1) Féng Yǐng shénme shíhou qù Jiùjīnshān?
(2) Féng Yǐng qù Jiùjīnshān lǚyóu ma?
(3) Féng Yǐng qù Jiùjīnshān gàn shénme?
(4) Féng Yǐng dǎsuàn zài Jiùjīnshān dāi duō jiǔ?
(5) Jiùjīnshān de xiàtiān zěnme yàng?
(6) Féng Yǐng de gēge zhù zài Měiguó ma?

(CD1; 48)

II Read aloud the following phrases or words and add on the correct tone marks. If you have access to the audio material, listen first, and then add on the correct tone marks.

(1) **yiyue** (January)
(2) **san ge yue** (three months)
(3) **tebie da de fandian** (extremely large hotel)
(4) **xingqi'er** (Tuesday)
(5) **feichang leng** (extremely cold)
(6) **dasuan** (to plan)

Lesson Seven
Wèn lù 问路
Asking for directions

By the end of this lesson, you should be able to:

- ask how to get to certain destinations
- understand some expressions regarding directions
- distinguish between **kàn**, **kàn jiàn** and **kàn de jiàn**
- distinguish between the use of **kàn bú jiàn** and **méi (yǒu) kàn jiàn**
- say ordinal numbers (e.g. first, second, etc.)
- write and recognize more characters

Dialogue 1

. . . zài nǎr? . . . 在哪儿? Where is . . . ? **(CD2; 2)**

Imagine that you are in a place where Chinese is spoken and you do not know your way around very well. Below are three situations you may find yourself in.

(a) *Inside a hotel*

YOU	Qǐng wèn, cèsuǒ/jiǔbā/diàntī/gōngyòng diànhuà zài nǎr?
CHINESE SPEAKER	Zài cāntīng de zuǒ biān.

(b) *In the street*

YOU	Qǐng wèn, fùjìn yǒu chāoshì ma?
CHINESE SPEAKER	Yǒu. Nǐ kàn de jiàn qiánmian hónglǜ dēng ma?
YOU	Kàn de jiàn.
CHINESE SPEAKER	Zǒu dào hónglǜ dēng, wǎng yòu guǎi. Wǒ jìde nàr yǒu.

(c) *In the street*

YOU	Nǐ néng gàosu wǒ zuò jǐ lù chē qù huǒchē zhàn ma?
CHINESE SPEAKER	Bú yòng zuò chē. Zǒulù shí fēnzhōng jiù dào le.
YOU	Zěnme zǒu?
CHINESE SPEAKER	Dì yī ge lùkǒu wǎng dōng guǎi.

(a) *Inside a hotel*

| YOU | 请问，厕所/酒吧/电梯/公用电话在哪儿？ |
| CHINESE SPEAKER | 在餐厅的左边。 |

(b) *In the street*

| YOU | 请问，附近有超市吗？ |
| CHINESE SPEAKER | 有。你看得见前面红绿灯吗？ |

| YOU | 看得见。 |
| CHINESE SPEAKER | 走到红绿灯，往右拐。我记得那儿有。 |

(c) *In the street*

YOU	你能告诉我坐几路车去火车站吗？
CHINESE SPEAKER	不用坐车。走路十分钟就到了。
YOU	怎么走？
CHINESE SPEAKER	第一个路口往东拐。

(CD2; 1)

Vocabulary

cèsuǒ	厕所	toilet
jiǔbā	酒吧	bar
diàntī	电梯	lift
gōngyòng	公用	public
diànhuà	电话	phone
zuǒ	左	left
biān	边	side
fùjìn	附近	nearby/close by
chāoshì	超市	supermarket
kànjiàn	看见	to see/to have seen
kàn de jiàn	看得见	to be able to see/can see
qiánmiàn	前面	ahead
hónglǜ dēng	红绿灯	traffic light
zǒu	走	to walk
dào	到	until/up to
wǎng yòu guǎi	往右拐	to turn right
jìde	记得	to remember
nàr	那儿	there
zuò	坐	to take/to catch
lù	路	route/road
chē	车	car/bus
huǒchē zhàn	火车站	railway station [*lit.* 'fire car stop']

bú yòng	不用	no need/do not need
zǒulù	走路	to walk, on foot [*lit.* 'walk road']
jiù . . . le	就 . . . 了	[see Note 13]
zěnme zǒu?	怎么走？	How do I get there?/how do I get to . . .? [*lit.* 'how to walk?']
dì yī	第一	first
lùkǒu	路口	crossroads/junction
dōng	东	east

Notes on Dialogue 1 (CD2; 4)

■ 1 **Zuǒ** and **yòu**

Do you remember the term **zuǒyòu** we learnt in Lesson 2, which means 'approximately'? On its own, **zuǒ** means 'left' and **yòu** right. If you want to say 'A is on the left/right', you must use the word **biān** and say **A zài zuǒ/yòu biān**. For example:

Nán cèsuǒ zài *zuǒ biān*. Nǚ cèsuǒ zài *yòu biān*.
The men's toilet is *on the left* and the women's is *on the right*.

There are two other commonly used terms for 'toilet':

wèishēng jiān 卫生间 (*lit.* 'hygiene room') and
xǐshǒu jiān 洗手间 (*lit.* 'wash hand room').

If you want to say 'A is on B's left/right' or 'A is to the left/right of B', you must say **A zài B de zuǒ/yòu biān**. For example:

Diàntī zài cāntīng de *yòu biān*.
The lift is *to the right* of the dining-room.
(Looking at a photograph)
Wǒ mèimei zài wǒde *zuǒ biān*.   My sister is *on my left*.

■ 2 Other direction words

Dōng, nán, xī and **běi** (east, south, west, north) are often used to give directions. For example:

Bǎihuò shāngdiàn *zài* **Běijīng Fàndiàn** *de dōng biān*.
The department store is *to the east* of the Beijing Hotel.

The combinations of these direction words are different in order from English. See below:

dōngběi	northeast	**dōngnán**	southeast
xīběi	northwest	**xīnán**	southwest

■ 3 More on **yǒu**

We learnt **yǒu** (to have) in Lesson 4 in saying, for example, **Běijīng Fàndiàn yǒu yī ge yóuyǒng chí**. **Yǒu** can also be used without a noun preceding it to mean 'There is/are . . .'. The adverb **fùjìn** (nearby) is often used in front of **yǒu** in this case. For example:

    Fùjìn *yǒu* **yī jiā hěn dà de yínháng.**
Lit.   Nearby have one very large bank.
    There is a very large bank nearby.

    Fùjìn *yǒu* **cèsuǒ ma?**   Is there a toilet nearby?

■ 4 Use of **kàn de jiàn**

When the word **jiàn** is put after the verbs **kàn** (to see) or **tīng** (to listen), it indicates the result of those verbs. With **de** inserted between

kàn or **tīng** and **jiàn**, i.e. **kàn de jiàn** or **tīng de jiàn**, the emphasis is on whether one is able, for example, to see or hear. For example:

A: **Nǐ *kàn de jiàn* ma?**   Can you see?
B: ***Kàn de jiàn.***   Yes, I can.

To negate, replace **de** with **bù** (pronounced with a neutral tone). For example:

Wǒ kàn *bu* jiàn hónglǜ dēng.   I ca*n't* see the traffic lights.

(On the phone)
Wǒ tīng bu jiàn nǐ shuō shénme.   I can't hear what you are saying.

If you want to say 'to have seen/heard', there is no need to use **de**, simply say **kàn jiàn *le*** or **tīng jiàn *le***, which again is different from **kàn le** and **tīng le** because the latter means 'looked at' or 'listened' respectively. For example:

Wǒ *kàn jiàn le* càidān.   I've seen the menu./I saw the menu.
Wǒ *kàn le* yīxià càidān.   I looked at the menu.

Note that to negate the above, place **méi** or **méi yǒu** in front of the verb. Let us compare the two negations:

Wǒ *méi* (*yǒu*) kàn jiàn cèsuǒ.   I *didn't* see the toilet.
Wǒ kàn *bu* jiàn cèsuǒ.   I *can't* see the toilet.

■ 5 Use of **wǎng . . . guǎi**

The Chinese equivalent of 'to turn left' is **wǎng zuǒ guǎi**. Simply put the direction words (see Notes 1 and 2 above) between **wǎng** and **guǎi**. For example:

Zǒu dào hónglǜ dēng, *wǎng* dōng *guǎi*.
Walk as far as the traffic lights, then *turn* east.

■ 6 Use of **jìde**

The verb **jìde** is used to indicate things that you now remember or have remembered. For example:

Nǐ *jìde* tā tàitai de míngzi ma?   Do you *remember* his wife's name?
Wǒ *jìde* nǐ.   I *remember* you.

To negate, use **bù** in front of the verb. For example:

Wǒ *bú* jìde tā duō dà le.   I *don't remember* how old he is.

Note that the verb **jìde** cannot be used to express a notion of future time. For example, it cannot be used to say 'Please remember something' or 'I will remember something'.

■ 7 Position of **nàr** and **zhèr**

Do you remember the two pronouns **nà** (that) and **zhè** (this)? Once **ér** is added to them, we have **nàr** (there) and **zhèr** (here), which are always placed either before the verb or after **zài** (to be at/to be in). For example:

> *Nàr* **yǒu yī ge gōngyòng diànhuà.**
> *There's* a public telephone there.

> (Looking at a map)
> **Wǒde dàxué zài *zhèr*.**
> My university is *here*.

■ 8 Difference between **huì** and **néng**

In Lesson 2 we learnt the auxiliary verb **huì** which means 'can' or 'to be able to'. **Huì** emphasizes ability whereas **néng** emphasizes willingness. For example:

> **Wǒ gēge bú *huì* yóuyǒng.**
> My elder brother *cannot* swim.

> **Nǐ *néng* jiǎngjiang nǐde qingkuàng ma?**
> *Could* you tell me about yourself?

■ 9 Some means of transport

Anything that has got wheels is a **chē**. Thus we have:

zìxíng*chē*	bicycle (**zìxíng** means 'self-pedalling')
xiǎo*chē*	car (**xiǎo** means 'small')
huǒ*chē*	train (**huǒ** means 'fire')
chūzū*chē*	taxi (**chūzū** means 'on rent')
mǎ*chē*	horse-drawn carriage (**mǎ** means 'horse')

However, **gōnggòng qìchē** (**gōnggòng** means 'public together' and **qìchē** means 'vehicle') is often shortened to **chē** in mainland China. **Gōng jiāo chē** (*lit.* 'public transport car') is another frequently used term.

■ 10 Use of **zuò** (to take)

Zuò literally means 'to sit'. Except with bicycle, **zuò** can be used with all of the above forms of transport:

zuò **gōnggòng qìchē**	to take a bus
zuò **huǒchē**	to take the train
zuò **chūzūchē**	to take a taxi (see Note 1, Lesson 11)

■ 11 More on the question word **jǐ**

This question word has appeared earlier in various questions that have to do with numbers. **Jǐ** is also used to ask which number bus to take. For example:

Qǐng wèn, zuò *jǐ* lù chē qù huǒchē zhàn?
Could you tell me please *which* number bus to catch to get to the railway station?

■ 12 Use of **bú yòng**

Basically, **bú yòng** means 'there is no need to' or 'do not need'. For example:

Nǐ *bú yòng* gěi wǒ mǎi lǐwù.
You *don't need* to buy me any presents.

Bú yòng xiè. **Zánmen shì hǎo péngyou.**
Lit. No need to thank. We are good friends.
Don't mention it. We're good friends.

■ 13 Construction **jiù . . . le**

One usage of this construction is to emphasize the verb or predicative adjective which is inserted between **jiù** and **le**. It implies that it takes little time, effort, or money to get something done. Let us look at some examples:

Zǒulù shí fēnzhōng *jiù* **dào** *le*.
Lit.   Walk   ten minutes   get there.
It's only ten minutes' walk, and you'll be there.

Shí kuài qián *jiù* **gòu** *le*.
Ten yuan will be enough.

■ 14 **Zěnme zǒu?**

This is a very common way of asking how to get to somewhere, although literally the phrase means 'How to walk?' You can put your desired destination in front of **zěnme zǒu**. For example:

Huǒchē zhàn *zěnme zǒu***?**
How do I get to the railway station?

You can also place the verb **qù** (to go) before the destination. For example:

Qù **nǐmende dàxué** *zěnme zǒu***?**
How do I get to your university?

■ 15 Ordinal numbers (e.g. first, second, etc.)

It is very easy to form ordinal numbers in Chinese. Simply put **dì** in front of a numeral (e.g. **yī, èr, sān**, etc.). For example:

dì **yī**	first	*dì* **èr**	second
dì **shíyī**	eleventh	*dì* **èrshísān**	twenty-three

If you want to say, for example, 'the first junction', the measure word **gè** needs to be inserted between the ordinal number and the noun. Thus we have **dì yī** *ge* **lùkǒu**.

Exercises

Exercise 1

You want to find out the following from a Chinese speaker:

(a)   Where the toilet is.
(b)   If there is a supermarket nearby.

(c)   Where the No. 10 bus is.
(d)   How to get to the railway station.
(c)   Which number bus to catch to go to the Beijing Hotel.

Exercise 2

Look at the picture below and then complete the sentences describing the position of each person in relation to someone else in the picture:

2 Amy

3 Xiao Fang

1 Lao Zhang

4 Anna

(a)   Lǎo Zhāng _____.
(b)   Àimǐ _____.
(c)   Ānnà _____.

Exercise 3

Look at the following two pictures and answer the questions (see page 149 for new signs):

I A plan of a corner of the ground floor of a hotel

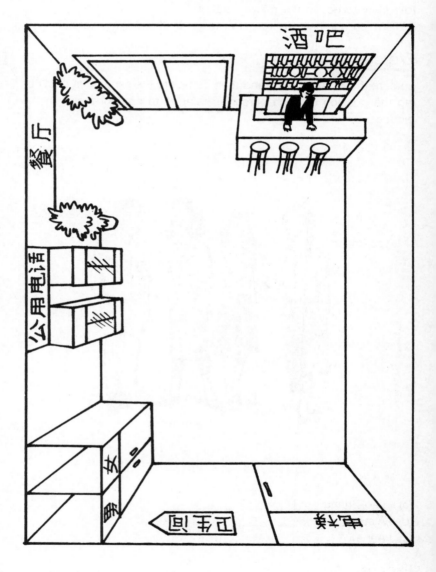

(a)   Cèsuǒ zài nǎr?
(b)   Gōngyòng diànhuà zài nǎr?
(c)   Cāntīng zài nǎr?
(d)   Diàntī zài nǎr?

II A map of a corner of Beijing

Suppose the following two destinations are both within walking distance:

(a) Huǒchē zhàn zěnme zǒu?
(b) Qù Běijīng Fàndiàn zěnme zǒu?

Exercise 4

Negate the following sentences and then translate the negated sentences into English:

(a) Tā jìde wǒde míngzi.
(b) Nǐ děi (*have to*) gěi wǒ mǎi lǐwù.
(c) Fùjìn yǒu chāoshì.
(d) Wǒ kàn jiàn le huǒchē zhàn.
(e) Wǒ kàn de jiàn hónglǜ dēng.

Exercise 5

Translate the following sentences into Chinese:

(1) There is a hotel there.
(2) She can speak Chinese.
(3) I can't tell you about him.
(4) Turn right at the first junction. You'll get there in about 15 minutes.
(5) Which bus shall I take to go to the railway station?

Dialogue 2

Jiè zìxíngchē 借自行车 Borrowing a bike (CD2; 6)

This dialogue is between David, who is teaching English in Beijing, and his friend Linlin.

DAVID   Wǒ kěyi jiè yīxià nǐde zìxíngchē ma?
LÍNLIN Dāngrán kěyi. Nǐ yào qù nǎr?
DAVID   Qù Jiànguó Lù de Zhōngguó Yínháng huàn yīxiē qián.
LÍNLIN Nǐ zhīdào zěnme zǒu ma?
DAVID   Bù zhīdào. Dànshì, wǒ xiǎng wǒ néng zhǎo dào.
LÍNLIN Wǒ bù xiāngxìn. Nǐ zuìhǎo xiān chá yīxià dìtú.
DAVID   Hǎo zhǔyi. Qí chē dàyuē xūyào duō jiǔ?
LÍNLIN Bàn ge xiǎoshí zuǒyòu. Rúguǒ nǐ lùguò yóujú, néng bāng wǒ jì fēng xìn ma?
DAVID   Méi wèntí.

DAVID   我可以借一下你的自行车吗？
LÍNLIN 当然可以。你要去哪儿？
DAVID   去建国路的中国银行换一些钱。
LÍNLIN 你知道怎么走吗？
DAVID   不知道。但是，我想我能找到。
LÍNLIN 我不相信。你最好先查一下地图。
DAVID   好主意。骑车大约需要多久？
LÍNLIN 半个小时左右。如果你路过邮局，能帮我寄封信吗？
DAVID   没问题。

(CD2; 5)

Vocabulary

jiè	借	to borrow
zìxíngchē	自行车	bicycle
yào	要	to be going to/will
Jiànguó Lù	建国路	Jianguo Road
yínháng	银行	bank
huàn	换	to change
qián	钱	money
dànshì	但是	but
wǒ xiǎng . . .	我想. . .	I think . . .
zhǎo dào	找到	to find something (successfully)
xiāngxìn	相信	to believe
nǐ zuì hǎo . . .	你最好. . .	you'd better
chá	查	to check
dìtú	地图	map
hǎo zhǔyì	好主意	good idea
qí	骑	to ride
xūyào	需要	to need/take
xiǎoshí	小时	hour
rúguǒ . . . dehuá	如果. . . 的话	if
lùguò	路过	to go by/to pass by
yóujú	邮局	post office
bāng	帮	to help
jì	寄	to post
fēng	封	[measure word]
xìn	信	letter
méi wèntí	没问题	no problem

Notes on Dialogue 2

■ 16 Use of **jiè**

In Chinese, the word for 'to borrow' is the same as the word for 'to lend', which will be introduced in Lesson 9. Let us see an example of **jiè** when used to mean 'to borrow':

Wǒ xiǎng *jiè* yīxià nǐde zìxíngchē.
I'd like to *borrow* your bike.

Note that here **yīxià** does not have any specific meaning except reducing the abruptness of the tone. **Yīxià** usually follows **jiè** when it means 'to borrow'. For example:

Wǒ kěyi *jiè* yixià nǐde dìtú ma?
Could I *borrow* your map for a while?

■ 17 Use of **yào**

Here, **yào** is used in front of verbs to indicate that something, often a planned action, is happening in the near future. For example:

Sūshān *yào* qù Zhōngguó lǚyóu.
Susan is going to China to travel.

Wǒ fùmǔ liùyuè *yào* lái Yīngguó.
My parents are coming to Britain in June.

■ 18 Verb phrase **zhǎo dào**

When the phrase **zhǎo dào** is preceded by **néng** or **kěyi**, it means 'to be able to find'. If you cannot find something, put **bù** between **zhǎo** and **dào**. For example:

A: **Nǐ *néng zhǎo dào* huǒchē zhàn ma?**
    Can you find the railway station?

B: **Zhǎo *bú* dào.**
    I *can't*.

When **zhǎo dào** is followed by **le**, it means 'to have found' or 'found', and if you have not found or did not find something, put the negation word **méi(yǒu)** in front of **zhǎo dào**. For example:

A: **Nǐ *zhǎo dào* nǐde qiánbāo *le* ma?**
    Have you found your wallet?

B: ***Méiyǒu* zhǎo dào.**
    No, I *haven't* found it.

■ 19 Verb **xiāngxìn**

If you want to say 'I don't believe it', you can either say **Wǒ bù xiāngxìn** or **Wǒ bú xìn**. In spoken Chinese, **xiāng** is often omitted from **xiāngxìn**. For example:

A: **Wǒ jīnnián sānshíwǔ suì.**   A: I'm thirty-five this year.
B: **Wǒ bú xìn.**   B: I don't believe it.

■ 20 Use of **qí**

When **qí** is followed by **zìxíngchē**, it means 'to ride a bike', 'by bike' or 'go cycling'. For example:

Nǐ huì *qí* zìxíngchē ma?
Can you ride a bike?

Zuótiān, wǒ *qí zìxíngchē* qù le Tiān'ānmén.
I *went* to Tian'anmen *by bike* yesterday.

Nǐ xǐhuan *qí zìxíngchē* ma?
Do you like *cycling*?

■ 21 Use of **xūyào**

The verb **xūyào** means 'to require' or 'to need'. It can also be trans-lated as 'It takes . . .' in certain contexts. For example:

Tā *xūyào* yī jiàn máoyī.
He *needs* a jumper.

Qí zìxíngchē qù Běijīng Dàxué *xūyào* èrshí fēnzhōng.
It *takes* twenty minutes to get to Beijing University by bike.

■ 22 Difference between **xiǎoshí** and **diǎn**

Xiǎoshí (hour) is used for the duration of time and **diǎn** is used to tell the time. For example:

A: **Cāntīng jǐ *diǎn* kāimén?**
What *time* does the restaurant open?

B: **Hái yǒu yī ge *xiǎoshí*.**
Still an *hour* to go.

Let us compare the use of **bàn** (half) in combination with **diǎn** and **xiǎoshí**:

yī diǎn *bàn*	half past one
yī ge *bàn* xiǎoshí	one hour and a half
bàn ge xiǎoshí	half an hour

■ 23 Construction **rúguǒ . . . dehuà**

The word **rúguǒ**, meaning 'if', is used either at the very beginning of a sentence or after the subject so that it makes the sentence conditional. For example:

Rúguǒ nǐ bú rènshi Xiǎo Wáng, wǒ gěi nǐ jièshào.
If you don't know Xiao Wang, I'll introduce you to her.

Nǐ *rúguǒ* méi yǒu dìtú, nǐ kěyi jiè wǒde.
If you don't have the map, you can borrow mine.

Rúguǒ is often used together with **dehuà** (it has no specific meaning and the first syllable carries no tones) in the first half of a conditional sentence. For example:

Rúguǒ nǐ lùguò yóujú *dehuà*, qǐng bāng wǒ jì fēng xìn.
If you pass by the post office, please post a letter for me.

Exercises

Exercise 6

What do you say if you want to know how long it takes to:

(a)   cycle to the Bank of China
(b)   walk to the railway station
(c)   get to Tian'anmen by bus?

Exercise 7

Pair work – one person asks questions in Chinese based on Dialogue 2, and the other person answers them. For example:

A: Línlin yǒu zìxíngchē ma?
B: Yǒu.

Exercise 8

Translate the following sentences into Chinese:

(a) I don't believe that you don't have a bike.
(b) I'm going to Shanghai next Saturday.
(c) David didn't find the Bank of China.
(d) You'd better check the map.
(e) It takes more than an hour to cycle to my university.
(f) This is a good idea.

Characters

In this lesson, we have come across some important words that are often used for signs. Let us try to recognize them:

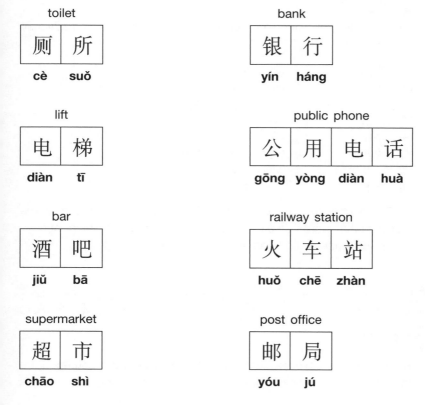

toilet
厕 所
cè   suǒ

bank
银 行
yín   háng

lift
电 梯
diàn   tī

public phone
公 用 电 话
gōng yòng diàn huà

bar
酒 吧
jiǔ   bā

railway station
火 车 站
huǒ   chē   zhàn

supermarket
超 市
chāo   shì

post office
邮 局
yóu   jú

As Chinese roads often run from north to south or east to west, the following four characters are important in telling the directions and in recognizing road signs:

Character	Pinyin	Stroke order	English
东	dōng	东 一 左 车 矢 东	east
南	nán	南 一 十 广 占 內 內 丙 南 南	south
西	xī	西 一 广 币 厅 西 西	west
北	běi	北 丨 ㇀ 丬 北 北	north

Exercise 9

(1) Match the following signs on the left with the English equivalent on the right:

(a) 邮局   (i)   railway station
(b) 银行   (ii)   post office
(c) 超市   (iii) supermarket
(d) 厕所   (iv)   bank
(e) 酒吧   (v)   bar
(f) 火车站   (vi)   public phone
(g) 公用电话   (vii) toilet
(h) 电梯   (viii) lift

(2) Some province and city names in Chinese contain one of the four direction words discussed above. Get a map of China, and try to find province or city names that contain 东, 南, 西, 北.

Reading/listening comprehension

 (CD2; 7)

Below are five Chinese sentences. Underneath each sentence are three English sentences. Read or listen to (if you have access to the audio material) the Chinese sentence first and tick the English sentence which is closest in meaning to the Chinese sentence.

(1) **Gōngyòng diànhuà zài shí lù gōnggòng qìchē zhàn de zuǒ biān.**

(a) There is no public telephone nearby.
(b) The number 10 bus stop is on the left of the public telephone.
(c) The public telephone is on the left of the number 10 bus stop.

(2) **Nǐ zuìhǎo zuò èrshí lù chē qù huǒchē zhàn.**

(a) You should walk to the bus station.
(b) You'd better go to the station by bus.
(c) You'd better go to the station by bike.

(3) **Qí zìxíngchē dào Běijīng Fàndiàn xūyào bàn ge xiǎoshí zuǒyòu.**

(a) It takes about an hour and a half to get to the Beijing Hotel by bike.
(b) It takes half an hour to get to the Beijing Hotel by bus.
(c) It takes half an hour to get to the Beijing Hotel by bike.

(4) **Wǒ méi zhǎo dào wǒde zìxíngche.**

(a) I found my bike.
(b) I didn't find my bike.
(c) I can't find my bike.

(5) **Tā bú jìde qù Běijīng Dàxué zěnme zǒu.**

(a) She can't remember Beijing University.
(b) She remembers Beijing University.
(c) She can't remember how to get to Beijing University.

Lesson Eight
Mǎi dōngxi (I) 买东西
Shopping (I)

By the end of this lesson, you should be able to:

- tell someone the price of a product
- ask about prices
- tell the shop-assistant what and how many you want to buy
- do some bargaining
- use the question words **duō shǎo**
- write more characters and recognize more signs

Dialogue 1

Duō shǎo qián? 多少钱？ How much is it?
(CD2; 9)

Anne is working in Chengdu. Today, she is doing her shopping. She goes into a fruit and vegetable shop where customers are served by shop-assistants.

SHOP-ASSISTANT	Nǐ hǎo. Nǐ xiǎng mǎi shénme?
ANNE	Wǒ xiǎng mǎi yīxiē shuǐguǒ.
SHOP-ASSISTANT	Nǐ kàn, wǒmen yǒu xīnxiān de cǎoméi, Hǎinán Dǎo xiāngjiāo, gè zhǒng píngguǒ.
ANNE	Zhèxiē shì shénme?
SHOP-ASSISTANT	Lìzhī.
ANNE	Duō shǎo qián yī jīn?
SHOP-ASSISTANT	Shíwǔ kuài bā máo.
ANNE	Wǒ yào yī jīn lìzhī. Cǎoméi zěnme mài?

SHOP-ASSISTANT	Shí'er kuài wǔ yī jīn.
ANNE	Yào bàn jīn cǎoméi. Yǒu méi yǒu táozi?
SHOP-ASSISTANT	Méi yǒu, duìbuqǐ. Hái yào biéde ma?
ANNE	Bú yào, xièxie.
SHOP-ASSISTANT	Yīgòng èrshí'èr kuài líng wǔ fēn.
ANNE	Gěi nǐ sān shí kuài.
SHOP-ASSISTANT	Hǎo de. Zháo nǐ bā kuài qī máo wǔ.
ANNE	Xièxie.

SHOP-ASSISTANT	你好。你想买什么？
ANNE	我想买一些水果。
SHOP-ASSISTANT	你看，我们有新鲜的草莓，海南岛香蕉，各种苹果。
ANNE	这些是什么？
SHOP-ASSISTANT	荔枝。
ANNE	多少钱一斤？
SHOP-ASSISTANT	十五块八毛。
ANNE	我要一斤荔枝。草莓怎么卖？
SHOP-ASSISTANT	十二块五一斤。
ANNE	要半斤草莓。有没有桃子？
SHOP-ASSISTANT	没有，对不起。还要别的吗？
ANNE	不要，谢谢。
SHOP-ASSISTANT	一共二十一块两毛五分。
ANNE	给你三十块。
SHOP-ASSISTANT	好的。找你八块七毛五。
ANNE	谢谢。

(CD2; 8)

Vocabulary

mǎi	买	to buy
yīxiē	一些	some
shuǐguǒ	水果	fruit
nǐ kàn	你看	have a look [*lit.* 'you look']
xīnxiān	新鲜	fresh
cǎoméi	草莓	strawberry
Hǎinán Dǎo	海南岛	Hainan Island
xiāngjiāo	香蕉	banana

gè zhǒng	各种	various kinds
píngguǒ	苹果	apple
zhèxiē	这些	these
lìzhī	荔枝	lychee
duō shǎo	多少	how much; how many
duō shǎo qián	多少钱	how much is it?
jīn	斤	[unit of weight, equivalent of half a kilo]
kuài; máo; fēn	块；毛；分	[currency words, see Note 1]
yào	要	to want
mài	卖	to sell
táozi	桃子	peach
biéde	别的	anything else
zhǎo	找	to return [see Note 8]

Notes on Dialogue 1

■ 1 Currency terms **(CD2; 10)**

In mainland China and Taiwan, the currency word is **yuán**, for which the informal term is **kuài**. One **yuán** consists of ten **jiǎo**, the informal term for which is **máo**. And one **jiǎo** or one **máo** consists of ten **fēn**. Let us list them separately:

Informal	*Formal*
kuài	**yuán**
máo	**jiǎo**
fēn	**fēn**

The sign for Chinese yuan is ¥. Let us look at the following prices expressed with informal currency terms:

¥ 0.05	**wǔ** *fēn*
¥ 0.80	**bā** *máo*
¥ 0.23	**liǎng** *máo* **sān** *fēn*
¥ 1.50	**yī** *kuài* **wǔ** *máo*
¥ 2.95	**liǎng** *kuài* **jiǔ** *máo* **wǔ** *fēn*
¥ 12.30	**shí'èr** *kuài* **sān** *máo*
¥ 6.05	**liù** *kuài* **líng wǔ** *fēn*

Note that if there is more than one currency term involved in a price, the last one can always be omitted. Thus, it is correct to express four of the above prices in the following way:

¥ 1.50	**yī** *kuài* **wǔ**
¥ 2.95	**liǎng** *kuài* **jiǔ** *máo* **wǔ**
¥ 12.30	**shí'èr** *kuài* **sān**
¥ 6.05	**liù** *kuài* **líng wǔ**

Since most currencies have only two terms (e.g. pounds and pence; dollars and cents), it is very easy to make the mistake of saying **bāshí fēn** (eighty fen) for ¥ 0.80, for example. You must remember to say **bā máo** or **bā jiǎo**.

■ 2 Unit of weight

The official unit of weight is **gōngjīn** (kilogram). However, **jīn** (half a kilo) is most commonly used in dealing with small quantities of goods, especially in shops. As **jīn** itself is a unit of weight, measure words are not needed in between a number and **jīn**. For example:

A: **Nǐ yào jǐ *jīn* píngguǒ?**
How many *half-kilos* of apples do you want?

B: **Wǒ yào liǎng *jīn* píngguǒ.**
I want a *kilo* of apples.

■ 3 Use of place names

Place names (e.g. names of cities and countries) can be used as adjectives in front of nouns. For example:

Zhōngguó fàn   *Chinese* food
Yīngguó gōngsī   *British* company
Měiguó péngyou   *American* friends
Hǎinán Dǎo xiāngjiāo *Hainan* bananas

■ 4 Asking the price

The most important phrase to remember is **Duō shǎo qián?** You can specify the goods and the quantity. For example:

Píngguǒ *duō shǎo qián*   yī jīn?
Lit.   Apple   how much money   one jin?
How *much* is a half-kilo of apples?

Duō shǎo qián   yī jīn   píngguǒ?
Lit.   How much money one jin apple?
How *much* is a half-kilo of apples?

If the context makes clear what you are talking about – for example, bananas – you can simply say:

Duō shǎo qián?   *or*   **Duō shǎo qián yī jīn?**

Another common way of asking the price is **Zěnme mài?**, which can be broadly translated as 'How is it sold?' If you want to specify the goods, they should always be placed at the beginning of the question. For example:

Lìzhī   *zěnme mài?*   *How* are lychees *sold?*
Lit.   Lychee how   sell?

■ 5 Difference between **duō shǎo** and **jǐ**

As we learnt before, when the question word **jǐ** (how many?) is used, the questioner expects a small quantity (fewer than twenty) in the reply. Another thing to remember about **jǐ** is that in most cases either a measure word or unit word must be used. **Duō shǎo** (how many?/how much?) does not have such restrictions. For example:

Nǐ yào *jǐ jīn* xiāngjiāo?
How many jins of bananas do you want?

Nǐ yào *duō shǎo* xiāngjiāo?
What quantity of bananas do you want?

6 Difference between **yào** and **xiǎng**

Look at these three sentences:

Wǒ *yào* **kāfēi.**
Lit. I want coffee.

Wǒ *yào* **hē kāfēi.**
Lit. I want drink coffee.

Wǒ *xiǎng* **hē kāfēi.**
Lit. I want drink coffee.

The verb **yào** can be followed by nouns or verbs whilst **xiǎng** must be followed by another verb if the meaning 'to want' is intended. When **xiǎng** is followed by a noun or a sentence, it means 'to miss' or 'to think'. For example:

Wǒ *xiǎng* **kāfēi.**   I *miss* coffee.
Wǒ *xiǎng*, **tā èrshí zuǒyòu.**   I *think* he's about twenty.

There is also a subtle difference in meaning between **yào** and **xiǎng**. **Xiǎng** is more like the English 'would like' when followed by another verb whilst **yào** is a straightforward 'to want' showing a certain degree of determination. For example:

Wǒ *xiǎng* **mǎi yīxiē shuíguǒ.**   I'd *like* to buy some fruit.
Wǒ *yào* **mǎi yīxiē shuíguǒ.**   I *want* to buy some fruit.

■ 7 Verbs **mǎi** and **mài**

Although **mǎi** (to buy) and **mài** (to sell) share the same pronunciation, they differ in tones and character representation (see characters on page 166). Do not worry if you cannot get the tone right, because the context will always help.

■ 8 Use of **zhǎo**

This verb has several meanings. The meaning 'to return' is only re-stricted to situations where someone gives someone else the change. For example:

A: **Gěi nǐ wǔ kuài.**
Here is five kuai.

B: *Zhǎo* **nǐ yī kuài bā máo.**
Here is one kuai and eight mao change.

(A being the customer, and B the shop-assistant.) Remember that **zhǎo** cannot be used to mean 'to return' other things (e.g. books).

■ 9 Extra vocabulary on fruit

You may find the following words useful:

lízi	pear	**júzi**	tangerine
xìngzi	apricot	**bōluó**	pineapple
chénzi	orange	**xī guā**	water melon

■ 10 Construction **yǒu méi yǒu**

Like . . . **shì bú shì** . . . **?** (see Note 8 of Lesson 5), . . . **yǒu méi yǒu** . . . **?** is an alternative pattern to . . . **yǒu** . . . **ma?** For example:

> **Nǐ *yǒu* Zhōngguó chá *ma?***
> *becomes* **Nǐ *yǒu méi yǒu* Zhōngguó chá?**
> Do you have any Chinese tea?

Exercises

Exercise 1

Look at the following drawings, paying attention to the price next to each drawing, and answer the questions using complete sentences:

¥8.75 / **yī jīn**

¥9.00 / **yī jīn**

¥14.65 / **yī jīn**

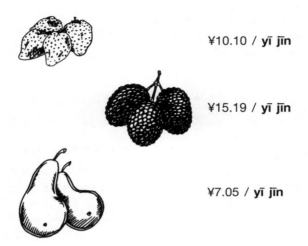

¥10.10 / **yī jīn**

¥15.19 / **yī jīn**

¥7.05 / **yī jīn**

(a) Píngguǒ duō shǎo qián yī jīn?
(b) Shénme jiǔ kuài yī jīn?
(c) Xiāngjiāo zěnme mài?
(d) Cǎoméi duō shǎo qián yī jīn?
(e) Shénme qī kuài líng wǔ yī jīn?
(f) Duō shǎo qián yī jīn lìzhī?

Exercise 2

Fill in the blanks using **yào** or **xiǎng**, and in some cases either can be used:

(a) (When asked what David wants to drink, his mum says:)
    Dàwèi _____ yī bēi júzi zhī (**júzi zhī** means 'orange juice').
(b) Wǒ bù _____ hē kāfēi.
(c) (In a shop) Wǒ _____ sān jīn cǎoméi.
(d) Tā _____ xiān chī wǔfàn.

Exercise 3

Translate the following sentences into Chinese:

(a) I'd like to buy some Hainan Island bananas.
(b) He doesn't want strawberries.
(c) I bought a kilo of apples.
(d) Do you want anything else?

(e) I don't know how much it is.
(f) A: Here is five kuai.
    B: Here is two mao and five fen change.

Dialogue 2

Tài guì le 太贵了 It's too expensive **(CD2; 12)**

David is in Guangzhou on a business trip. After a week's tough negotiations, he suddenly remembers that he wants to do some shopping. So he asks his Chinese colleague Fan Ting.

DAVID	Xiǎo Fàn, xīngqītiān shāngdiàn guānmén ma?
FÀN TÍNG	Bù guānmén. Suóyǒude shāngdiàn, yínháng, yóu jú dōu kāimén. Zěnme, nǐ xiǎng mǎi dōngxi ma?
DAVID	Shì de. Wǒ xiǎng gěi wǒ tàitai mǎi jǐ tiáo zhēn sī wéijīn, gěi xiǎohái hē péngyou mǎi yīxiē lǐwù.
FÀN TÍNG	Nà bù nán. Wǒ kěyǐ dài nǐ qù bǎihuò shāngdiàn.
DAVID	Nǐ tài hǎo le. Duō xiè.

(*As they could not find everything David would like to buy in the big department stores, they decide to go to a nearby market where bargains are to be found. David sees a nice silk tie.*)

DAVID	Xiǎojie, zhè tiáo lǐngdài zěnme mài?
STREET-VENDOR	Liǎng bái wǔshí kuài yī tiáo.
DAVID	Tài guì le.
STREET-VENDOR	Liǎng bǎi kuài, xíng ma?
DAVID	Sān bái wǔshí kuài mǎi liǎng tiáo, zěnme yàng?
STREET-VENDOR	Hǎo ba, hǎo ba.
DAVID	Wǒ yào le.

DAVID	小范，星期天商店关门吗？
FÀN TÍNG	不关门。所有的商店、银行、邮局都开门。怎么？你想买东西吗？
DAVID	是的。我想给我太太买几条真丝围巾，给小孩和朋友买一些礼物。
FÀN TÍNG	那不难。我可以带你去百货商店。
DAVID	你太好了。多谢。

. . . .

DAVID	小姐，这条领带怎么卖？
STREET-VENDOR	两百五十块一条。
DAVID	太贵了。
STREET-VENDOR	两百块，行吗？
DAVID	三百五十块买两条，怎么样？
STREET-VENDOR	好吧，好吧。
DAVID	我要了。

(CD2; 11)

Vocabulary

xīngqītiān	星期天	Sunday
shāngdiàn	商店	shop
guānmén	关门	to be closed/to close
suǒyǒude	所有的	all
dōngxi	东西	things
mǎi dōngxi	买东西	to go shopping/to do shopping [*lit.* 'buy things']
jǐ	几	several
tiáo	条	[measure word, see Note 14]
zhēn sī	真丝	pure silk
wéijīn	围巾	scarf
xiǎo hái	小孩	small children
lǐwù	礼物	presents/gifts
nán	难	to be difficult/difficult
dài	带	to take
bǎihuò shāngdiàn	百货商店	department store [*lit.* 'hundred goods shop']
duō xiè	多谢	many thanks
xiǎojiě	小姐	Miss [*lit.* 'little sister']
lǐngdài	领带	tie
guì	贵	to be expensive
bǎi	百	hundred

Notes on Dialogue 2

■ 11 Use of **suóyǒude . . . dōu . . .**

If you want to say 'all the banks' inclusively, use **suóyǒude** and **dōu** at the same time. Put **suóyǒude** in front of nouns and **dōu** in front of verbs. For example:

Zài Yīngguó, suóyǒude yínháng xīngqītiān dōu guānmén.
In Britain, *all* the banks are closed on Sunday.

Suóyǒude dōngxi dōu hěn guì.
All the things are very expensive.

■ 12 Verbal phrase **mǎi dōngxi**

Literally, **mǎi dōngxi** means 'to buy things'; idiomatically, it means 'to do shopping'. If you want to say 'to go shopping', the verb **qù** (to go) must be used before **mǎi dōngxi**. Phrases such as **yīxiē** (some), **yīdiǎnr** (a little) are inserted in between **mǎi** and **dōngxi**. For example:

Wǒ xiānsheng bù xǐhuan mǎi dōngxi.
My husband does not like *going shopping*.

Māma qù mǎi dōngxi le.
Mum has *gone shopping*.

Tā mǎi le yīxiē dōngxi.
He *did* some *shopping*.

■ 13 Construction **gěi . . . mǎi . . .**

In English, you say *I buy something for somebody*; in Chinese, you say 'for somebody I buy something'. For example:

Tā xiǎng gěi tāde xiǎohái mǎi yīxiē lǐwù.
Lit.   She want for her   children buy some presents.
She wants to buy some presents for her children.

Wǒ gěi wǒde tàitai mǎi le yī tiáo wéijīn.
Lit.   I   for my   wife bought a   scarf.
I bought a scarf for my wife.

■ 14 Measure word **tiáo**

This measure word is used for things such as a scarf, tie, trousers, etc. For example:

Zhè *tiáo* lǐngdài hěn piàoliang.
This tie is very beautiful.

Tā mǎi le sān *tiáo* zhēn sī wéijīn.
She bought three pure silk scarves.

■ 15 Adjective **jǐ**

This is the same **jǐ** as the question word **jǐ** (how many?/which?). However, in this context, it means 'several' and is used to refer to any number that is more than one but less than ten. Let us compare **jǐ** as a question word to **jǐ** as an adjective in the following two sentences:

A: **Māma, wǒ yǒu *jǐ* tiáo lǐngdài?**
Mum, *how many* ties do I have?
B: **Wǒ zěnme zhīdào?**
How could I know?

A: **Nǐ qù nǎr?**
Where are you going?
B: **Mǎi dōngxi. Wǒ xiǎng mǎi *jǐ* jīn shuíguǒ.**
Going shopping. I'd like to buy *several* jins of fruit.

■ 16 Construction **dài . . . qù/lái**

If you want to take someone from where you are to somewhere else, you use the verb **dài** with **qù** (to take); and if you want to bring someone from somewhere else to where you are, you use the verb **dài** with **lái** (to bring). The words **qù** and **lái**, originally meaning 'to go' and 'to come' respectively, are directional words in this context. There is always a person's name or a personal pronoun in between **dài** and **qù/lái**. Let us look at some examples:

Fàn Tíng *dài* Dàwèi *qù* mǎi dōngxi.
Fan Ting *takes* David to do the shopping.

Nǐ kěyi *dài* wǒ *qù* yínháng ma?
Could you *take* me to the bank?

Tā bù xiǎng *dài* tāde xiǎohái *lái*.
She doesn't want to *bring* her children along.

Note the direction words **qù** and **lái** are often pronounced with a
neutral tone.

■ 17 **Nǐ tài hǎo le**

The phrase **Nǐ tài hǎo le**, literally meaning 'You are extremely good',
is equivalent to the English expressions *It's very kind of you* or *You
are too kind*.

■ 18 Use of **Xiǎojie**

As China opens up to the West, the term **xiǎojie** (which is like the
French word *mademoiselle*) is becoming more and more popular to
address, for example, female shop-assistants instead of the term
tóngzhì (comrade). It is also a way of attracting a lady's attention.
Xiǎojie can also be used as a title to mean 'Miss'. For example:

Customer: ***Xiǎojie*, nǐmen yóu cǎoméi ma?**
Miss, do you have strawberries?

(On the phone) **Wáng *xiǎojie* zài ma?**
Is *Miss* Wang in?

■ 19 **Wǒ yào le**

This is a commonly used phrase in shops when you have decided
that you want to buy something, which can be broadly translated
as 'I'll take it'.

■ 20 Extra vocabulary on things to buy

Chinese	English
yī tào míngxìnpiàn	a set of postcards
yóupiào	stamp
Yīng Hàn cídiǎn	English–Chinese dictionary

Exercises

Exercise 4

You tell the shop-assistant that you would like to buy

(a) a pure silk tie
(b) one kilo of bananas
(c) two scarves
(d) half a kilo of apples
(e) a map of Beijing
(f) two postcards

Exercise 5

You ask your Chinese friend if he/she can take you to

(a) a department store
(b) a bank
(c) a post office
(d) a swimming pool

Exercise 6

What would you say on the following occasions based on what we have learnt:

(a) A street-vendor approaches you and asks you if you would like a silk scarf; you see the price tag and you think it is too expensive.
(b) After some bargaining, you have decided to make a purchase.
(c) You are in a fruit shop, but the shop-assistant is not aware of your presence. You want to attract her attention and also ask her if they have lychees.
(d) You are new in a city and a colleague of yours has offered to take you shopping; you want to express your gratitude using a more sophisticated expression.

Exercise 7

Complete the following sentences using the expressions in the brackets, and then translate them into English:

(a) Tā _____ (*for his girl-friend*) mǎi le yī tiáo zhēn sī wéijīn.
(b) Wǒ yīnggāi qù bǎihuò shāngdiàn _____ (*do some shopping*).
(c) Xīngqītiān (*all banks*) _____ kāimén.
(d) Xiǎo Wáng hē le _____ (*several cups of*) kāfēi.
(e) Wǒ gēge huì _____ (*bring my mother*) kàn wǒmen.

Exercise 8

Pair work – one person asks questions in Chinese based on Dialogue 2, and the other person answers them. For example:

A: Dàwèi wèishénme xiǎng qù shāngdiàn?
B: Tā xiǎng gěi tàitai hé xiǎohái mǎi lǐwù.

Characters

When shopping, it is very useful to recognize the Chinese currency words:

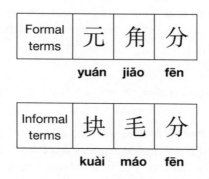

Formal terms	元	角	分
	yuán	jiǎo	fēn

Informal terms	块	毛	分
	kuài	máo	fēn

Let us learn to write the following three characters:

Character analysis	Head component and its meaning	Stroke order	Pinyin	English
⁊ + 头 tóu	(one)	买 ⁊ ⁊⁊ ⁊ᐧ ⁊ 买	mǎi	to buy
十 + 买	十 (ten)	卖 一 十 士 卉 去 走 卖 卖	mài	to sell
西 + 女	西 (west)	要 一 ⼧ ⼧ 襾 襾 西 要 要 要	yào	to want

(Unexplained component - 头 **tóu**: head)

In Lesson 7, we learnt the direction words 东 (**dōng**, east) and 西 (**xī**, west). The interesting thing is that when we put 东西 together, it means 'things' and 西 is pronounced with a neutral tone. So 买东西 literally means 'buy things'.

Exercise 9

(1) If you see the following prices, how much are they? Give the English translation.

(a) 十五元
(b) 三块七毛
(c) 六十八元一角
(d) 二十五块

(2) Use the character analysis table above and make up a story each about 买，卖 and 要 to help you memorize them.

(3) Put pinyin underneath the following sentences and then translate them into English:

(a) 我要买东西。
(b) 我们不卖早饭。

(4) Find the component that is shared by these two characters:

要，好

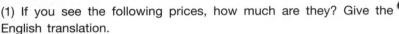

Reading/listening comprehension

(CD2; 14)

Read the following dialogue, and then answer the questions in English below. If you have access to the audio material, listen first, and then answer the questions in Chinese.

B Vocabulary

hěnduō	a lot of/many	**shuìyī**	night gown [*lit.* 'sleep clothes']
jiàn	[measure word for clothes]	**zhuōbù**	table-cloth
kuài	[measure word]	**kànkan**	to take a look

David is going back to Toronto after working in Beijing for a couple of weeks, and he has just done some shopping. A Chinese friend of his, Xiao Li, has come to see him and asks about his shopping.

XIĂO LĬ	Nǐ mǎi le yīxiē shénme?
DAVID	Hěnduō dōngxi. Wǒ gěi wǒ tàitai mǎi le yī jiàn shuìyī.
XIĂO LĬ	Zhēn piàoliang. Shì zhēn sī de ma?
DAVID	Shì de.
XIĂO LĬ	Duō shǎo qián?
DAVID	Liǎng bǎi bāshí wǔ kuài. Guì ma?
XIĂO LĬ	Zhēnde bú guì. Zhèxiē shì shénme?
DAVID	Jǐ kuài zhuōbù.
XIĂO LĬ	Wǒ kěyi kànkan ma?
DAVID	Dāngrán kěyi.
XIĂO LĬ	Tài piàoliang le.

QUESTIONS

(1) Dàwèi gěi tā tàitai mǎi le shénme?
(2) Zhè ge dōngxi duō shǎo qián?
(3) Xiǎo Lǐ juéde Dàwèi mǎi de dōngxi zěnme yàng?
(4) Dàwèi hái mǎi le shénme biéde dōngxi?

Lesson Nine
Mǎi dōngxi (II) 买东西
Shopping (II)

By the end of this lesson, you should be able to:

- say some colour words
- make simple comparisons
- ask to borrow things from somebody
- ask someone's opinion about two things
- write more characters

Dialogue 1

Nǎ jiàn hǎo? 哪件好？ Which is better?
(CD2; 16)

Paul is studying Chinese at a university in Beijing. Today, he is going shopping with his flatmate Liu Hong. They are looking at some sweaters.

PAUL   Xiǎo Liú, nǐ shuō zhè liǎng jiàn máoyī, nǎ jiàn hǎo?
LIÚ HÓNG Wǒ juéde lǜde bǐ huángde hǎo. Nǐ chuān lǜ yánsè
           bǐjiào hǎo.
PAUL   Hǎo ba, wǒ tīng nǐde.

(Paul has decided to take the green sweater and as he is reaching for his wallet . . .)

PAUL	Zāogāo! Wǒ wàng le dài qiánbāo. Xiǎo Liú, nǐ kěyi jiè gěi wǒ yīxiē qián ma?
LIÚ HÓNG	Méi wèntí. Nǐ yào duō shǎo?
PAUL	Sān bǎi kuài, xíng ma?
LIÚ HÓNG	Xíng. Gòu ma?
PAUL	Gòu le.
LIÚ HÓNG	Gěi nǐ.
PAUL	Tài xièxie nǐ le. Míngtiān wǒ yīdìng huán gěi nǐ qián.
LIÚ HÓNG	Bù jí. Zánmen qù shūdiàn kànkan, hǎo ma? Wǒ xiǎng mǎi jǐ běn shū.
PAUL	Hǎo de.

PAUL	小刘，你说这两件毛衣，哪件好？
LIÚ HÓNG	我觉得绿的比黄的好。你穿绿颜色比较好。
PAUL	好吧，我听你的。
...	
PAUL	糟糕！我忘了带钱包。小刘，你可以借给我一些钱吗？
LIÚ HÓNG	没问题。你要多少？
PAUL	三百块，行吗？
LIÚ HÓNG	行。够吗？

PAUL	够了。
LIÚ HÓNG	给你。
PAUL	太谢谢你了。明天我一定还给你钱。
LIÚ HÓNG	不急。咱们去书店看看，好吗？我想买几本书。
PAUL	好的。

(CD2; 15)

Vocabulary

jiàn	件	[measure word for clothes]
máoyī	毛衣	sweater/jumper
juéde	觉得	to think/to feel
lǜ	绿	green
bǐ	比	to be compared with
huáng	黄	yellow
chuān	穿	to wear
yánsè	颜色	colour
bǐjiào	比较	quite/rather/relatively
tīng	听	to listen to
zāo gāo	糟糕	Oh, no!
wàng	忘	to forget
dài	带	to bring/to take
qiánbāo	钱包	wallet/purse
jiè	借	to lend
gòu	够	to be enough
gěi nǐ	给你	here you are [*lit.* 'for you']
yīdìng	一定	definitely/must
huán	还	to return
jí	急	urgent/hurry
shū	书	book
shūdiàn	书店	bookshop
běn	本	[measure word for books]

Notes on Dialogue 1

■ 1 **Nǐ shuō . . .**

This is one of the ways to ask someone's advice. Literally, **nǐ shuō** means 'you say' or 'you speak', which can be broadly translated as 'What do you think . . . ?' or 'What would you say . . . ?'. For example:

> **Nǐ shuō zánmen jǐ   diǎn qù yóuyǒng?**
> *Lit.* You say we   what time go swimming?
> What time *do you think* we shall go swimming?

> **Nǐ   shuō Běijīng dà háishì Lúndūn dà?**
> *Lit.* You say Beijing big or   London big?
> *What would you say?* Is Beijing bigger or is London bigger?

■ 2 Colours **(CD2; 17)**

Below are some commonly used colour words:

Chinese	English	Chinese	English
hóng	red	**bái**	white
hēi	black	**lán**	blue
huī	grey	**jīnhuáng**	golden
júhuáng	orange	**hè**	brown
zǐ	purple	**fěn**	pink

The above colour words are adjectives. If you want to say 'the red' or 'the blue one', simply add **de** (see Note 15, Lesson 3) to the appropriate colour adjective. If you want to say 'the white colour', add **yánsè** (colour) or **sè** (the same **sè** as in **yánsè**) to the adjective **bái** (white). For example:

> A: **Nǐ yào nǎ zhǒng yánsè?**   A: Which colour do you want?
> B: **Hóng*de*.**   B: The red.
> A: **Nǐ xǐhuan shénme yánsè?**   A: What colour do you like?
> B: **Lán *yánsè*./Lán sè.**   B: The blue colour.

If you want to say, for example, 'dark blue' or 'light blue', place **shēn** (dark) or **qiǎn** (light) in front of **lán** (blue). Thus we have **shēn lán** or **qiǎn lán**.

■ 3 Comparing two things

If you compare A with B and want to say 'A is better than B', or 'A is more beautiful than B', use the construction:

A + **bǐ** + B + *adjective*

For example:

Lìzhī *bǐ* píngguǒ guì.
Lychees are *more* expensive *than* apples.

Dōngtiān, Běijīng *bǐ* Lúndūn lěng.
In winter, Beijing is colder *than* London.

Zhè jiàn lǜ máoyī *bǐ* hēide hǎo.
This green jumper is *better than* the black one.

When asking someone's opinion about two things, you list the two things first, and then ask the question in the usual order. For example:

Lǜ máoyī *hé* hēi máoyī, nǎ jiàn hǎo?
Lit. Green jumper and black jumper, which [measure word] be good?
Which is better, the green jumper or the black jumper?

Nǐ *hé* nǐ gēge, shéi gāo?
Lit. You and your elder brother who be tall?
Who is taller, you or your elder brother?

■ 4 Use of **bǐjiào**

This adverb is very often used in front of adjectives to modify them. It can mean 'relatively', 'quite' or 'rather'. It is one of those favourite words people use when they express their opinions or give advice to somebody so that it does not sound too aggressive or bossy. For example:

Wǒ juéde nǐ chuān hēi yánsè *bǐjiào* hǎo.
Lit. I think you wear black colour quite well.
I think black suits you *quite* well.

Zhōngwén *bǐjiào* nán.
The Chinese language is *rather* difficult.

■ 5 Verb **tīng**

The verb **tīng** (to listen to) can be followed by a noun, a phrase or a sentence. For example:

Yuēhàn xǐhuan *tīng* Zhōngguó yīnyuè.
John likes *to listen to* Chinese music.

Qǐng *tīng* tā shuō.
Please *listen to* what he says.

The expression **Wǒ tīng nǐde** (*lit.* 'I listen to yours'), which occurs in Dialogue 1, can be taken to mean 'I'll take your advice'.

■ 6 Verb **wàng**

This is a very useful word to remember. It is often used together with the past indicator **le** to mean 'to forget' or 'to have forgotten'. For example:

Wǒ *wàng* le gěi xiǎohái mǎi lǐwù.
I *forgot* to buy presents for the children.

A: **Zhōngwén zěnme shuō 'lychee'?**
How do you say 'lychee' in Chinese?

B: **Duìbuqǐ, wǒ *wàng* le.**
Sorry, I *forgot*.

■ 7 More on the verb **dài**

In Note 16 of Lesson 8, we came across this verb. In that context, it meant 'to bring' or 'to take' *somebody* to somewhere. Here, it means 'to bring' or 'to take' *something*. For example:

Wǒ wàng le *dài* qiánbāo.   I forgot to *bring* the wallet.
Nǐ *dài* qián le ma?   *Have you got* some money on you?

When the verb **dài** is used without any directional words, it is ambiguous. For example, the sentence **Wǒ mèimei *dài* le yīxiē shuǐguǒ** can mean 'My younger sister *brought* some fruit' or 'My younger sister took some fruit'. To make it clear that it means 'to bring', you can use the directional word **lái** either after the verb **dài** or after the object. For example:

Tā fùmǔ *dài lái* le yīxiē Zhōngguó chá.
Her parents *brought* some Chinese tea.

or **Tā fùmǔ *dài* le yīxiē Zhōngguó chá *lái*.**
Her parents *brought* some Chinese tea.

Note the position of the past indicator **le** in the above two sentences.

■ 8 Verb **jiè**

When **jiè** is used to mean 'to lend', it is almost always used together with the prepositional phrase **gěi** + somebody (to somebody). For example:

Liú Hóng *jiè gěi* le Bǎoluó sānshí kuài qián.
Liu Hong *lent* thirty yuan to *Paul*.

Note that the past particle **le** is placed after the preposition **gěi**. Let us compare **jiè** (to borrow) with **jiè** (to lend):

Wǒ xiǎng jiè yīxià nǐde zìxíngchē.
I'd like to borrow your bike.

Nǐ kěyi *jiè gěi* wǒ yīxiē qián ma?
Could you *lend me* some money?

■ 9 Verb **huán**

The verb **huán**, meaning 'to return' or 'to give . . . back' can only be followed by things or money which you have borrowed. It cannot be used to mean 'to return home', for example. If you want to say 'to return something to somebody' or 'to return somebody something', use the phrase **gěi** + somebody after the verb **huán**. For example:

Nǐ   shénme shíhou *huán gěi* wǒ qián?
Lit.   You when   return to me money?
When are you going to *give me* the money *back*?

When the preposition **gěi** is used in a statement, the past indicator **le** is usually placed after **gěi** instead of after the verb; when **gěi** occurs in a yes/no question, **le** is placed immediately before the question word **ma**. For example:

Tā huán *gěi le wǒ* yī běn shū. She has *returned* one book to me.
Tā huán *gěi* nǐ shū *le* ma?   Has she *returned* any books
                              to you?

The preposition **gěi** is sometimes omitted in the spoken language.
For example:

    Wǒ wàng le *huán* tā qián.
    I forgot to *return* the money to him.

■ 10 Use of **gòu**

This is a very useful phrase, especially at the dinner table. Until you
say **Gòu le** (That's enough) food will be offered to you again and
again. The phrase tends to be repeated to show that it is the truth,
not simply said out of politeness. For example:

    A: **Gòu ma?**   Is it enough?
    B: ***Gòu le, gòu le.***   Yes, it's enough.

Remember that although **le** has no significant meaning, it must be
used together with **gòu** to mean 'Yes, it's enough'. However, when the
negation word **bù** is used, **le** is usually omitted. For example:

    A: **Gòu ma?**   Is it enough?
    B: ***Bú gòu.***   *No, it's not.*

■ 11 Omission of **yǒu** in **méi wèntí**

The verb **yǒu** (to have) is usually omitted when it is negated by **méi**
in phrases or sentences. For example:

Méi *yǒu* wèntí.   *becomes*   **Méi wèntí.**   No problem.
Méi *yǒu* guānxi.   *becomes*   **Méi guānxi.**   It doesn't matter.
Wǒ méi yǒu kāfēi.   *becomes*   **Wǒ méi kāfēi.**   I don't have any coffee.

Exercises

Exercise 1

Compare the following two things or people in each drawing and
make up sentences using **bǐ**:

(a) USA   China

(b) ¥15.90   ¥8.45

(c) John   Wang Lin

(d)

(e) PASSPORT   PASSPORT
NAME Amy Smith AGE: 43
PASSPORT   PASSPORT
NAME Wong Lin Lin AGE: 36

Some adjectives you may need in making comparisons:

gāo   tall   **dà**   old (age only)
ǎi   short   **xiǎo**   young (age only)

Exercise 2

The following questions do not have a *single* correct answer. Answer them in Chinese using your own opinions. Then translate the answers into English:

(a) Nǐ zuì xǐhuan shénme yánsè?
(b) Nǐ bǐjiào xǐhuan shénme fàn?
(c) Zhōngwén hé Fǎwén (French), nǎ ge nán?
(d) Fǎguó fàn bǐ Yīngguó fàn hǎo ma?

Exercise 3

Match the colour words in the left-hand column with the nouns in the right-hand column (one colour word may go with more than one noun):

(a) lán   1   píngguǒ
(b) lǜ   2   xiāngjiāo
(c) huáng   3   chá (tea)
(d) hóng   4   tiān (sky)

Exercise 4

Translate the following sentences into Chinese:

(a) Could you lend me two apples?
(b) He doesn't like lending money to friends.
(c) When is she going to give me the money back?
(d) I forgot to bring my wallet.
(e) Thank you for bringing some Chinese tea.
(f) Did she take her jumper with her?
(g) Liu Hong looks younger than Xiǎo Fāng.

Exercise 5

What does the verb **jiè** mean in the following sentences? Write 'borrow' or 'lend':

(a) Wǒ xiǎng jiè yīxià nǐde zìxíngchē.
(b) Nǐ kěyi jiè gěi wǒ yīxiē qián ma?
(c) Wǒ bù xiǎng jiè wǒ fùmǔ de qián.
(d) Xiǎo Fāng jiè gěi le Lǎo Wáng wǔshí kuài qián.

Dialogue 2

Zhēn hésuàn 真合算 It's a bargain (CD2; 19)

Jane and Yuan Yi work for a joint-venture company in Guangzhou and they have become very good friends. Yuan Yi speaks a little English. Jane has invited Yuan Yi to her place for a meal. When Jane arrives home, she finds Yuan Yi waiting outside her flat.

JANE	Duìbuqǐ. Wǒ chí dào le.
YUÁN YÌ	Méi guānxi. Wǒ gāng lái.
JANE	Jīntiān xià bān zǎo. Wǒ qù guàng le guàng fúzhuāng shìchǎng.
YUÁN YÌ	Yǒu shénme hǎo dōngxi ma?
JANE	Yǒu hěnduō. Kěxī wǒ méi dài zúgòu de qián. Wǒ mǎi le yī jiàn . . . Zhōngwén zěnme shuō 'jumper'?
YUÁN YÌ	'Máoyī'.
JANE	Duì. Wǒ mǎi le jiàn máoyī.
YUÁN YÌ	Ràng wǒ kànkan. (*after she has had a look and felt it*) Zhēn bú cuò. Mōshangqu hěn shūfu. Duō shǎo qián?
JANE	Bāshí duō kuài.
YUÁN YÌ	Zhème piányi! Zhēn hésuàn. Wǒ hěn xǐhuan zhè zhǒng yánsè. Hái yǒu ma?
JANE	Shēn hóng sè de mài guāng le. Zhè shì zuìhòu yī jiàn. Búguò, hái yǒu hěnduō qítā hǎokàn de yánsè.
YUÁN YÌ	Wǒ míngtiān bú shàng bān, chōu kòng qù kànkan.

JANE	对不起。我迟到了。
YUÁN YÌ	没关系。我刚来。
JANE	今天下班早。我去逛了逛服装市场。
YUÁN YÌ	有什么好东西吗？

JANE	有很多。可惜我没带足够的钱。我买了一件 ... 中文怎么说 'JUMPER'？
YUÁN YÌ	'毛衣'。
JANE	对。我买了件毛衣。
YUÁN YÌ	让我看看。... 真不错。摸上去很舒服。多少钱？
JANE	八十多块。
YUÁN YÌ	这么便宜，真合算。我很喜欢这种颜色。还有吗？
JANE	深红色的卖光了。这是最后一件。不过，还有很多其他好看的颜色。
YUÁN YÌ	我明天不上班，抽空去看看。

(CD2; 18)

Vocabulary

chí dào	迟到	to be late [*lit.* 'late arrive']
gāng	刚	just
xià bān	下班	to finish work
guàng	逛	to look around
fúzhuāng	服装	clothing
shìcháng	市场	market
shénme	什么	any/anything
hěn duō	很多	many
zúgòude	足够的	enough
bú cuò	不错	not bad
mōshangqu	摸上去	it feels ...
shūfu	舒服	nice/comfortable
duō	多	more than/over
zhème	这么	so
piányi	便宜	to be cheap/cheap/inexpensive
hé suàn	合算	good bargain
zhǒng	种	kind
shēn	深	dark [e.g. colour]
mài guāng le	卖光了	to be sold out
zuìhòu	最后	last
qítā	其他	other

hǎokàn	好看	good-looking/nice [*lit.* 'good see']
shàng bān	上班	to go to work/be at work
chōu kòng	抽空	to make time/to find time

Notes on Dialogue 2

■ 12 Verbs **lái** and **dào**

The verb **lái** can mean both 'to come' or 'to arrive', whilst the verb **dào** can only mean 'to arrive'. They are interchangeable when the meaning of 'to arrive' is intended. For example:

| **Wǒ gāng *lái*.** | I've just *arrived*. |
| **Wǒ gāng *dào*.** | I've just *arrived*. |

Note that when the word **gāng** (just) is used, **le** is not needed.

■ 13 Adverbs **chí** and **zǎo**

Regarding the verb **lái** (to arrive/come), **chí** (late) and **zǎo** (early) are placed *after* it. For example:

Xiǎo Wáng lái *chí* le wǔ fēnzhōng.
Xiao Wang arrived five minutes *late*.

Wǒ lái *zǎo* le.
I arrived *earlier*.

However, **chí** must be placed *before* **dào** in **Wǒ *chí* dào le** (*lit.* 'I *late* arrived'). The expression **Wǒ chí dào le** is used more frequently than **Wǒ lái chí le** if the meaning of 'I'm late' is intended. An alternative to **chí** is **wǎn**, which is often used after the verb.

■ 14 Verb **guàng**

The verb **guàng** can be broadly translated as 'look around' (usually followed by shopping places). The phrase **guàng shāngdiàn** has slightly different implications from **mǎi dōngxi**. When you **guàng shāngdiàn**, there is nothing specific you want to buy, whereas the phrase **mǎi dōngxi** suggests that you know what you want to buy. For example:

Wǒ xǐhuān *guàng* shìchǎng.
I like to *look around* markets.

Tā bù xǐhuān *guàng* shāngdiàn.
She doesn't like to *look around* shops.

■ 15 Shìchǎng

In mainland China, **shìchǎng**, meaning 'markets', are places where bargains are expected. There are all kinds of markets. Here are some useful words:

shū huà shìchǎng	calligraphy and art market
nóng mào shìchǎng	fruit and vegetable market
yú shìchǎng	fish market
sīchóu shìchǎng	silk market

■ 16 Repetition of some one-syllable verbs

When some one-syllable verbs are repeated, a touch of informality is added to the expression. For example:

Wǒ qù kàn*kan*.
I'll go and have a look.

Nǐ xiǎng guàng*guang* shìchǎng ma?
Would you like to have a look around the market?

If the past indicator **le** is used when the verb is repeated, it is placed between the two verbs, *not* after the second verb. For example:

Wǒ kàn *le* kàn nà běn shū, méi yìsi.
I had a read of that book. Not interesting.

Wǒ tīng *le* tīng tāde Zhōngwén, hái bú cuò.
I had a listen to her Chinese. Not bad.

Note that because **le** is toneless, the repeated verb following it must keep its original tone.

■ 17 Phrases **shàng bān** and **xià bān**

The verb **shàng** in **shàng bān** is the same **shàng** as in **shàng xué** (to go to school) (see Note 10 of Lesson 5). The verb **xià** in **xià bān** can also be used to form the expression **xià xué** (to finish school). **Shàng bān** means 'to go to work' and **xià bān** means 'to finish work':

Míngtiān nǐ *shàng bān* zǎo ma?
Are you *going to work* early tomorrow?

Nǐ jīntiān jǐ diǎn *xià bān*?
What time do you *finish work* today?

When adverbs **chí** (late) and **zǎo** (early) are used to modify the verbal phrases **shàng bān** and **xià bān** (usually to describe the past action), (a) they are placed after **shàng bān** and **xià bān**; and (b) if no other expressions such as 'five minutes', 'half an hour', etc. follow **chí** and **zǎo**, the past particle **le** is omitted. For example:

Wǒ jīntiān shàng bān *chí le* yī kè zhōng.
I was fifteen minutes *late* for work today.

Wǒmen jīntiān xià bān hěn *zǎo*.
We finished work very early today.

■ 18 Use of **shénme**

Shénme can also be used in front of nouns in questions and negative sentences to mean 'any'. For example:

Fúzhuāng shìchǎng yǒu *shénme* hǎo dōngxi ma?
Is there *any* good stuff in the clothing market?

Tā méi yǒu *shénme* péngyou.
He doesn't have *any* friends.

■ 19 More on the question word **zěnme**

We saw this word previously in **Zěnme yàng?**, **Zěnme mài?**, etc. Let us see how it is used in asking more complex questions. For example:

Zhōngwén (nǐ) zěnme shuō 'TV'?
How do you say 'TV' in Chinese?

Nǐde míngzi (nǐ) zěnme xiě?
How do you write your name?

Note that the pronoun **nǐ** in the above sentences can be omitted.

■ 20 Omission of **yī** before measure words

The number **yī** (one) is usually omitted before measure words that precede nouns. However, if the noun following the measure word is omitted, the number word **yī** must remain. For example:

> **Wǒmende dàxué yǒu** *ge* **Fǎguórén.**
> *Lit.* Our university   have [measure word] France person.
> There is a French person at our university.

> **Xiǎo Wáng mǎi le liǎng jiàn máoyī. Wó mǎi le** *yī jiàn*.
> Xiao Wang bought two jumpers and I bought one.

■ 21 Use of **bú cuò**

Literally, **bú cuò** means 'not bad'. However, the Chinese **bú cuò** actually means 'quite good' or 'quite well'. For example:

Zhè ge fàndiàn *bú cuò*.
This hotel is *quite good*.

A: **Nǐ fùmǔ zuìjìn zěnme yàng?**
    How are your parents these days?

B: *Bú cuò*, **xièxie.**
    Quite well, thank you.

■ 22 Use of **duō**

The word **duō** is used after a number to mean 'more than' or 'over'. If there is a measure word in the sentence, **duō** must be placed before the measure word. For example:

Wǒde Zhōngwén lǎoshī sānshí *duō* **suì.**
My Chinese teacher is *over* thirty.

Tā yǒu èrshí *duō* **ge shūshu hé ā'yí.**
He has *more than* twenty uncles and aunts.

■ 23 Use of **hěn** before the verb

When **hěn** is used before the adjective, it means 'very' (see Lesson 1). Here, it is used before the verb and it means 'very much'. Let us compare the following two sentences:

Tā *hěn* hǎokàn.   She is very good-looking.
    adjective
Wǒ *hěn* xǐhuan Zhōngguó fàn.   I like Chinese food very much.
    verb

■ 24 Verbal phrase **chōu kòng**

The verb **chōu** literally means 'to draw/pull'. When it is used together with **kòng** (*lit.* 'space/vacancy'), we have the phrase **chōu kòng** meaning 'to make time'. For example:

Wǒ yīdìng *chōu kòng* qù kàn nǐ.
I'll definitely *make time* to go to see you.

Nǐ kěyi *chōu kòng* qù mǎi dōngxi ma?
Could you *make time* to go shopping?

Another expression which also means 'to make time' is **chōu shíjiān**. For example:

Nǐ *chōu shíjiān* gěi wǒ jiǎngjiang nǐde qíngkuàng, hǎo ma?
Will you *make some time* to tell me about yourself?

■ 25 Difference between **gòu** and **zúgòu de**

The word **gòu** (followed by **le** in affirmative sentences) is used *after* nouns to mean 'there is enough . . .' or 'be enough' whereas **zúgòu de** is used *before* nouns to mean 'enough'. For example:

A: **Qián *gòu* ma?**   Is there *enough* money?
B: **Gòu le.**   It's *enough*.

Tā yǒu *zúgòu de* qián.   He has *enough* money.

Exercises

Exercise 6

Fill in the blanks with **qù**, **shàng**, or **guàng**:

(a) Wǒ jīntiān bú _____ bān.
(b) Nǐ xiǎng qù _____ fúzhuāng shìchǎng ma?
(c) Zhū Mǐn xià ge yuè _____ Zhōngguó.
(d) Nǐde érzi _____ xiǎo xué le ma?

Exercise 7

Based on what we have learnt so far, what do you say in the following situations:

(a) You are late for your appointment and you apologize.
(b) You want to assure your friend that there is absolutely no prob-
     lem if he wants to borrow some money from you.
(c) You do not know how to say the phrase 'good bargain' in
     Chinese and you ask your Chinese teacher.
(d) You have just borrowed some money from your friend, and you
     want to assure her that you will definitely give it back to her
     tomorrow.

Exercise 8

Re-arrange the word order of the following so that each set of words
becomes a meaningful sentence. Then translate the sentences into
English:

(a) zhè tiáo lǐngdài, shūfu, mōshangqu, hěn
(b) shāngdiàn, wǒ, le, guàng, guàng
(c) gěi le wǒ, Tāng Bīn, èrshí kuài qián, jiè
(d) dào, tā, jīntiān zǎoshang, chí, èrshí fēnzhōng, le

Exercise 9

Fill in the blanks with **gòu** or **zúgòu de**:

(a) Sìshí kuài _____ ma?
(b) Wǒ méi yǒu _____ shíjiān qù yóuyǒng.

(c) A: Bàn jīn cǎoméi _____ ma?
     B: _____ le.
(d) Tāmen yǒu _____ qián qù Zhōngguó lǚyóu.

Exercise 10

Translate the following sentences into Chinese:

(a) She doesn't have any good friends.
(b) I'm not working tomorrow. I can find some time to go swimming.
(c) I guess he is over fifty.
(d) I'm sorry. The dark blue jumpers are sold out. Will black do?
(e) It's a really good bargain. Any more of these?
(f) My parents are in quite good health.

Characters

Let us learn two more head components: 纟 in 绿 (**lǜ**, green) and 钅 in 钱 (**qián**, money):

Character analysis	Head component and its meaning	Stroke order	English
纟 + 录 **lǜ**	纟 (silk)	绿 ㇙ 纟 纟 纟 纟 纟 纟 纟 纟 绿 绿	green
钅 + 戋 **jiān**	钅 (metal)	钱 ㇒ ㇀ ㇐ ㇐ 钅 钅 钅 钅 钱 钱 钱	money

(Unexplained components - 录 **lù**: acting as phonetic; 戋 **jiān**: spear)

Exercise 11

(1) Find out from the Vocabulary for both dialogues which characters use the silk and metal head components.

(2) Check the Vocabulary for both Dialogue 1 (p. 171) and Dialogue 2 (pp. 180–1) and list the characters that share the following components. Then learn to write those characters.

(a) 宀　　(b) 口　　(c) 心　　(d) 扌

(3) Choose the right character (see page 187) to fill in the blanks and then translate the sentences into English.

(a) 她没有_____。

　　 i) 钱　　ii) 银　　iii) 钢

(b) 我想买_____电话。

　　 i) 级　　ii) 禄　　iii) 绿

Reading/listening comprehension

(CD2; 20)

Below are seven Chinese sentences. Underneath each sentence are three interpretations. Read or listen to (if you have access to the audio material) each sentence first and then decide which interpretation is closest in meaning to the original sentence.

(1) Duìbuqǐ. Yìdàlì kāfēi mài guāng le. Hǎinán Dǎo kāfēi xíng ma?
　　(a) Yǒu hěnduō Yìdàlì kāfēi.
　　(b) Yǒu Hǎinán Dǎo kāfēi.
　　(c) Wǒmen méi yǒu kāfēi.

(2) Míngtiān, wǒ qī diǎn shàng bān.
　　(a) Wǒ míngtiān bú shàng bān.
　　(b) Wǒ míngtiān qī diǎn xià bān.
　　(c) Wǒ míngtiān qī diǎn kāishǐ gōngzuò.

(3) Xiǎo Fāng jiè gěi le Dàwèi wǔshí kuài qián.
　　(a) Dàwèi wèn Xiǎo Fāng jiè le wǔshí kuài qián.
　　(b) Dàwèi jiè gěi le Xiǎo Fāng wǔshí kuài qián.
　　(c) Xiǎo Fāng méi yǒu wǔshí kuài qián.

(4) Zāogāo! Wǒ wàng le huán Línlin qián.
　　(a) Wǒ wàng le dài Línlin de qián.
　　(b) Wǒ wàng le gěi Línlin qián.
　　(c) Línlin wàng le gěi wǒ qián.

(5) Wǒ mèimei bǐ wǒ hǎokàn.
　　(a) Wǒ juéde wǒ mèimei hěn hǎokàn.
　　(b) Wǒ juéde wǒ hé wǒ mèimei yīyàng hǎokàn.
　　(c) Wǒ juéde wǒ mèimei bù hǎokàn.

(6) Dàwèi bù zhīdào Zhōngwén zěnme shuō 'toilet'?
　　(a) Dàwèi huì yòng Zhōngwén shuō 'toilet'.
　　(b) Dàwèi bú huì yòng Zhōngwén shuō 'toilet'.
　　(c) Dàwèi bù zhīdào cèsuǒ zài nǎr.

(7) Chén Lìli chuān huáng sè bǐjiào hǎo.
　　(a) Chén Lìli chuān huáng sè hǎokàn.
　　(b) Chén Lìli chuān hóng sè bǐjiào hǎo.
　　(c) Chén Lìli xǐhuān huáng sè.

Lesson Ten
Zài cān'guǎn 在餐馆
At the restaurant

By the end of this lesson, you should be able to:

- name a few Chinese dishes
- order some food and drinks in a restaurant
- use two more measure words
- use **guo** to describe a past experience
- position some adverbs correctly by using **de**
- write and recognize more characters

 Dialogue 1

 Diǎn cài ma? 点菜吗？ Ready to order?
(CD2; 22)

Daniel and Janet are on an intensive Chinese language programme in Qingdao. Li Youde is their Chinese friend and he is taking them out for a meal tonight. They've just entered a restaurant . . .

WAITRESS Wǎnshang hǎo. Jǐ wèi?
LǏ YŎUDÉ Sān wèi.
WAITRESS Qǐng gēn wǒ lái.
(they follow the waitress to a table . . .)
WAITRESS Qǐng zuò. Nǐmen xiǎng xiān hē yīdiǎnr shénme?
DANIEL Wǒ yào yī píng Qīngdǎo píjiǔ.

LǏ YǑUDÉ   Wǒ yě yīyàng.
WAITRESS   Xiǎojie xiǎng hē shénme?
JANET   Yī bēi chéngzi zhī.
WAITRESS   Hǎo de. Qǐng kàn càidān.
(*after some discussion, they've decided to go for warm dishes
only, and now the waitress comes to take the order . . .*)
WAITRESS   Diǎn cài ma?
LǏ YǑUDÉ   Diǎn. Wǒ lái diǎn. Yī ge hǎixiān tāng, yī ge jīdīng chǎo
            shícài, yī ge . . .
DANIEL   Zài lái yī fènr xiǎo lóng bāozi ba. Yī fènr yǒu jǐ gè?
WAITRESS   Liù ge.
DANIEL   Nà, lái liǎng fènr ba. Wǒ è sǐ le.
WAITRESS   Hǎo de. Qǐng shāo děng.
LǏ YǑUDÉ   Hái yǒu, cài lǐ qǐng bú yào fàng wèijīng.
WAITRESS   Zhīdào le.

WAITRESS   晚上好。几位？
LǏ YǑUDÉ   三位。
WAITRESS   请跟我来。
 . . .
WAITRESS   请坐。你们想先喝一点儿什么？

DANIEL	我要一瓶青岛啤酒。
LǏ YǑUDÉ	我也一样。
WAITRESS	小姐想喝什么？
JANET	一杯橙子汁。
WAITRESS	好的。请看菜单。
. . .	
WAITRESS	点菜吗?
LǏ YǑUDÉ	点。我来点。一个海鲜汤，一个鸡丁炒时菜，一个...
DANIEL	再来一份儿小笼包子吧。一份儿有几个？
WAITRESS	六个。
LǏ YǑUDÉ	那，来两份儿吧。我饿死了。
WAITRESS	好的。请稍等。
LǏ YǑUDÉ	还有，菜里请不要放味精。
WAITRESS	知道了。

(CD2; 21)

Vocabulary

wèi, píng	位, 瓶	[measure word, see Note 1]
gēn	跟	to follow
zuò	坐	to sit/to sit down
píjiǔ	啤酒	beer
yīyàng	一样	to be the same/same
chéngzi zhī	橙子汁	orange juice
càidān	菜单	menu
diǎn cài	点菜	to order (+ food)
wǒ lái diǎn	我来点	let me do the ordering
hǎixiān	海鲜	seafood
tāng	汤	soup
jī dīng	鸡丁	diced chicken
shí cài	时菜	seasonal vegetables
fèn	份	[measure word, often pronounced with an 'r' sound attached to it]
xiǎo lóng	小笼	small steamer
bāozi	包子	steamed bun with filling

è sǐ le	饿死了	to be starving
shāo děng	稍等	it won't be long [*lit.* 'a while wait']
hái yǒu	还有	another thing; also
fàng	放	to put
wèijīng	味精	MSG

Notes on Dialogue 1

■ 1 Measure words **wèi** and **píng**

Wèi is only used in front of people. It is a polite form of the measure word **gè**. For example:

Zhōngwén Xì yǒu liǎng *wèi* jiàoshòu.
There are two professors in the Chinese Department.

Waiter: **Jǐ wèi?**   Waiter: How many of you?
Customer: **Sì wèi.**   Customer: Four.

Píng is used to indicate bottles and jars. For example:

Wǒ mǎi le sān *píng* píjiǔ.
I bought three bottles of beer.

■ 2 Use of **gēn**

In English, you say *Follow me*; in Chinese, you must say 'Follow me walk', 'Follow me read', 'Follow me come', etc. depending on the activity. For example:

| | **Qǐng** | ***gēn*** | **wǒ** | ***lái.*** |
| *Lit.* | Please follow me come. |

Please follow me./This way, please.

| | **Qǐng** | ***gēn*** | **tā** | ***dú.*** |
| *Lit.* | Please follow him read. |

Please follow him./Please read after him.

■ 3 **Wǒ yě yīyàng**

This phrase can be used if you wish to show that you agree with someone else's choice or opinion of a kind of drink, a film, etc. It can be broadly translated as 'Same for me, please', 'I think the same' or 'Me too', depending on the context. For example:

A: **Wǒ yào yī bēi chénzi zhī.**
I'd like a glass of orange juice.
B: **Wǒ yě yīyàng.**
Same for me, please.

A: **Wǒ hěn xǐhuan Zhōngguó fàn.**
I like Chinese food very much.
B: **Wǒ yě yīyàng.**
Me too.

■ 4 Phrase **diǎn cài**

The phrase **diǎn cài**, literally meaning 'choose dish', can only be used in restaurant situations. For example:

Waiter: **Xiānsheng, diǎn cài ma?**   Ready to order, sir?
Customer: **Diǎn.**   Yes, please.

The verb **diǎn** can be followed by dish names. For example:

Wǒ *diǎn* le yī ge tángcù yú.
I've ordered a sweet and sour fish.

■ 5 Phrase **wǒ lái diǎn**

In China, when your hosts take you out for a meal, they usually do the ordering, as they do not want their guests to feel uncomfortable about choosing expensive dishes. The phrase **wǒ lái diǎn** means 'Let me do the ordering'. Literally it means 'let me come to choose' (the word **ràng**, meaning 'let', is omitted here).

■ 6 Eating out

A typical Chinese meal at a restaurant consists of some cold dishes, and sometimes soup to start with, followed by some hot dishes (in terms of temperature), together with rice, noodles or other flour-based food such as dumplings. If you order one soup, it comes in a large bowl which is enough for the number of people at the table. The dishes are ordered together, and shared among people at the table. There's no separate course for dessert. However, there are some sweet dishes, which are served at the same time as other main dishes. Larger restaurants may serve pieces of fruit at the end. Most Chinese people have tea with their meal.

■ 7 More dish names and vegetarian dishes (CD2; 23)

Most restaurants in China offer the menu in Chinese characters only. So here are some common dish names in both character and pinyin to help with your menu reading:

牛肉炒面	**niúròu chǎo miàn**	beef fried noodles
春卷	**chūn juǎn**	spring roll
猪肉饺子	**zhūròu jiǎozi**	dumplings with pork filling
蛋炒饭	**dàn chǎo fàn**	egg-fried rice
白米饭	**bái mǐfàn**	boiled rice
酸辣豆腐汤	**suān là dòufu tāng**	hot and sour tofu soup
馄吞汤	**húntūn tāng**	wen-ton soup
古老肉	**gǔ lǎo ròu**	sweet and sour pork
葱爆羊肉	**cōng bào yángròu**	stir-fried lamb with spring onions
牛肉炒青椒	**niúròu chǎo qīngjiāo**	stir-fried beef with green pepper
麻辣豆腐	**málà dòfu**	tofu in Sichuan style
糖醋鱼	**táng cù yú**	sweet and sour fish
炸大虾	**zhá dàxiā**	deep fried king prawn
素菜	**sù cài**	vegetarian dishes
炒豆芽	**chǎo dòu yá**	stir-fried bean sprouts
清炒什菜	**qīng chǎo shí cài**	stir-fired mixed vegetables
素饺子	**sù jiǎozi**	vegetarian dumpling
素春卷	**sù chūn juǎn**	vegetarian spring roll

■ 8 Use of *lái*

This is the same **lái** as in '**lái Zhōngguó**' (come to China), but here it means 'to bring'. It is used to order food and drinks. For example:

Qǐng *lái* yī píng píjiǔ.
One bottle of beer please.

■ 9 Common drinks (CD2; 24)

Below are the names for some common drinks which you may wish to order:

shuǐ	water	**píngguǒ zhī**	apple juice
kuàngquán shuǐ	mineral water	**bōluó zhī**	pineapple juice
chá	tea	**yēzi zhī**	coconut juice
huā chá	jasmine tea	**kékóu kělè**	Coca Cola
lǜ chá	green tea	**pútao jiǔ**	wine

(You can add **hóng** or **bái** in front of **pútao jiǔ** to make it 'red wine' or 'white wine'.)

mǐ jiǔ   rice wine   **bái jiǔ**   spirits (*lit.* 'white alcohol')

■ 10 Predicative adjectives + **sǐ le**

This is a very useful combination to remember. It can be used whenever you want to exaggerate things. Literally, **sǐ le** means 'to have died' or 'died'. For example:

> **Wǒ gāoxìng *sǐ le*.**
> *Lit.*   I   be happy died.
>   I'm so happy.

> **Wǒ è   *sǐ le*.**
> *Lit.*   I   be hungry died.
>   I'm starving.

■ 11 Verb **děng**

The expression **Qǐng shāo děng** (*lit.* 'Please a while wait') is a more formal way of saying 'Just a second'. On casual occasions, you can say ***Děng* yīxià** (*lit.* 'Wait a second') or ***Děngdeng*** (*lit.* 'Wait wait').

Exercises

Exercise 1

What do you say if you want to order the following?

(a)   a glass of orange juice
(b)   a bottle of beer
(c)   two glasses of white wine
(d)   some Chinese tea

Exercise 2

Look at the menu below and say what you would like to order (go back to Note 7 if necessary):

菜单 càidān		
		价格 jiàgé
汤	**Tāng**	
酸辣豆腐汤	suān là dòufǔ tāng	¥ 4.20
海鲜汤	hǎixiān tāng	¥ 5.50
馄吞汤	húntūn tāng	¥ 3.80
热菜	**Rè cài**	
古老肉	gǔ lǎo ròu	¥ 8.80
糖醋鱼	táng cù yú	¥ 15.00
鸡丁炒什菜	jī dīng chǎo shí cài	¥ 12.20
牛肉炒青椒	niúròu chǎo qīngjiāo	¥ 8.90
炸大虾	zhá dà xiā	¥ 25.00
鱼头烧豆腐	yú tóu shāo dòufu	¥ 28.00
清炒什菜	qīng chǎo shí cài	¥ 6.60
主食	**Zhǔ shí**	
蛋炒饭	dàn chǎo fàn	¥ 3.00
白米饭	bái mǐfàn	¥ 1.50
小笼包子（一份6个)	xiǎo lóng bāozi (yī fèn 6 ge)	
猪肉	zhūròu	¥ 3.50
海鲜	hǎixiān	¥ 6.00
素	sù	¥ 2.40
饺子（一份15个)	jiǎozi (yī fèn 15 ge)	
猪肉	zhūròu	¥ 4.50
海鲜	hǎixiān	¥ 6.60
素	sù	¥ 5.00
牛肉炒面条	niúròu chǎo miàntiáo	¥ 7.00

New words:

价格 **jiàgé**   price
热菜 **rè cài**   hot dishes (in terms of temperature)
主食 **zhǔ shí** rice and flour-based food

Exercise 3

Translate the following phrases and sentences into Chinese:

(a) Please sit down.
(b) I'd like to have a look at the menu.
(c) This way, please. (uttered by a waiter in a restaurant)
(d) I'm starving.
(e) Just a second.

Dialogue 2

Nǐ chī guo kǎo yā ma?   你吃过烤鸭吗？
Have you ever had roast duck? (CD2; 26)

Gao Xiaohua lives in Taiwan. This is her first visit to mainland China since she left in the early 1940s. She is now visiting some of her school friends in Beijing and Liu Chenggang is one of them. They are discussing which restaurant to go to.

CHÉNGGĀNG	Nǐ chī guo Běijīng kǎo yā ma, Xiǎohuá?
XIǍOHUÁ	Méiyǒu.
CHÉNGGĀNG	Shì ma? Nà, nǐ yīdìng děi chángchang. Nǐ jīntiān wǎnshang yǒu kòng ma?
XIǍOHUÁ	Yǒu kòng.
CHÉNGGĀNG	Nà, wǒ jīnwǎn qǐng nǐ chī kǎo yā, zěnme yàng?
XIǍOHUÁ	Tài hǎo le. Zánmen qù nǎ jiā cān'guǎn?
CHÉNGGĀNG	Běijīng Kǎo Yā Diàn.

(Later that evening, Xiaohua and Chenggang are enjoying their meal at the Beijing Roast Duck Restaurant)

XIǍOHUÁ	Nǐ tài duì le. Zhēn hǎochī.
CHÉNGGĀNG	Wǒ zhēn gāoxìng nǐ xǐhuān kǎo yā. Duō chī yīxiē.
XIǍOHUÁ	Hǎo de. Qǐng dì gěi wǒ jiàng.

CHÉNGGĀNG	Bǐng gòu ma?
XIǍOHUÁ	Gòu le. Wǒ kuài chī bǎo le.
CHÉNGGĀNG	Wǒ yǐjing chī bǎo le. Wǒ bǐ nǐ chī de kuài. Nà, wǒ mǎi dān le.
XIǍOHUÁ	Hǎo ba. Duō xiè!
CHÉNGGĀNG	Fúwùyuán, qǐng mǎi dān.

CHÉNGGĀNG	你吃过北京烤鸭吗，小华？
XIǍOHUÁ	没有。
CHÉNGGĀNG	是吗？那，你一定得尝尝。你今晚有空吗？
XIǍOHUÁ	有空。
CHÉNGGĀNG	那，我今晚请你吃烤鸭。怎么样？
XIǍOHUÁ	太好了。咱们去哪家餐馆？
CHÉNGGĀNG	北京烤鸭店。
...	
XIǍOHUÁ	你太对了。真好吃。
CHÉNGGĀNG	我真高兴你喜欢烤鸭。多吃一些。
XIǍOHUÁ	好的。请递给我酱。
CHÉNGGĀNG	饼够吗？
XIǍOHUÁ	够了。我快吃饱了。
CHÉNGGĀNG	我已经吃饱了。我比你吃得快。那，我买单了。
XIǍOHUÁ	好吧。多谢！
CHÉNGGĀNG	服务员，请买单。

(CD2; 25)

Vocabulary

guo	过	[see Note 12]
kǎo yā	烤鸭	roast duck
shì ma?	是吗	is that so?
nà	那	in that case
děi	得	to have to/must
cháng	尝	to taste/try (food)
jīnwǎn	今晚	tonight
yǒu kòng	有空	to have time/to be free
qǐng	请	to invite/take someone out
cān'guǎn	餐馆	restaurant

hǎochī	好吃	tasty/delicious [*lit.* 'good eat']
duō	多	more
dì	递	to pass
jiàng	酱	sauce
bǐng	饼	pancake
kuài	快	nearly
bǎo	饱	to be full
de	得	[see Note 21]
mǎi dān	买单	to settle the bill
qǐng mǎi dān	请买单	bill please
fúwùyuán	服务员	waiter/waitress

Notes on Dialogue 2

■ 12 Use of **guo**

Guo is inserted after some verbs to indicate that something happened in the definite past, but not with a specific date. The emphasis is on the past experience as opposed to when it happened. Expressions denoting past times (e.g. last year, yesterday) are usually not used together with **guo**. A verb plus **guo** is the equivalent of the English expressions *to have been to . . .* or *to have done something*. For example:

| **Nǐ qù** *guo* **Zhōngguó ma?** | Have you ever been to China? |
| **Wǒ chī** *guo* **Yìdàlì fàn.** | I have had Italian food. |

To negate verbs with **guo** following them, use **méiyǒu** or **méi**. For example:

Xiǎohuá *méiyǒu* **chī guo Běijīng kǎo yā.**
Xiaohua hasn't had Beijing roast duck before.

■ 13 Use of **děi**

Děi is a colloquial word meaning 'to have to' or 'must'. If you want to be very persistent, the adverb **yīdìng** (definitely/must) can be placed before **děi**. For example:

Wǒ *děi* zǒu le.   I've *got to* leave.
Nǐ yīdìng *děi* lái wǒmen You've *got to* come to ours for
jiā chī fàn.   a meal.

The negation of **děi** is **bú yòng** or **bú bì** *not* **bú děi** (for **bú yòng**, see Note 12 of Lesson 7). For example:

Nǐ *bú yòng* lái.   You *don't have to* come.
Nǐ *bú bì* mǎi píjiǔ.   You *don't have to* buy any beer.

Note this is the same character as the one in Note 21, but with different pronunciation and a different meaning. (see Characters on page 206.)

■ 14 Forming time expressions with **jīntiān**

In English, you say *this morning*, *this afternoon* and *this evening*; in Chinese, you put **jīntiān** (today) in front of **zǎoshang**, **xiàwǔ** and **wǎnshang**. Thus we have:

jīntiān zǎoshang   this morning
jīntiān xiàwǔ   this afternoon
jīntiān wǎnshang   this evening

Note that **jīntiān zǎoshang** and **jīntiān wǎnshang** can be shortened to **jīnzǎo** and **jīnwǎn** (tonight).

■ 15 Use of **yǒu kòng**

The word **kòng** is the same **kòng** as in **chōu kòng** (to make time) which appeared in Lesson 9. **Yǒu kòng** means 'to have time' or 'to be free'. To negate **yǒu kòng**, put **méiyǒu** or **méi** in front of **kòng**. For example:

A: **Nǐ míngtiān wǎnshang *yǒu kòng* ma?**
   Will you *be free* tomorrow evening?

B: **Kǒngpà *méi* kòng.**
   I'm afraid *not*.

■ 16 Verb **qǐng**

We learnt this word back in Lesson 1, where it meant 'please'. When **qǐng** is used as a verb, it means 'to invite' or 'to treat someone to something'. If you want to say 'to invite someone to dinner', you must say 'to invite someone eat dinner'. For example:

> **Wǒ xiǎng *qǐng* nǐ *chī* wǎnfàn.**   I'd like to invite you to dinner.

If it is a past event, put the past indicator **le** after **chī** *not* **qǐng**. For example:

> **Zuówǎn Lǎo Lǐ *qǐng* wǒ chī *le* kǎo yā.**
> Lao Li treated me to some roast duck last night.

■ 17 **Duō chī yīxiē**

This expression is usually used in situations where a host/hostess insists that a guest has some more to eat or a parent asks the child to eat more. **Duō chī yīxiē** literally means 'more eat some'. Here the word **duō** is an adverb which describes the verb **chī**. It is put before the verb in sentences which make suggestions or give orders. For example:

> **Qǐng *duō* mǎi yīxiē shuǐguǒ.**   Please buy some *more* fruit.
> ***Duō* chī yīxiē dàxiā.**   Have some *more* prawns.
> ***Duō* hē yīxiē píjiǔ.**   Have some *more* beer.

■ 18 Verb **dì**

This verb is usually used together with the preposition **gěi** to mean 'to pass something to somebody'. For example:

> **Nǐ kěyi *dì gěi* wǒ táng ma?**   Could you *pass* me the sugar?
> **Qǐng *dì géi* wǒ bǐng.**   Please *pass* me the pancakes.

■ 19 **Wǒ gòu le**

Grammatically, this is not a correct sentence because it means 'I'm enough'. However, this has become an accepted expression to mean 'I've had enough' or 'It's enough for me'.

■ 20 **Chī bǎo le**

This is another very popular phrase at the dinner table. If you are already full and do not wish to have any more food put into your bowl, you can say one of these phrases:

Wǒ chī bǎo le.
Chī bǎo le. } I'm full./I've had enough to eat.
Wǒ bǎo le.

■ 21 Use of **de** to link verbs or predicative adjectives with their adverbs

The particle **de**, which is a different **de** (得) from the **de** (的) in **wǒde**, for example, is used to link verbs or predicative adjectives with adverbs if you wish to describe the degree of something. Adverbs such as **kuài** (fast), **duō** (more), **zǎo** (early), **chí** (late), **hǎo** (well), etc. are usually used for this purpose. Thus, the pattern is:

verb/predicative adjective + **de** + adverb

For example:

(a) **Lǎo Zhāng <u>chī</u> *de* hěn <u>duō</u>.**
verb adverb
Lao Zhang eats a lot.

(b) **Wǒ <u>chī</u> *de* bǐ nǐ   <u>kuài</u>.**
verb adverb
Lit. I eat compared with you fast.
I eat faster than you do.

With predicative adjectives, it does not matter whether the adverb is placed before the predicative adjective or after it. For example:

(c) **Běijīng de dōngtiān <u>lěng</u> *de* <u>hěn</u>.**
pred. adj. adverb
Beijing's winter is very cold.

(d) **Běijīng de dōngtiān <u>hěn</u>   <u>lěng</u>.**
adverb pred. adj.
Beijing's winter is very cold.

With verbs, the position of **kuài** depends on whether it is an order or describes one's manner. For example:

Qǐng *kuài* chī.   Please eat quickly.
Tā chī *de kuài*.   He eats fast.

To negate sentences (a) and (b) above, place **bù** *after* **de**. For example:

Lǎo Zhāng chī de *bù* **hěn duō.**
Lao Zhang does*n't* eat much.

Wǒ chī de *bù* **bǐ nǐ kuài.**
I'm not eating faster than you are.

To negate sentence (c) above, use the normal negation order, i.e. put **bù** before the predicative adjective and omit both **de** and the adverb. Alternatively, move the adverb before the predicative adjective and put **bù** before the adverb. For example:

Běijīng de dōngtiān *bù* **lěng.**
Beijing's winter is*n't* cold.

Běijīng de dōngtiān *bù* **hěn lěng.**
Beijing's winter is*n't* very cold.

Another thing to remember is that when this structure is used to describe a past event, do not use **le** or **guo** with **de**. In most situations, the context makes it clear if it was a past event. For example:

Jīntiān zǎoshang, tā lái *de* **hěn zǎo.**
She arrived very early this morning.

Exercises

Exercise 4

Translate the following sentences into Chinese using either **guo** or **le**:

(a)   Has Xiǎohuá ever been to China?
(b)   David went to London yesterday.
(c)   He has not had Chinese food before.
(d)   A: Have you had your breakfast?
      B: Not yet.

Exercise 5

What do you say in the following situations:

(a) You want to let your host know that you have had enough to eat.
(b) You would like to have some more pancakes.
(c) You want one of the people at the table to pass you the sauce.
(d) At the dinner table, you want to invite your guests to have some more food.
(e) You stop the waiter and ask for another bottle of beer.

Exercise 6

Complete the following sentences with the phrases provided in the brackets:

(a) _____ (*If you have time*), zánmen qù chī kǎo yā, hǎo ma?
(b) _____ (*you've got to*) lái kàn wǒmen.
(c) _____ (*This morning*) wǒ shàng bān chí dào le èrshí fēnzhōng.
(d) Rúguǒ nǐ chī bǎo le, _____ (*let's settle the bill*).
(e) Xiǎo Zhāng bù xiǎng _____ (*invite Lao Wang*).

Exercise 7

Translate the following sentences into Chinese using **de** to link verbs or predicative adjectives with adverbs where appropriate:

(a) The swimming pool opened very early this morning.
(b) Please come a bit early.
(c) I came in very late this morning.
(d) John speaks very quickly.

Exercise 8

Negate the following sentences:

(a) Nǐ shuō de duì.
(b) Wǒ mèimei lái de hěn zǎo.
(c) Yīngguó de xiàtiān rè de hěn.
(d) Tāde fùmǔ tuìxiū de hěn zǎo.
(e) Xiǎohuá gāoxìng de hěn.

Characters

Let us first learn two head components which are used in this lesson:
⁺⁺ in 菜 (**cài**, vegetable) and 火 in 烤 (**kǎo**, roast):

Character analysis	Head component and its meaning	Stroke order	English
⁺⁺ + 采 **cǎi**	⁺⁺ (grass)	菜 一 十 ⁺⁺ 艹 艹 艿 艿 苹 苹 菜	vegetable
火 + 考 **kǎo**	火 (fire)	烤 ′ ″ ヶ ヺ 火 火 炸 炸 炉 烤 烤	roast

(Unexplained components - 采 **cǎi**: acting as phonetic; 考 **kǎo**: acting as phonetic)

In Dialogue 2, we have also seen the character 得 having two pronunciations. When it is pronounced **děi**, it means 'to have to, must', and when it is pronounced **de**, it is a grammar word (see Note 21 above). Let us see how this character is written:

Character analysis	Head component and its meaning	Stroke order	English
彳 + 日 + 寸	彳 (step)	得 ′ ⁊ 彳 彳 彳⁷ 彳⁷ 彳⁷ 彳⁷ 彳⁷ 得 得	to have to, must; [grammar word]

Exercise 9

(1) Check the Vocabulary for both Dialogue 1 (pp. 192–3) and Dialogue 2 (pp. 199–200) and list the characters that use the ⁺⁺ and 火 head components.

(2) In Lesson 1, the character 喝 with the mouth head component 口 was introduced. And in Lesson 4, the food head component 饣 was introduced (e.g. 饭). Find other characters in this lesson (from both vocabulary lists) with the mouth head component 口 and the food head component 饣.

(3) Match the following characters with their English translations (use the Vocabulary lists of this lesson if you like):

(a) 菜单 (b) 餐馆 (c) 烤鸭 (d) 汤 (e) 啤酒

i) soup   ii) roast duck   iii) beer   iv) restaurant   v) menu

Reading/listening comprehension

(CD2; 27)

Read the passage (either in pinyin or character, or both) below, and then decide if the statements following are true or false. If you have access to the audio material, listen to the passage first, then listen to the statements, and then decide if the statements are true or false.

Vocabulary

B

běnlái	本来	originally
zhuōzi	桌子	table
biàn	便	then
fúwù	服务	service

Zuótiān wǎnshang, wǒde lǎo péngyou Wáng Píng hé tāde zhàngfu qǐng wǒ chī fàn. Wǒmen běnlái xiǎng chī kǎo yā, xiān qù le yī jiā Běijīng Kǎo Yā Diàn, kěxí méi yǒu zhuōzi. Wǒmen biàn qù le yī jiā Guǎngzhōu cān'guǎn chī hǎixiān. Wǒmen dōu juéde zhè jiā cān'guǎn fēicháng hǎo, fúwù yě hǎo. Wǒmen chī le zhá dà xiā, táng cù yú, hái yǒu qīng chǎo shí cài. Wáng Píng de zhàngfu hē le yī bēi píjiǔ, wǒ hé Wáng Píng hē le huā chá.

昨天晚上，我的老朋友王萍和他的丈夫请我吃饭。我们本来想吃烤鸭，先去了一家北京烤鸭店，可惜没有桌子。我们便去了一家广州餐馆吃海鲜。我们都觉得这家餐馆非常好，服务也好。我们吃了炸大虾，糖醋鱼，还有清炒什菜。王萍的丈夫喝了一杯啤酒，我和王萍了花茶。

TRUE OR FALSE?

(1) Zuótiān wǎnshang tāmen chī le kǎo yā.

昨天晚上他们吃了烤鸭。

(2) Yīgòng sān ge rén qù chī fàn.

一共三个人去吃饭。

(3) Zhè jiā Guǎngzhōu cān'guǎn yǒu hěnduō hǎixiān.

这家广州餐馆有很多海鲜。

(4) 'Wǒ' hé Wáng Píng méiyǒu hē píjiǔ.

'我'和王萍没有喝啤酒。

(5) Wáng Píng hé tā zhàngfu bù xǐhuān zhè jiā Guǎngzhōu cān'guǎn.

王萍和她丈夫不喜欢这家广州餐馆。

(6) Zhè jiā Guǎngzhōu cān'guǎn de fúwù bú cuò.

这家广州餐馆的服务不错。

Lesson Eleven
Zuò chūzūchē hé mǎi huǒchē piào 坐出租车和买火车票
Taking the taxi and buying train tickets

By the end of this lesson, you should be able to:

- take a taxi and buy train tickets
- say which train you wish to take
- use more sophisticated phrases to modify nouns by using **de**
- make more sophisticated comparisons
- write and recognize more characters

Dialogue 1

Qǐng dài wǒ qù . . .   请带我去 . . .
Please take me to . . . **(CD2; 29)**

John is doing his sight-seeing in Beijing. He's just hailed a taxi . . .

JOHN	Qǐng dài wǒ qù Tiān Tán.
TAXI DRIVER	Duìbuqǐ, wǒ bú qù Tiān Tán.
JOHN	Wéishénme?
TAXI DRIVER	Nà biān dǔchē dǔ de hěn lìhai. Nǐ zuò dìtiě ba.
JOHN	Dìtiě zhàn zài nǎr?
TAXI DRIVER	Wǒ dài nǐ qù.
JOHN	Xièxie!

(*John is now at the underground station.*)

JOHN   Wǒ mǎi yī zhāng qù Tiān Tán de piào. Qǐng
                    wèn, zuò jǐ hào xiàn?
TICKET ASSISTANT   Xiān zuò èr hào xiàn, wǎng Píngguǒyuán
                    fāngxiàng, zài Dōngdān xià chē, huàn wǔ hào xiàn.
JOHN   Xièxie.

(Now John is on Line 5, and he asks one of the passengers . . .)

JOHN   Qǐng wèn, qù Tiān Tán yīnggāi zài nǎ yī zhàn xià
                    chē?
PASSENGER   Nǐ zuò cuò chē le. Zhè shì qù fǎn fāngxiàng de.
JOHN   Zāogāo!
PASSENGER   Bié jí. Wǒ gānghǎo xià yī zhàn xià chē. Nǐ gēn
                    wǒ zǒu ba.
JOHN   Tài xièxie nǐ le.

JOHN   请带我去天坛。
TAXI DRIVER   对不起，我不去天坛。
JOHN   为什么？
TAXI DRIVER   那边堵车堵得很厉害。你坐地铁吧。
JOHN   地铁站在哪儿？
TAXI DRIVER   我带你去。
JOHN   谢谢！
. . .
JOHN   我买一张去天坛的票。请问，坐几号线？
TICKET ASSISTANT   先坐二号线，往苹果园方向，在东单下车，
                    换五号线。
JOHN   谢谢。

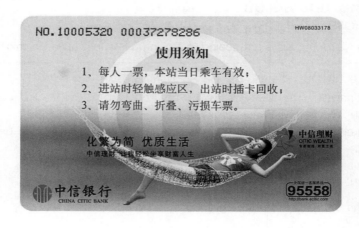

. . .

JOHN	请问，去天坛应该在哪一站下车？
PASSENGER	你坐错车了。这是去反方向的。
JOHN	糟糕！
PASSENGER	别急。我刚好下一站下车。你跟我走吧。
JOHN	太谢谢你了。

(CD2; 28)

B Vocabulary

Tiān Tán	天坛	Temple of Heaven
nà biān	那边	over there; that side
dǔchē	堵车	to have a traffic jam [*lit.* 'block cars']
lìhai	厉害	serious; severe
dìtiě	地铁	underground/subway [*lit.* 'ground iron']
jǐ hào xiàn?	几号线？	which line?
èr hào xiàn	二号线	No. 2 Line
wǎng . . . fāngxiàng	往 . . . 方向	toward the direction of . . .
Píngguǒyuán	苹果园	[a station name, *lit.* 'apple yard']
Dōngdān	东单	[a station name, *lit.* 'east single']
xià chē	下车	to get off
zhāng	张	[measure word]
piào	票	ticket

yīnggāi	应该	should/ought to
nǎ yī zhàn?	哪一站？	which stop?
cuò	错	wrong
fǎn fāngxiàng	反方向	opposite direction
bié jí	别急	don't worry
gānghǎo	刚好	it happens/coincidentally
xià yī zhàn	下一站	next stop

Notes on Dialogue 1

■ 1 Taking a taxi

Taxis are a convenient and inexpensive means of transport in various cities in China. Simply raise your hand to hail a taxi. The English word 'Taxi' together with the Chinese characters are on top of all taxis in major cities. The Chinese word for taxi is 出租车 (**chūzhūchē**), literally meaning 'for rent car'. There are a few expressions for 'to take a taxi' and 'to call a taxi':

zuǒ chūzūchē	to take a taxi (formal)
dǎ chē	to call a taxi; to take a taxi (colloquial)
dǎ dī	to call a taxi, to take a taxi (colloquial)

■ 2 Taking the subway (underground)

Only four Chinese cities have a subway system: Beijing, Shanghai, Guangzhou and Tianjin. You can buy either a ticket for the journey or a kind of pay-as-you-go card. The sign for 'subway' is always written in both Chinese characters (地铁) and English.

■ 3 More on **de** to link verbs with adverbs

In Lesson 10, Note 21, we saw the use of **de** to link a single syllable verb **chī** with **kuài**:

wǒ chī de kuài   I eat fast

If a verb consists of two syllables, when using **de** to link the adverb, the pattern is:

2-syllable verb + the first syllable of the same verb + de + adverb

For example:

Nà biān *dǔ*chē   *dǔ*   de hěn lìhai.
Lit.   That side block car block **de** very severe.
There is a big traffic jam over there.

Tā *yóuyǒng yóu*   de hěn kuài.
Lit.   He swim   swim **de** very fast.
He swims very fast.

Very often the structure of these 2-syllable verbs is 'verb + object' (e.g. **dǔchē** is 'block car' and **yóuyǒng** is 'swim a swim'). The above structure is also used with one-syllable verbs if those verbs take an object. For example:

Wǒ shuō   Yīngwén shuō   de bú cuò.
    verb   object
Lit.   I   speak English   speak **de** not bad.
I speak pretty good English.

■ 4 Measure word **zhāng**

The measure word **zhāng** is used before nouns such as **piào** (ticket), **bàozhǐ** (newspaper), **zhǐ** (sheets), etc. whenever required. For example:

liǎng *zhāng* gōnggòng qìchē piào   two bus tickets
yī *zhāng* dìtiě piào   one ticket

■ 5 Using **de** to link a verbal phrase with a noun

In English, prepositions such as 'in', 'to', etc. are used to specify nouns (e.g. a woman *in* a red jumper; a ticket *to* London). Also, in English, these modifying phrases or clauses come after the noun. The situation is very different in Chinese. Verbal phrases, not prepositions, are used to specify or modify nouns and they come before nouns. They are linked by **de**. For example:

Wǒ mǎi yī zhāng qù   Tiān Tán *de*   piào.
Lit.   I   buy one   go to the Temple of Heaven ticket.
A ticket to the Temple of Heaven, please.

Nà ge chuān hóng máoyī *de* rén   shì wǒ jiějie.
Lit.   That wear red jumper person is my elder sister.
The one in the red jumper is my elder sister.

■ 6 Use of **cuò**

When **cuò** is used to mean 'to be wrong', it must be followed by **le**. For example:

Duìbuqǐ, wǒ cuò le.   Sorry, *I'm wrong.*

Cuò can also be used as an adverb to modify verbs. For instance, in English the sentence *I got it wrong* can be used to refer to things one has said, seen, heard, etc. However, in Chinese, you must say **Wǒ shuō cuò le** (*lit.* 'I spoke wrong'), **Wǒ kàn cuò le** (*lit.* 'I saw wrong'), **Wǒ tīng cuò le** (*lit.* 'I heard wrong'), etc. depending on the context. For example:

(A to C): **Wǒmen xīngqīsì qù Shànghǎi.**
We are going to Shanghai on Thursday.

(B interrupts): **Nǐ shuō cuò le. Shì xīngqīsān.**
You *got it wrong*. It's Wednesday.

When a verb takes an object (e.g. 'to take the bus' – 'the bus' being the object of 'to take'), **cuò** is placed after the verb but before the object. **Le** can be put either after **cuò** or after the object providing that the object that follows the verb is not a very long phrase. For example:

Zāogāo, wǒ diǎn cuò le <u>cài</u>.   Oh, no! I ordered the *wrong*
                        object   dish.

Wǒ zuò cuò <u>chē</u> le ma?   Have I taken the *wrong* bus/
                   object   train/tube?

■ 7 Use of **bié**

The word **bié**, meaning 'do not', is only used in imperative sentences (e.g. 'Don't smoke'). It is always placed before the verb. For example:

Bié jí. Hái yǒu shíjiān.   *Don't* worry. There's still time.

Bié gàosu māma wǒ zài zhèr.   *Don't* tell Mum that I'm here.

■ 8 **Xià ge** and **xià yī . . .**

In Lesson 3, we learnt the phrase **xià ge** when it was used in **xià ge xīngqī** (next week) with **yī** omitted. The complete form is **xià yī**

ge xīngqī. Yī is usually omitted when it is followed by the measure word **gè**. Numbers other than **yī** cannot be omitted. For example:

xià *liǎng* ge xīngqī   next *two* weeks
xià *sān* ge yuè   next *three* months

We have also learnt that some nouns require measure words other than **gè**. In these cases, you must use **xià** + number + that measure word to mean 'next'. For example:

yī *liàng* zìxíngchē one bike   → **xià yī *liàng* zìxíngchē** *next* bike
sān *zhāng* piào three tickets   → **xià sān *zhāng* piào** *next* three tickets

There are a couple of nouns such as **zhàn** (stop), **bù** (step), etc., which can be used as measure words. In this case, you must use **xià** + number + **zhàn/bù** to mean 'next'. For example:

yī zhàn one stop   → **xià yī zhàn** next stop
liǎng bù two steps   → **xià liǎng bù** next two steps

■ 9 Use of **gānghǎo**

This phrase is always placed before verbs. For example:

Wǒ *gānghǎo* yào qù dìtiě zhàn. Wǒ dài nǐ qù.
I happen to be going to the underground station. I'll take you there.

Exercises

Exercise 1

Use **de** to form one complete sentence from the pairs of sentences below. Then translate them into English:

Example: **Chuān hóng máoyī** (wear red jumper).
   Nà ge rén shì wǒde gēge.
Change to: **Nà ge chuān hóng máoyī *de* rén shì wǒde gēge.**

(a)   Qù Tiān'ānmén. Wǒ mǎi sān zhāng piào.
(b)   Gāng dào (*just arrived*). Nà ge nánhái shì Lǎo Liú de érzi.
(c)   Chángcháng chí dào (*always be late*).
   Wáng jīnglǐ bù xǐhuan nàxiē rén (nàxiē *means 'those'*).

Exercise 2

Fill in the blanks with appropriate measure words:

(a) Tā mǎi le liǎng _____ zhēnsī lǐngdài.
(b) Yī _____ qù huǒchē zhàn de piào duō shǎo qián?
(c) Xià yī ___ bú shì Tiān Tán.
(d) Tā mǎi le wǔ _____ Qīngdǎo píjiǔ.

Exercise 3

What do you say to yourself when you realize that:

(a) you have taken the wrong bus
(b) you have ordered the wrong dish
(c) you have called someone the wrong name
(d) you have bought the wrong coffee

Exercise 4

You tell your friend not to:

(a) worry
(b) take a taxi
(c) tell Lao Wang how old you are
(d) speak English
(e) lend his bike to Liu Hong

Exercise 5

Translate the following sentences into Chinese:

(a) Next stop is Beijing University.
(b) I didn't know that you were going away for the next two weeks.
(c) You need to get off at the next stop and change to Line No. 1.
(d) The traffic is badly blocked up over there.
(e) At which stop should I get off for the Temple of Heaven?
(f) Please take me to the Beijing Roast Duck Restaurant.

Exercise 6

Pair work – one person asks questions in Chinese based on Dialogue 1, and the other person answers them. For example:

A: Yuēhàn yào qù nǎr?
B: Tiān Tán.

Dialogue 2

Mǎi huǒchē piào 买火车票 Buying train tickets
(CD2; 31)

Chen Xiaojuan, an American Chinese born in Taiwan, is travelling in China by herself. She wants to take a train journey from Chendu to Guilin.

CHÉN XIĂOJUĀN	Qǐng wèn, zhè shì shòupiào chù ma?
TICKET ASSISTANT	Shì de.
CHÉN XIĂOJUĀN	Wǒ yào mǎi yī zhāng qù Guìlín de huǒchē piào.
TICKET ASSISTANT	Shénme shíhou zǒu?
CHÉN XIĂOJUĀN	Xià ge xīngqīsān, jiù shì liùyuè sì hào.
TICKET ASSISTANT	Nǐ dǎsuàn chéng nǎ cì lièchē?
CHÉN XIĂOJUĀN	Wǒ bù qīngchu. Zuìhǎo shì wǎnshang liù dián zuǒyòu kāi de chē.
TICKET ASSISTANT	T-bāshíyī cì zěnme yàng? Shíjiǔ diǎn sìshíwǔ fāchē.
CHÉN XIĂOJUĀN	Shénme shíhou dào Guìlín?
TICKET ASSISTANT	Dì èr tiān shíliù diǎn èrshí fēn dào.
CHÉN XIĂOJUĀN	Shíjiān bù cuò. Wǒ jiù mǎi zhè cì chē de piào.
TICKET ASSISTANT	Nǐ yào yìngwò háishi ruǎnwò?
CHÉN XIĂOJUĀN	Wǒ bù dǒng.
TICKET ASSISTANT	Yìngwò bǐ ruǎnwò piányi wǔshí kuài, dànshì yìngwò méi ruǎnwò shūfu.
CHÉN XIĂOJUĀN	Wǒ yào yī zhāng yìngwò.

CHÉN XIĂOJUĀN	请问，这是售票处吗？
TICKET ASSISTANT	是的。
CHÉN XIĂOJUĀN	我要买一张去桂林的火车票。
TICKET ASSISTANT	什么时候走？
CHÉN XIĂOJUĀN	下个星期三，就是六月四号。
TICKET ASSISTANT	你打算乘哪次列车？
CHÉN XIĂOJUĀN	我不清楚。最好是晚上六点左右开的车。
TICKET ASSISTANT	T八十一次怎么样？十九点四十五发车。

CHÉN XIĂOJUĀN	什么时候到桂林？
TICKET ASSISTANT	第二天十六点二十分到。
CHÉN XIĂOJUĀN	时间不错。我就买这次车的票。
TICKET ASSISTANT	你要硬卧还是软卧？
CHÉN XIĂOJUĀN	我不懂。
TICKET ASSISTANT	硬卧比软卧便宜五十块，但是硬卧没软卧舒服。
CHÉN XIĂOJUĀN	我要一张硬卧。

(CD2; 30)

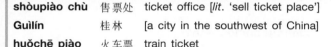

shòupiào chù	售票处	ticket office [*lit.* 'sell ticket place']
Guìlín	桂林	[a city in the southwest of China]
huǒchē piào	火车票	train ticket
zǒu	走	to leave
jiù shì	就是	that is
chéng	乘	to take/to catch (e.g. train, subway/ underground, bus, plane, etc.)
cì	次	number
lièchē	列车	train
qīngchǔ	清楚	to be clear/to be sure
zuìhǎo	最好	ideally
kāi	开	to leave/to depart
fāchē	发车	to depart/departure
dì èr tiān	第二天	the following day [*lit.* 'the second day']
yìngwò	硬卧	hard-sleeper
ruǎnwò	软卧	soft-sleeper
dǒng	懂	to understand

Notes on Dialogue 2

■ 10 Use of the verb **zǒu**

The verb **zǒu** has several meanings. In Dialogue 2, it means 'to leave'. However, it can also mean 'to get there', 'to walk', etc. depending on the context. For example:

Nǐ māma shénme shíhou zǒu?
When is your mother *leaving*?

Nǐ xiǎng zǒulù háishi zuò chē?
Do you want to *walk* or take the bus?

Qù nǐmende dàxué, zěnme zǒu?
How *do you get* to your university?

Zǒu dào dì yī ge lùkǒu, wǎng dōng guǎi.
Walk to the first junction, then turn east.

■ 11 Use of **jiù shì**

This phrase can be used to explain things further and sometimes to reinforce a certain piece of information. It can be broadly translated as 'that is . . .'. For example:

A: **Nǐ qīzi shénme shíhou dào?**
　　When is your wife arriving?

B: **Xià ge xīngqīliù, *jiù shì* sānyuè sān hào.**
　　Next Saturday, that is, 3 March.

Sometimes there is no need to translate **jiù shì** into English. For example:

Tiějūn, *jiù shì* Xiǎoméi de jiějie, jiè gěi le wǒ tāde zìxíngchē.
Tiejun, Xiaomei's elder sister, lent me her bike.

■ 12 Chinese trains and the use of **cì**

All passenger trains in China are numbered, with a roman letter in front of the number to indicate the category or the type of the train. The main types include: P-category (**pǔtōng lièchē**, ordinary trains), K-category (**pǔkuài lièchē**, fast ordinary trains), T-category (**tèkuài lièchē**, express fast trains), Z-category (**zhídá tèkuài**, express non-stop), D-category (**dònglì chēzǔ**, high-speed trains). On most long distance trains, you have three ticket choices: **ruǎnwò** (soft-sleepers), **yìngwò** (hard-sleepers) or **yìngzuò** (hard-seats). The word **cì**, meaning 'number', is used between the number of a particular train and the word **lièchē** or **chē** for train.

■ 13 Difference between **huǒchē** and **lièchē**

Huǒchē is a general term for trains whilst **lièchē** usually refers to a specific train. For example:

Wǒ bù xǐhuān zuò *huǒchē*.
I don't like taking *trains*.

D-shíyī cì *lièchē* shísì diǎn líng wǔ fāchē.
Train no. D-11 departs at 14:05.

It is inappropriate rather than wrong to use **huǒchē** for a specific train. The term **lièchē** is often shortened to **chē**. For example:

D-shíyī cì *chē* dào le ma?   Has the number D-11 *train* arrived?
Zhè shì qù Guìlín de *chē* ma?   Is this the *train* to Guilin?

■ 14 Difference between **chéng** and **zuò**

There is no difference in meaning between these two terms. Both **chéng** and **zuò** can be followed by road vehicles, planes and ships when the meaning 'to take' or 'to catch' is intended. The only difference is that **chéng** is more formal than **zuò**. For example:

(A train-conductor says to a customer)
Huānyíng nín *chéng* èrshíyī cì lièchē.
Welcome to [travel with] no. 21 train.

When the phrase **chéng/zuò** + means of transportation precedes the verb **qù** (to go), it means 'to go by train/bus, etc.'. For example:

Xiǎojuān *zuò* huǒchē *qù* Guìlín.
Xiaojuan *is going* to Guilin *by train*.

■ 15 Other useful train-related words:

站台	**zhàntái**	platform
候车室	**hòuchē shì**	waiting room
列车员	**lièchē yuán**	train attendant
餐车	**cān chē**	dining car

■ 16 More on making comparisons

In Lesson 9, we learnt to make simple comparisons. For example, we learnt how to say 'A is older than B', but we did not learn how to say 'A is five years older than B', 'B is not as old as A' or 'B is less expensive than A'. Let us compare these three sentences:

Pattern: A + **bǐ** + B + adjective

Dǒng Mín bǐ Gù Liáng dà.
Dong Min is older *than* Gu Liang.

Pattern: A + **bǐ** + B + adjective + *specifics*

Dǒng Mín bǐ Gù Liáng dà wǔ suì.
Dong Min is *five years* older than Gu Liang.

Pattern: B + **méi** or **méiyǒu** + A + adjective

Gù Liáng méi Dǒng Mín dà.
Gu Liang is *not* as old as Dong Min.

Let us see some more examples:

Yìngwò bǐ ruǎnwò guì wǔshí kuài.
Hard-sleepers are *fifty yuan* more expensive than soft-sleepers.

Xīn Qín bǐ Miáo Lán kuài yī fēnzhōng.
Xin Qin is *one minute* faster than Miao Lan.

Yìngwò méi ruǎnwò guì.
Hard-sleepers are *less* expensive than soft-sleepers.

Jīntiān méiyǒu zuótiān nàme lěng.
Today is not as cold as yesterday.

Exercises

Exercise 7

You want to tell the railway ticket-assistant that you want to buy:

(a) two tickets to Beijing
(b) one ticket to Shanghai on 8 March
(c) three hard-sleepers to Guilin
(d) two tickets for the number 26 train

Exercise 8

Make as many comparative sentences as possible based on the two sentences in each group:

Example: Yìngwò piào wǔshí wǔ kuài.   Ruǎnwò piào yī bǎi kuài.
        Yìngwò piào bǐ ruǎnwò piào piányì sìshíwǔ kuài.

   or Ruǎnwò piào bǐ yìngwò piào guì sìshíwǔ kuài.
   or Yìngwò méi yóu ruǎnwò guì.
(a) Qīngdǎo píjiǔ yī kuài qī máo yī píng.
     Běijīng píjiǔ yī kuài yī máo yī píng.
(b) Xiǎoméi sānshíyī suì.
     Dàwèi sānshí suì.
(c) Lǎo Wáng juéde Zhōngguó fàn hǎochī.
     Lǎo Wáng juéde xīcān ('Western food') bú tài hǎochī.
(d) Běijīng de xiàtiān hěn rè.
     Lúndūn (London) de xiàtiān bù tài rè.

Exercise 9

Translate the following sentences into Chinese:

(a) The train arrives in Guilin at 13:05 the following day.
(b) I leave on Friday, that is, 25 March.
(c) What time does this train arrive in Beijing?
(d) What time does the number 67 train depart?

Characters

Let us recognize the following signs:

subway

地	铁
dì	tiě

ticket office

售	票	处
shòu	piào	chù

taxi

出	租	车
chū	zū	ché

Let us learn to write the following three very useful verbs. They are also very interesting characters:

Character analysis	Head component and its meaning	Stroke order	Pinyin	English
人 + 人 + 土 **tǔ**	土 (earth)	坐 丿 亻 亻 从 丛 坐 坐	**zuò**	to sit, to take
土 + 厶 **sī**	厶 (private)	去 一 十 土 去 去	**qù**	to go
忄 + 董 **dǒng** (艹 重 **zhòng**)	忄 (heart)	懂 丶 忄 忄 忄 忄 忄 忄 忄 忄 忄 懂 懂 懂	**dǒng**	to understand

(Unexplained component - 董 **dǒng**: acting as phonetic; 重 **zhòng**: heavy)

To memorise 坐, you can imagine two people sitting on the soil, chatting to each other. For 懂, the head component is heart, but this is known as a vertical heart (different from the normal heart 心). So we can say that in order to understand something you need to use your heart in a special way!

Exercise 10

(1) Write down the head component common to the following words:

地坛，坐

(2) Fill in the blanks using one of the verbs in the brackets (坐，去，懂) and then translate the sentences into English:

(a)　我要买一张_____北京的票。
(b)　去火车站_____几号线？
(c)　_____天坛在哪儿下车？
(d)　我听不_____你说的什么。

Reading/listening comprehension

I Below is a departure timetable for some trains. Use it to answer the questions in Chinese which follow.

Vocabulary

chē cì	车次	train number
shǐfā zhàn	始发站	departure station
zhōngdiǎn zhàn	终点站	destination [*lit.* 'end station']
fāchē shíjiān	发车时间	departure time

车次	始发站	终点站	发车时间
D106	上海	广州	9:50
T56	广州	北京	20:10
Z86	桂林	西安	17:05
K25	广州	深圳	7:45

QUESTIONS

(1) Qù Guǎngzhōu de chē jǐ diǎn fāchē?
   去广州的车几点发车？
(2) Nǎ cì chē qù Běijīng?
   哪次车去北京？
(3) Qù Xī'ān de chē de shǐfā zhàn shì nǎr?
   去西安的车的始发站是哪儿？
(4) K25 cì chē qù nǎr?
   K25次车去哪儿？
(5) Z86 cì chē qù Shànghǎi ma?
   Z86次车去上海吗？

(CD2; 32)

II Below are four sentences. Read each sentence first and then decide if the interpretation below is correct or not by writing 'true' or 'false'. If you have access to the audio material, listen to the sentence first, and then decide if the interpretation is 'true' or 'false'.

(1) **Wó xiǎng mǎi sān zhāng qù Yúnnán de huǒchē piào.**
    I'd like to buy three train tickets to Yunnan.

(2) **Wǒ māma bù xiǎng zuò wǎnshang fāchē de huǒchē.**
    My mother doesn't like taking trains.

(3) **Rúguǒ méi yìngwò dehuà, wǒ jiù mǎi míngtiān de ruǎnwò.**
    If there aren't any hard-sleepers, I'm not going.

(4) **Qǐng zuò yī hào xiàn qù Běijīng Fàndiàn.**
    Please take Line 1 to get to the Beijing Hotel.

Lesson Twelve
Zài fàndiàn 在饭店
At the hotel

By the end of this lesson, you should be able to:

- ask about the availability of hotel rooms
- describe the kind of room you would like to have
- use ordinal numbers with appropriate measure words
- make some complaints
- recognize more characters

Dialogue 1

Yǒu kòng fángjiān ma? 有空房间吗？
Any rooms available? **(CD2; 34)**

Jane (Zhēnní) has just finished attending a conference in Beijing, and she would like to stay on for a couple of days in a hotel near the centre of the city. She goes into a downtown hotel.

JANE	Qǐng wèn, nǐmen yǒu kòng fángjiān ma?
RECEPTIONIST	Yào kàn qíngkuàng. Nǐ yào shénme yàng de fángjiān?
JANE	Yào yī jiān yǒu liǎng zhāng chuáng de fángjiān.
RECEPTIONIST	Òu, nà shì biāozhǔn jiān. Nǎ tiān rù zhù? Zhù jǐ tiān?
JANE	Jīntiān jiù rù zhù, zhù sān tiān.
RECEPTIONIST	Ràng wǒ chácha. Zhēn qiǎo! Yǒu yī jiān kòng fángjiān.
JANE	Duō shǎo qián yī tiān?
RECEPTIONIST	Wǔ bǎi sānshí yuán.

JANE	Hán zǎocān ma?
RECEPTIONIST	Hán zǎocān.
JANE	Wǒ yào le.

(After Jane has filled in all the necessary forms . . .)

RECEPTIONIST	Zhè shì nǐde yàoshi. Fángjiān zài dì sān céng.

JANE	请问，你们有空房间吗？
RECEPTIONIST	要看情况。你要什么样的房间？
JANE	要一间有两张床的房间。
RECEPTIONIST	噢，那是标准间。哪天入住？住几天？
JANE	今天就入住，住三天。
RECEPTIONIST	让我查查。真巧！有一间空房间。
JANE	多少钱一天？
RECEPTIONIST	五百三十元。
JANE	含早餐吗？
RECEPTIONIST	含早餐。
JANE	我要了。
. . .	
RECEPTIONIST	这是你的钥匙。房间在第三层。

(CD2; 33)

Vocabulary

kòng	空	vacant/available
shénme yàng de	什么样的	what kind of . . .
fángjiān	房间	room
yào kàn qíngkuàng	要看情况	it depends [*lit.* 'will see situation']
chuáng	床	bed
biāozhǔn	标准	standard
rù zhù	入住	to check in (for hotels only)
chácha	查查	to check
zhēn qiǎo!	真巧	what a coincidence!/what good luck!
jiān	间	[measure word for rooms]
hán	含	to include
yàoshi	钥匙	key
céng	层	floor

Notes on Dialogue 1

■ 1 Hotels and hotel rooms

There are several terms for 'hotel' in Chinese and they are mostly interchangeable. Luxury hotels are called 饭店 (**fàndiàn**), 酒店 (**jiǔdiàn**) or 宾馆 (**bīn guǎn**). 旅店 (**lǚdiàn**) or 旅馆 (**lǚguǎn**) are mid-to bottom-range hotels. In hotels with 4 stars and above, rooms are classified as 标准间 (**biāozhǔn jiān**, standard room with two beds), 商务间 (**shāngwù jiān**, executive room usually with a king-size bed and facilities such as a fax machine) and 豪华套房 (**háohuá tàofáng**, deluxe suite with a sitting-room). In small and medium-sized hotels, you can find single rooms (单人间 **dānrén jiān**) and double rooms (双人间 **shuāngrén jiān**).

■ 2 Use of **kòng fángjiān**

Literally, **kòng fángjiān** means 'unoccupied room'. The word **kòng** used here is the same **kòng** as in **yǒu kòng** (to have time) in Lesson 10. In the context of booking into a hotel, **kòng fángjiān** can mean 'vacancy' or 'rooms available'. For example:

Duìbuqǐ. Wǒmen méi yǒu *kòng fángjiān*.
Sorry. We don't have any *vacancies*.

Nǐ zhīdào Běijīng Fàndiàn yǒu *kòng fángjiān* ma?
Do you know if there are any *rooms* available in the Beijing Hotel?

■ 3 Phrase **kàn qíngkuàng**

This is a very useful phrase. We actually learnt the term **qíngkuàng** in Lesson 5 in sentences such as **jiǎngjiang nǐ jiā de *qíngkuàng*** (Tell me about your family). The phrase **Kàn qíngkuàng** or **Yào kàn qíngkuàng** means 'It depends'. For example:

A: **Nǐ míngtiān qù yóuyǒng ma?**
   Are you going swimming tomorrow?
B: **Kàn qíngkuàng.**
   It depends.

If you want to say 'It depends on something', you must say **Yào kàn** + something. For example:

A: **Nǐ xiǎng mǎi zhēnsī lǐngdài ma?**
    Do you want to buy some silk ties?
B: **Yào kàn jiàgé.**
    It depends on the price.
A: **Nǐ qí zìxíngchē shàng bān ma?**
    Do you go to work by bike?
B: **Yào kàn tiānqì.**
    It depends on the weather.

■ 4 Shortening of noun phrases

Some noun phrases or proper nouns sometimes get shortened by omitting certain parts. Unfortunately, there are no rules to follow. Below are a few phrases we have already learnt which can be shortened:

biāozhǔn fángjiān	→ **biāo jiān**	standard room
Běijīng Dàxué	→ **Běi Dà**	Beijing University
gōnggòng qìchē	→ **gōng chē**	bus

■ 5 **Duō shǎo qián yī tiān?**

When you ask about the hotel tariff in English, you say *How much is it per night?* In Chinese, you say 'How much is it per day?' For example:

Biāozhǔn jiān *duō shǎo qián yī tiān?*
How much is it per night for a standard room?

Běijīng Fàndiàn de shāngwù jiān qī bǎi yuán *yī tiān*.
Executive rooms in the Beijing Hotel cost seven hundred yuan
    per night.

■ 6 Use of ordinal numbers with measure words

In Lesson 7, we learnt how to say ordinal numbers, e.g. **dì yī** (first), **dì èr** (second). When ordinal numbers precede nouns that require a measure word, you must put the measure word after the ordinal number. For example:

liǎng *ge* cāntīng two dining-rooms **dì èr ge** the second one

sān *liàng* three bikes → **dì sān *liàng*** the third bike
zìxíngchē
liù *céng* six floors → **dì liù *céng*** the seventh floor

Note that the word **céng** is only used to refer to different floors in a building. It cannot be used to mean the 'floor' in, for example, 'wooden floor'. When counting floors, the Chinese equivalent of 'ground floor' in English is the first floor; the second floor is the first floor, etc.

Nouns such as **tiān** (day), **nián** (year), etc., which do not require measure words, must follow the ordinal number. For example:

yī *tiān* one *day* → **dì yī *tiān*** the first *day*
sì *nián* four *years* → **dì sì *nián*** the fourth *year*

Exercises

Exercise 1

Match the question with an appropriate answer:

(a) Nǐ yào shénme yàng de fángjiān?
(b) Nǐ shénme shíhòu rù zhù?
(c) Nǐmen jīnwǎn yǒu kòng fángjiān ma?
(d) Duō shǎo qián yī tiān?
(e) Nǐ yào zhù jǐ tiān?

(i) Sì bǎi liùshí yuán yī tiān.
(ii) Liǎng tiān.
(iii) Duìbuqǐ, méi yǒu fángjiān le.
(iv) Liǎng jiān biāozhǔn jiān.
(v) Bā yuè shí hào.

Exercise 2

You tell the receptionist at a hotel that you would like:

(a) a standard room for 3 days
(b) a room with two beds
(c) two standard rooms for one night

Exercise 3

Translate the following sentences into Chinese:

(a)   Do you have any rooms available?
(b)   My room does not have a telephone.
(c)   Your room is on the fourth floor.
(d)   The third bike on the left is mine.

Exercise 4

Pair work – one person asks questions in Chinese, based on Dialogue 1, and the other person answers them. For example:

A: Zhēnní xiǎng yào shénme yàng de fángjiān?
B: Yǒu liǎng zhāng chuáng de.

Dialogue 2

Diàndēng huài le   电灯坏了   The light is not working (CD2; 36)

The following morning, Jane bumps into the duty manager of the hotel.

DUTY MANAGER	Zǎoshang hǎo. Nín zuówǎn shuì de hǎo ma?
JANE	Lǎoshí shuō, shuì de bù hǎo.
DUTY MANAGER	Zěnme huí shì?
JANE	Zuótiān wǎnshang, gébì fángjiān hěn chǎo. Chǎo dào bànyè liǎng diǎn.
DUTY MANAGER	Zhēn bàoqiàn. Wǒ huì chǔlǐ zhè jiàn shì.
JANE	Xièxie. Ò, duì le. Wǒde fángjiān lǐ yǒu ge diàndēng huài le.
DUTY MANAGER	Shì ma? Wǒ yīdìng ràng rén qù xiū. Hái yǒu biéde wèntí ma?
JANE	Zànshí méi yǒu. Huí jiàn.
DUTY MANAGER	早上好。您昨晚睡得好吗？
JANE	老实说，睡得不好。
DUTY MANAGER	怎么回事？

JANE	昨天晚上，隔壁房间很吵。吵到半夜两点。
DUTY MANAGER	真抱歉。我会处理这件事。
JANE	谢谢。噢，对了。我的房间里有个电灯坏了。
DUTY MANAGER	是吗？我一定让人去修。还有别的问题吗？
JANE	暂时没有。回见。

(CD2; 35)

B Vocabulary

lǎoshi shuō	老实说	frankly speaking/to be honest
shì	事	thing/matter
zěnme huí shì?	怎么回事？	what's the matter?
gé bì	隔壁	next door
chǎo	吵	to be noisy
bàn yè	半夜	early hours of the morning
zhēn bàoqiàn	真抱歉	many apologies
chǔlǐ	处理	to see to/to handle
zhè jiàn shì	这件事	this matter
jiàn	件	[measure word, see Note 10]
duì le	对了	right/by the way
lǐ	里	inside/in
diàndēng	电灯	light [*lit.* 'electric light']
huài le	坏了	to have broken down/does not work
ràng rén	让人	to send for someone
xiū	修	to repair/fix
wèntí	问题	problem
zànshí	暂时	at the moment/temporarily

Notes on Dialogue 2

■ 7 **Zěnme huí shì?**

This is a very colloquial phrase. The complete phrase should be **Zěnme yī huí shì?** (*lit.* 'How one thing?' – **huí** is another measure word for matters). This phrase is usually used if something has gone wrong and you want to find out about it. It means 'What's the matter?', 'What's the problem?' or 'What happened?' The word **shì**, which is a different word from **shì** (be), is a general term used to refer to abstract things. For example:

Wǒ míngtiān yǒu *shì*.
I've got *things* to do tomorrow.

Shénme *shì*?
What is it?

Wǒ yǒu liǎng jiàn *shì* gàosu nǐ.
I've got two *things* to tell you.

■ 8 More on past particles

So far, we have learnt two different ways to indicate a past event or an event which is related to the past by using **le** or **guo** after some verbs. However, you must not use either of the above two particles in sentences which describe a stable state of affairs in the past as opposed to momentary action. In the former case, the past tense is indicated by time-related phrases such as **zuótiān** (yesterday), **shàng ge xīngqī** (last week), etc. In particular, **le** or **guo** must not be used in the following three sentence types:

(a) Sentences with static verbs such as **shì** (to be), **yǒu** (to have), **xiǎng** (when it means 'to want'), **xǐhuān** (to like), **zhīdào** (to know), etc. For example:

Liǎng nián qián, **tā *yǒu* yī liàng zìxíngchē.**
He *had* a bike *two years ago*.

Qù nián, **tā *shì* dǎoyóu.**
She *was* a tourist guide *last year*.

Zuówǎn, **wǒ bù *xiǎng* chī fàn.**
I *didn't* want to eat *last night*.

(b) Sentences with predicative adjectives or the word **zài** (to be at/in). For example:

Zuówǎn, **gébì hěn *chǎo*.**
Next door *was* very noisy *last night*.

Zuótiān, wǒ bàba *zài* jiā.
My father *was* at home *yesterday*.

(c) Sentences with verbal phrases followed by **de**. For example:

Zuówǎn, wǒ shuì de hěn hǎo.
I slept very well last night.

You may have noticed that verbs other than **yǒu** (to have) used in the above sentences cannot be negated by **méi yǒu** or **méi**. For example:

Qù nián, tā bú shì dǎo yóu.
She wasn't a tourist guide last year.

■ 9 Use of **dào**

Dào (until) can be used after a verbal phrase, verb or predicative adjective to describe the duration of an event. For example:

Wǒ děng tā *dào* shí'èr diǎn.
I waited for him *until* twelve o'clock.

Tāmen chǎo *dào* hěn wǎn.
They were noisy all night.

Usually, if the verb is a two-syllable word, put **dào** after the first syllable and omit the second syllable. Let us take **kāimén** (to open) as an example:

Cāntīng *kāi* dào wǎnshang shí diǎn.
The restaurant *is open* until ten o'clock.

■ 10 Measure word **jiàn**

This is the same **jiàn** as in **yī *jiàn* máoyī** (one jumper) in Lesson 9, but it is different from the **jiān** as in **yī *jiān* fángjiān** (one room). Let us see how these two measure words differ in the following phrases:

	Tone	Character	English
yī *jiàn* shì	fourth tone	件	one matter
liǎng *jiàn* máoyī	fourth tone	件	two jumpers
sān *jiān* fángjiān	first tone	间	one room

■ 11 Use of **duì le**

This is used when the current topic of conversation reminds you of
something. It has the same effect as 'Oh, yes/right' in English when
used in those circumstances. For example:

A: **Xiǎo Lǐ qǐng wǒ chī wǎnfàn.**
Xiao Li has invited me to dinner.

B: **Duì le. Wǒ wàng le gàosu nǐ...**
Oh, right. I forgot to tell you...

A: **Wǒ mǎi le yī zhāng qù Shànghǎi de huǒchē piào.**
I bought a train ticket for Shanghai.

B: **Duì le. Lǐ Bīng shuō tā yě qù Shànghǎi.**
Oh, yes. Li Bing says she is going to Shanghai as well.

■ 12 Use of **lǐ**

The word **lǐ**, meaning 'inside' or 'in', indicates the position of an
object. It is always placed *after* the noun. For example:

Nǐmende fángjiān *lǐ*   yǒu wèishēng jiān ma?
Lit. Your   room   inside have bathroom   [question word]?
Is there a bathroom *in* your room?

Wǒde qiánbāo *lǐ*   méi yǒu qián.
Lit. My   wallet   inside not have money.
There is no money in my wallet.

Note that **lǐ** usually changes to neutral tone when used in the middle
of sentences.

■ 13 Something + **huài le**

Literally, **huài** means 'bad'. So we can say **huài rén** (bad person),
huài zhǔyi (bad idea), etc. When **huài le** follows a noun, it means
something 'does not work', 'is broken' or 'has gone bad'. For
example:

Tāde fángjiān lǐ yǒu ge diàndēng *huài le*.
One of the lights in his room *is not working*.

Wǒde zìxíngchē *huài le*.
My bike *is broken*.

Māma, wǒ juéde kǎo yā *huài le*.
Mum, I think the roast duck *has gone off.*

■ 14 Construction **ràng** + somebody + do something

In this context, the verb **ràng** means 'to ask' (see **ràng** in Lesson 3). For example:

Lǎo Wáng *ràng* wǒ dài nǐ qù yínháng.
Lao Wang *asked* me to take you to the bank.

Yuéhàn *ràng* wǒ wèn nǐde fùmú hǎo.
John *asked* me to say hello to your parents.

When **rén** (person) follows **ràng**, **rén** in this context means 'somebody'. Thus **ràng rén** can mean 'to send for somebody' or 'to ask someone'. For example:

Wǒ yīdìng *ràng rén* qù xiū nǐde dēng.
I'll definitely *send someone* to fix your light.

Mù Yīng huì *ràng rén* géi wǒ mǎi yī zhāng huǒchē piào de.
Mu Ying will *ask somebody* to buy me a train ticket.

■ 15 Useful expressions for hotel facilities

dàtáng	大堂	lobby
hùliánwǎng	互联网	internet
jiàoxǐng fúwù	叫醒服务	wake-up call
kèfáng fúwù	客房服务	room service
kōngtiáo	空调	air-conditioning
línyù	淋浴	shower
mínǐ bā/xiǎo bīngxiāng	迷你吧/小冰箱	mini-bar/small fridge
qiántái	前台	reception
tuì fáng	退房	to check out [*lit.* 'return room']
wèishēngjiān	卫生间	bathroom, toilet
wǐxiàn liánjiē	无线连接	wireless connection
xǐshǒuchí	洗手池	sink
yīng'ér chuáng	婴儿床	cot
yùndǒu	熨斗	iron
yùpén	浴盆	bath

Exercises

Exercise 5

Which is the odd word out in each group below?

(a) hē kāfēi   chī kǎo yā   chī zǎofàn   diàndēng
(b) chǔlǐ   biāozhǔn jiān   dānrén jiān   wèishēng jiān
(c) Yīngguórén   Zhōngguórén   Měiguórén   fàndiàn

Exercise 6

Pair off the verbs on the left with nouns on the right:

(a) xiū   1 zhè jiàn shì
(b) chǔlǐ   2 lǐwù
(c) yǒu   3 diàndēng
(d) mǎi   4 gōnggòng qìchē
(e) kàn   5 kòng fángjiān
(f) děng   6 péngyou

Exercise 7

You complain to the duty manager in your hotel that:

(a) the light in your room is not working
(b) the people next door are very noisy
(c) your room is too cold

Exercise 8

Translate the following into Chinese:

(a) Many apologies.
(b) Frankly speaking, . . .
(c) Did you sleep well?
(d) It depends.
(e) Sifang asked me to tell you that she is leaving next Thursday.
(f) There is no money in my wallet.
(g) A: Any other problems?
     B: Not for the moment.

Exercise 9

Describe the following in the past tense (see Note 15 for new words):

(a) your room was cold yesterday
(b) you were not in a going-out mood last night
(c) your next door neighbour was being noisy last night
(d) the room you had did not have a bath
(e) you did not know the air-conditioning in the room wasn't working.

Characters

Distinguish between 事 (**shì**, thing/matter) and 是 (**shì**, is/am/are; yes; correct):

Character analysis	Head component and its meaning	Stroke order
一 + 口 + ⇒ + 亅	一 (one)	事　一　一　一　一　一　一　事
日 + 疋 **pǐ**	日 (sun)	是　丨　冂　冃　日　旦　早　杲　杲　是

(Unexplained component - 疋 **pǐ**: cloth)

事 consists of four different components. The second component is a squashed version of 口, which means 'mouth'. Perhaps we can make up the following story for 事: 'we need to speak in order to sort things out'. For 是, there are only two components. The component 疋 originally means 'correct', which was associated with the character 正 (**zhèng**, correct). So we can make up the following story for 是: 'if something is true, you have to swear it under the sun'.

Exercise 10

(1) Fill in the gaps using either 事 (**shì**, thing/matter) or 是 (**shì**, is/am/are;

(a)   这不____ 我房间的钥匙。
      Zhè bù _____ wǒ fángjiān de yàoshi.
(b)   我____ 饭店经理。你有什么____？
      Wǒ _____ fàndiàn jīnglǐ. Nǐ yǒu shénme____？
(c)   这件____ 我不能处理，真抱歉。
      Zhè jiàn____ wǒ bù néng chǔlǐ, zhēn bàoqiàn.

(2) Fill in the gaps using appropriate words/phrases from the vocabulary lists for both dialogues.

From Dialogue 1 Vocabulary:
(a)   你的_____在 第十九层。
      Nǐde_____zài dì shíjiǔ céng.
(b)   你们明天有_____房间吗？
      Nǐmen míngtiān yǒu_____fángjiān ma?
(c)   你想什么时候_____我们饭店？
      Nǐ xiǎng shénme shíhòu_____wǒmen fàndiàn?

From Dialogue 2 Vocabulary:
(d)   我房间里的电话_____。
      Wǒ fángjiān lǐ de diànhuà_____.
(e)   他的车坏了，可是他不会_____。
      Tāde chē huài le, kěshì tā bú huì_____.
(f)   我有一个_____想问你。你有时间吗？
      Wǒ yǒu yī ge _____xiáng wèn nǐ. Nǐ yǒu shíjiān ma?

Reading comprehension

There are a few odd things in the following dialogue between a hotel receptionist (A) and a customer (B). Pick out the strange word(s) or phrase(s). Then you need to decide whether to cross them out or to replace them with more suitable words or phrases.

A   Nǐ hǎo!
B   Xièxie. Nǐmen yǒu kōng fángjiān ma?
A   Yào kàn qíngkuàng. Nǐ yào biāozhǔn jiān háishì píjiǔ?
B   Yào biāozhǔn jiān. Biāozhǔn jiān yǒu wèishēngjiān ma?
A   Yǒu. Nǐ dǎsuàn zhù jǐ tiān?
B   Liǎng ge tiān.

A Ràng nǐ chácha. Gānghǎo yǒu yī jiān biāozhǔn jiān.
B Duō shǎo qián yī jīn?
A Sān bǎi yuán. Xíng ma?
B Xíng. Wǒ yào le.

A 你好！
B 谢谢！你们有空房间吗？
A 要看情况。你要标准间还是啤酒？
B 要标准间。标准间有卫生间吗?
A 有。你打算住几天？
B 两个天。
A 让你查查。刚好有一间标准间。
B 多少钱一斤？
A 三百元。行吗？
B 行。我要了。

Lesson Thirteen
Dǎ diànhuà 打电话
Making telephone calls

By the end of this lesson, you should be able to:

- use some appropriate expressions on the telephone
- use the **shì . . . de** construction to express the time or manner of a past action
- indicate that you have completed an action by using **wán . . . le**
- distinguish the usage between **yī** and **yāo**
- recognize more characters

Dialogue 1

Wèi 喂 Hello (CD2; 39)

Alan is in Beijing to do some research. He is going to call his old friend Li Bin, who went to the same university as Alan . . .

ALAN	Wèi, qǐng zhǎo yīxià Lǐ Bīn.
LǏ BĪN	Wǒ jiù shì. Nǐ shì shéi'a?
ALAN	Wǒ shì Àilún, nǐ zài Yīngguó shàng xué shí de tóngxué.
LǏ BĪN	Zhēn de! Nǐ shì shénme shíhou lái de? Wǒ zěnme bù zhīdao?
ALAN	Shàng ge xīngqīsì lái de. Shì línshí juédìng.

LǏ BĪN	Wǒ tài jīdòng le. Nǐ shénme shíhou kěyǐ lái wǒ jiā?
ALAN	Shénme shíhou dōu xíng. Nǐ juédìng.
LǏ BĪN	Jīntiān wǎnshang xíng ma? Míngtiān wǒ yào qù Xiǎng Gǎng chūchāi.
ALAN	Dāng rán xíng. Nǐ zhù zài shénme dìfang?
LǏ BĪN	Wǒ jiā bù hǎo zhǎo. Wǒ lái jiē nǐ ba.
ALAN	Tài bàng le!

ALAN	喂，请找一下李彬。
LǏ BĪN	我就是。你是谁啊？
ALAN	我是爱伦，你在英国上学时的同学。
LǏ BĪN	真的！你是什么时侯来的？我怎么不知道？
ALAN	上个星期四来的。是临时决定。
LǏ BĪN	我太激动了。你什么时候可以来我家？
ALAN	什么时候都行。你决定。
LǏ BĪN	今天晚上行吗？明天我要去香港出差。
ALAN	当然行。你住在什么地方？
LǏ BĪN	我家不好找。我来接你吧。
ALAN	太棒了！

(CD2; 38)

B Vocabulary

wèi	喂	hello [only used on the telephone]
zhǎo	找	to look for
zài . . . shí	在 . . . 时	when
tóngxué	同学	classmate; school friend
shàng ge	上个	last
línshí	临时	last-minute/temporary
juédìng	决定	to decide/decision
jīdòng	激动	to be excited/exciting
shénme shíhou	什么时候	any time/whenever
dōu	都	[emphatic word, see Note 6]
nǐ juédìng	你决定	you decide
Xiǎng Gǎng	香港	Hong Kong
chūchāi	出差	to go on a business trip

shénme dìfang	什么地方	whereabouts [*lit.* 'what place']
bù hǎo zhǎo	不好找	not easy to find
jiē	接	to collect/to meet
tài bàng le!	太棒了!	wonderful!

Notes on Dialogue 1

■ 1 Use of **wèi**

This word is only used to begin a telephone conversation. It is basically a way of catching the attention of the person on the other end of the phone. For example:

Wèi, nǐ shì Běijīng Fàndiàn ma? *Hello.* Is that the Beijing Hotel?
Wèi, Xiǎo Liú zài ma?   *Hello.* Is Xiao Liu there?

■ 2 Some telephone expressions

If you want to speak to someone, you can say one of the following:

    Qǐng   zhǎo yīxià Lǐ Bīn?
Lit. Please look for   Li Bin.
    Could you get Li Bin please?

Note that the expression **yīxià** has the same effect, i.e. mitigating the abruptness, as it had in Lesson 3.

Qǐng wèn, Lǐ Bīn zài ma?   Is Li Bin around please?

If you happen to be the one who answers the telephone and speak first, you can say one of the following:

    Qǐng   wèn, nǐ zhǎo   shéi?
Lit. Please ask, you look for who?
    Whom do you want to speak to, please?

    Wèi, nǐ   shì nǎli?
Lit. Hello, you are whereabout?
    Hello, who is calling?

■ 3 More on the link word **de**

In the dialogue, Alan explains who he is by saying **Nǐ zài Yīngguó de tóngxué** (your classmate when you were in the UK). The word

de links the verbal phrase with the noun (see Note 5 in Lesson 11). The complete sentence should be:

Wǒ shì nǐ zài Yīngguó shàng xué shí de tóngxué.
I am your classmate when you were attending a college in Britain.

Note that this sentence can be taken apart into two simple sentences:

(a) **Wǒ shì nide tóngxué.**
(b) **Nǐ zài Yīngguó.**

■ 4 Construction **shì . . . de**

This construction has many usages. Let us look at two of them here. First, it is used in interrogative sentences which ask about the time, the place or manner of an action that happened in the past. The word **shì** is placed before the phrase that is being emphasized and **de** comes either at the end of the sentence or after the verb. For example:

Nǐ *shì* shénme shíhou lái Běijīng *de*? **Nǐ *shì* shénme shíhou lái *de* Běijīng?**	When did you arrive in Beijing?
Nǐ *shì* zěnme lái *de*?	How did you get here?

Without **shì . . . de**, the above first two sentences become:

Nǐ shénme shíhou lái Běijīng?
When are you coming to Beijing?

And the last sentence becomes **Nǐ zěnme lái?**, which means 'How do you get here?' or 'How are you going to get here?'

Second, the construction is used in positive sentences that emphasize the time or manner of a past action. For example:

Wǒ *shì* líng qī nián kāishǐ xué Zhōngwén *de*.
I started to learn Chinese in 2007.

Wǒ *shì* qí zìxíngchē lái *de*.
I came by bike.

Note that **shì** is often omitted in the above two cases. Thus we have:

> **Tā jǐ diǎn xià bān *de*?**
> What time did he leave/finish work?

> **Wǒ zuò gōnggòng qìchē lái *de*.**
> I came by bus.

Let us compare the use of **le** and **shì** . . . **de** in describing a past action:

> **Tā zuótiān lái *le*.**   She turned up yesterday.
> **Tā *shì* zuótiān lái *de*.**   She arrived yesterday.

Tā zuótiān lái le is merely a statement about a past event (i.e. to confirm that something happened yesterday), whilst **Tā shì zuótiān lái de** emphasizes the time 'yesterday' as opposed to any other time.

■ 5 Use of **shì** at the beginning of sentences

You may have noticed that the pronoun 'it' is seldom used in Chinese. Thus, the structure 'It is/was . . .' is sometimes replaced by **Zhè shì** . . . (This is/was . . .). For example:

> ***Zhè shì* línshí juédìng ma?**   *Was it* a last-minute decision?

The pronoun **zhè** is often omitted. So **shì** occurs at the beginning of a sentence:

> ***Shì* línshí juédìng.**   *It was* a last-minute decision.
> ***Shì* Wáng Fāng ma?**   *Is that* Wang Fang?

■ 6 More on question words used in statements

Certain question words, when used in statements, especially in conjunction with the emphatic word **dōu**, function as indefinite pronouns. Note how the meaning changes accordingly:

Word item	In questions	In statements
shénme shíhou	when	whenever / at any time
nǎr	where	wherever
zěnme	how	by whatever means

For the moment, let us concentrate on how to use **shénme shíhou** in conjunction with **dōu**, which can be placed after **shénme shíhou**. For example:

> **Shénme shíhou dōu xíng.**
> *Lit.* Whenever   be fine.
> *Whenever* you like.

Dōu can also be placed after the verb, that is, if a verb is used. For example:

> **Zánmen shénme shíhou <u>yóuyǒng</u> dōu xíng.**
>   verb
> *Lit.* We   whenever   swim   be fine.
> It's fine with me *whenever* we go swimming.

You can also use **shénme shíhou** in the first part of a sentence, and **dōu** in the second part. For example:

> **Nǐ shénme shíhou lái,   wǒ dōu zài.**
> *Lit.* You whenever   come, I   be in.
> *Whenever* you come, I'll be in.

If you want to negate the sentences with **shénme shíhou** and **dōu**, put the negation word after **dōu**. For example:

> **Xiǎo Lǐ shénme shíhou dōu *méi yǒu* kòng.**
> *Lit.* Xiao Li whenever   not have time.
> Xiao Li *never has* time.

■ 7 Question word **shénme dìfang**

Literally, **shénme dìfang** means 'what place'. In addition to 'what place', it also means 'whereabouts' or 'where exactly'. For example:

> **Nǐ zhù zài Běijīng *shénme dìfang*?**
> *Where exactly* in Beijing do you live?

> **Nǐ qù le Měiguó *shénme dìfang*?**
> *What places* in America did you go to?

■ 8 Use of **jiā**

Depending on the context, **jiā** can mean either 'home' or 'family'. For example:

Nǐ fùmǔ de *jiā* **zài shénme dìfang?**
Whereabouts is your parents' *home*?

Wǒ *jiā* **yǒu hěnduō rén. Wǒ yǒu yī ge dà** *jiā*.
There are many people in my *family*. I have a big *family*.

■ 9 Use of **bù hǎo** + verb

As you know, **bù hǎo** means 'not good'. However, when you have
the pattern 'something + **bù hǎo** + verb', it means 'It is not easy to
do something'. For example:

       Huǒchē zhàn   **bù hǎo** <u>zhǎo</u>.
                               verb
Lit.   Railway station not easy find.
      It's not easy to find the railway station.

       Zhōngwén bù hǎo <u>xué</u>.
                               verb
Lit.   Chinese   not easy learn.
      It's not easy to learn Chinese.

■ 10 Use of **jiē**

Jiē means 'to collect' or 'to meet', usually somebody. For example:

Jīntiān wǎnshang bā diǎn bàn, wǒ yào qù huǒchē zhàn *jiē* **wǒ
māma.**
I'm going to go to the station *to meet* my mother at half past
eight tonight.

Nǐ xūyào wǒ qù *jiē* **nǐ ma?**
Do you need me to go and *collect* you?

Exercises

Exercise 1

Complete the following telephone dialogues in as many ways as you
can think of:

(a) A: _____?
      B: Wǒ jiù shì Lǐ Bīn.

(b) A: Nǐ shì Běijīng Dàxué Zhōngwén Xì ma?
    B: _____?
    A: Qǐng zhǎo yīxià Hú Xīnháng.
(c) A: _____?
    B: Duìbuqǐ. Zhēnní bú zài.
(d) A: _____?
    B: Wǒ shì nǐde lǎo tóngxué Àilún.

Exercise 2

Combine the two sentences in each group to make them into one
sentence by using **de**:

> *Example*: Wǒ shì nǐde tóngxué. Nǐ zài Yīngguó shàng xué.
> → Wǒ shì nǐ zài Yīngguó shàng xué shí de tóngxué.

(a) Sīfāng shì Zhōngguórén.   Sīfāng zhù zài Xīnjiāpō.
(b) Línlin shì dà xuéshēng.   Línlin xué Zhōngwén.
(c) Wǒde Zhōngwén lǎoshī shì Zhōngguórén.
    Tā cóng Zhōngguó dàlù lái. (**dàlù** means 'mainland China')

Exercise 3

Translate the following sentences into Chinese:

(a) When did David leave?
(b) I came to work by bike this morning.
(c) Whenever you like. You decide.
(d) He does not like to take a bus, no matter when.
(e) Could you come to collect me?
(f) What time and where exactly shall we meet?
(g) When I was studying at Beijing University my parents went to
    China and travelled for 3 months.

Exercise 4

How do you ask Xiao Li the following in Chinese:

(a) What time did you leave work yesterday?
(b) How did you get to work yesterday?
(c) Was it last night that your younger sister arrived?
(d) When did your younger sister start learning English?

Exercise 5

Make up as many sentences as you can using **bù hǎo** to mean 'It is not easy to . . .' and write the English translation after each sentence.

Dialogue 2

 Shǒujī hàomǎ   手机号码   Mobile phone numbers (CD2; 41)

John works in the Shanghai office of a Canadian telecommunications company. It is a busy day today and all the phones in the office are engaged.

JOHN	Yǒngméi, nǐ yòng wán diànhuà le ma?
YǑNGMÉI	Yòng wán le.
JOHN	Wǒ děi gěi zánmen lǎobǎn dǎ ge diànhuà.
YǑNGMÉI	Tā jīntiān bú zài bàngōngshì. Yěxǔ qù jīchǎng jiē nà ge zhòngyào de kèhù le.
JOHN	Shì ma? Nǐ yǒu tāde xīn shǒujī hàomǎ ma?
YǑNGMÉI	Méi yǒu. Nǐ kěyǐ dǎ diànhuà wèn tāde mìshū.
JOHN	Hǎo zhǔyì.
SECRETARY	Èr liù bā fēnjī. Qǐng wèn, nǎ yī wèi?
JOHN	Wǒ shì Yuēhàn. Wǒ yǒu yī jiàn jí shì tóng Fāng jīnglǐ shāngliang. Tīngshuō tā jīntiān bú zài bàngōngshì. Tāde shǒujī hàomǎ shì duō shǎo?
SECRETARY	Qǐng děng yīxià. Tīng hǎo. Hàomǎ shì yāo sān bā bā qī sì liù èr yāo bā sān.
JOHN	Yāo sān bā bā qī sì liù èr yāo bā sān.
SECRETARY	Duì.

JOHN	永梅，你用完电话了吗？
YǑNGMÉI	用完了。
JOHN	我得给咱们老板打个电话。
YǑNGMÉI	他今天不在办公室。也许去机场接那个重要的客户了。
JOHN	是吗？你有他的新手机号码吗？
YǑNGMÉI	没有。你可以打电话问他的秘书。
JOHN	好主意。
SECRETARY	二六八分机。请问，哪一位？

JOHN	我是约翰。我有一件急事同方经理商量。听说他今天不在办公室。他的手机号码是多少？
SECRETARY	请等一下。听好。号码是一三八八七四六二一八三。
JOHN	一三八八七四六二一八三。
SECRETARY	对。

(CD2; 40)

Vocabulary

yòng	用	to use
wán	完	[see Note 11]
lǎobǎn	老板	boss
dǎ diànhuà	打电话	to make telephone calls/to telephone
bàngōngshì	办公室	office
yěxǔ	也许	perhaps
jīchǎng	机场	airport
zhòngyào	重要	important
kèhù	客户	client
xīn	新	new
shǒujī	手机	mobile phone
hàomǎ	号码	number
mìshū	秘书	secretary
fēnjī	分机	extension
nǎ yī wèi?	哪一位？	who is calling/speaking?
jíshì	急事	urgent matter
tóng	同	with/and
shāngliàng	商量	to discuss/to consult
tīng hǎo	听好	to listen carefully [*lit*. 'listen well']
yāo	一（幺）	one

Notes on Dialogue 2

■ 11 Use of **wán** after the verb

When you put **wán** after a verb, it indicates that the action is completed. It is similar to the English phrase 'to have finished with/doing something'. Whenever **wán** is used after a verb, **le** must be placed after whatever has been finished. For example:

> **Nǐ chī *wán* wǎnfàn *le* ma?**
> *Lit.* You eat finish supper [question word]?
> Have you *finished* having your supper?

> **Wǒ yòng *wán* wèishēng jiān *le*. Nǐ qù yòng ba.**
> *Lit.* I use finish bathroom.   You go use please.
> I've *finished* with the bathroom. Do go and use it.

■ 12 More on the preposition **gěi**

A phrase beginning with **gěi** . . . is always placed before the verbal phrase (see Lessons 8 and 15). Thus, if you want to say 'to telephone somebody' or 'to make a phone call to somebody', you say **gěi** + somebody + **dǎ diànhuà**. For example:

> **Bié wàng le *gěi nǐ māma* dǎ diànhuà.**
> Don't forget to phone your mum.

> **Míngtiān wǒ yídìng *gěi nǐ* dǎ diànhuà.**
> I'll definitely give you a call tomorrow.

If you want to mention the number of phone calls made or to be made, put the numerals together with the measure word **gè** before **diànhuà**. For example:

> **Zuótiān wǒ gěi zánmen lǎobǎn dǎ le *liǎng ge* diànhuà.**
> Yesterday, I made two phone calls to our boss.

■ 13 More on the omission of **de**

The word **de**, which indicates the ownership relationship, is usually omitted before **jiā** (home/family). For example:

> **Nǐ jiā bù hǎo zhǎo.**
> It's not easy to find *your home*.

> **Wǒ fùmǔ jiā zài Xiāng Gǎng.**
> *My parents' home* is in Hong Kong.

However, it is not wrong to use **de**. For example, it is perfectly right to say **Nǐde jiā bù hǎo zhǎo**. But **de** must be kept before **diànhuà**

hàomǎ (telephone number). The reason is that the concept of **jiā** is associated with people whilst **diànhuà hàomǎ** is just an object (see Note 4 in Lesson 5). For example:

Wǒde diànhuà huài le.
My telephone has been out of order.

Nǐ jiā de diànhuà hàomǎ shì shénme?
What is *your home* telephone number?

■ 14 More on the measure word **wèi**

We learnt this measure word in Lesson 10. The question **Nǎ yī wèi?** (*lit.* 'Which one?') is actually a polite way of asking 'Who is it?' on the telephone. For example:

Wèi, nǎ yī wèi? Hello. *Who is it, please?*

It is also appropriate to ask **Nǐ shì nǎ yī wèi?** (*lit.* 'You are which one?').

■ 15 Preposition **tóng**

You may have noticed by now that prepositional phrases (e.g. see Note 12 above) appear before verbal phrases. **Tóng**, meaning 'with' or 'and', is a preposition. Thus **tóng** + somebody is a prepositional phrase. This phrase must be placed before the verbal phrase. For example:

Wǒ xiǎng *tóng nǐde mèimei* shāngliang yī jiàn shì.
Lit. I want with your younger sister discuss one matter.
I'd like to discuss something *with your younger sister.*

Nǐ xiǎng *tóng wǒ* qù yóuyǒng ma?
Lit. You want with me go swim [question word]?
Would you like to go swimming *with me*?

Note that **tóng** and **hé** (and/with) are interchangeable.

■ 16 **Qǐng tīng hǎo**

Literally, this phrase means 'Please listen well'. It is like a sort of warning before you pass on a piece of important information on the telephone. It is similar in meaning to the English phrase 'Here it is' or 'Ready?' For example:

A: **Qǐng gàosu wǒ Xiǎo Lǐ de diànhuà hàomǎ?**
    Please tell me Xiao Li's telephone number.

B: **Qǐng tīng hǎo.**   **Bā-sì-líng-wǔ-liù-yāo.**
    Here it is: eight-four-zero-five-six-one.

■ 17 Asking for a telephone number

To ask 'What's your telephone number?', you literally say in Chinese 'Your telephone number is how many': **Nǐde diànhuà hàomǎ shì duō shǎo?**

■ 18 Use of the number **yāo**

Yāo is a substitute for **yī** (one). **Yāo** is used when the number 'one' occurs in telephone numbers, room numbers, bus and train numbers, etc. The reason is that the pronunciation of **yī** is likely to be mixed up with **qī** (seven) when a series of numbers is uttered. For example, **yāo** is used in the following:

> *yāo*-**líng-qī fángjiān**
> room *107*

> *yāo-yāo*-**sān lù diànchē**
> tram no. *113*

> **Wǒ jiā de diànhuà hàomǎ shì qī-qī-líng-wǔ-bà-*yāo*.**
> My home telephone number is *770581*.

Exercises

Exercise 6

Decide which **de** (if any) can be omitted in the following sentences. Rewrite the sentence if a **de** can be omitted:

(a) Wǒde jiějie shì dǎoyóu.
(b) Wǒmende jīnglǐ de bàngōngshì zài èr céng.
(c) Wǒde diànhuà huài le.

(d) Tāde fùmǔde jiā hěn piàoliang.
(e) Wáng Píng shì wǒ zài Běijīng shàng xué shí de tóngxué.

Exercise 7

Fill in the blanks using the prepositions **tóng** or **gěi**:

(a) Tā méi _____ tāde nǚ péngyou mǎi lǐwù.
(b) Qǐng _____ wǒ jièshào yīxià nǐde tàitai.
(c) Wǒ méi yǒu kòng _____ nǐ qù yóuyǒng.
(d) Qǐng yīdìng _____ wǒ dǎ diànhuà.
(e) Xiǎo Lǐ xiǎng _____ Lǐ jīnglǐ shāngliang yī jiàn shì.

Exercise 8

Rewrite the following sentences using **wán**. Then translate the rewritten sentences into English:

(a) Nǐ chī wǎnfàn le ma?
(b) Tā yòng diànhuà le.
(c) Tā diǎn cài le.
(d) Xiǎo Lǐ xiū diàndēng le.

Exercise 9

Translate the following sentences into Chinese:

(a) It is very expensive to make phone calls in the UK.
(b) What is your mobile phone number?
(c) Your father telephoned you last night.
(d) Is there a telephone at your home?

Exercise 10

Re-arrange the words in each group below so that they make meaningful sentences and then translate them into English:

(a) gěi lǎobǎn, wàng le, Jane, dǎ diànhuà
(b) diànhuà, kěyǐ, wǒ, hàomǎ, nǐde, nǐ, gàosu, ma [question word]
(c) tā, bàngōngshì, jīntiān, zài, bù

Characters

Let us first recognize the following two place names:

Hong Kong   Britain

香 | 港   英 | 国

xiāng gǎng   **yīng guó**

Literally, 香港 means 'fragrance harbour/port'. The translation of 'Britain' (英国) is based on the original pronunciation of 'England', hence the first syllable **yīng**.

Exercise 11

(1) Read the following dialogue in characters and then answer the questions in English:

A: 请问，小李在吗？我是他的朋友，叫张文。
B: 对不起，他不在家。他去银行了。
A: 他几点回来？
B: 六点左右。

(a) Who is calling whom?
(b) Where is Xiao Li?
(c) What time will he be back?

(2) Find characters in the Vocabulary of Dialogue 1 that have the water head component 氵.

Reading/listening comprehension

(CD2; 43)

Read the conversation below, and then answer the questions in Chinese. If you have access to the audio material, listen to the conversation first, and then answer the questions in Chinese.

Vocabulary

| **tīng qìng le ma?** | Have you got it? [*lit.* 'you hear clearly?'] |

The following telephone conversation is between two Chinese speakers.

A Qǐng wèn, Wáng Yǔ zài ma?
B Duìbuqǐ, tā bù zài. Qǐng wèn, nín shì nǎ yī wèi?
A Wǒ shì Wáng Yǔ de māma.
B Nín hǎo. Wǒ shì Xiǎo Liú.
A Nǐ hǎo, Xiǎo Liú. Wáng Yǔ jīntiān shàng bān ma?
B Shàng bān. Tā qù chī wǔfàn le. Yī diǎn bàn zuǒyòu huílai.
A Qǐng nǐ gàosu tā, wǒ zuò T-shíliù cì chē míngtiān wǎnshang liù diǎn shí fēn dào Shànghǎi. Tīng qīng le ma?
B Tīng qīng le. Nín xūyào tā qù huǒchē zhàn jiē nín ma?
A Tài xūyào le.
B Wǒ yīdìng gàosu tā.
A Duō xiè.

QUESTIONS
(1) Wáng Yǔ zài bàngōngshì ma?
(2) Shéi gěi Wáng Yǔ dǎ diànhuà le?
(3) Wáng Yǔ de māma shénme shíhou dào Shànghǎi?
(4) Wáng Yǔ de māma chéng jǐ cì lièchē dào Shànghǎi?
(5) Wáng Yǔ de māma xiǎng yào tāde érzi qù jiē tā ma?

Lesson Fourteen
Shèjiāo 社交
Socializing

| By the end of this lesson, you will be able to:

- express the number of times you have done certain things
- describe a past event in a more sophisticated manner
- differentiate between the verbs **lái/qù** and the directional words **lai/qu**
- ask a question requiring a yes or no answer and indicate that it is your guess by using **le**
- use **le** to indicate that a new situation has arisen and is still happening
- negate sentences with the adverb **yě**
- recognize some place names

 Dialogue 1

 Xiàyǔ le 下雨了 It's raining **(CD2; 45)**

Patrick is American and his wife, Meifang, is Taiwan Chinese. They are currently visiting Meifang's family in Taibei. Today, they have been invited to a barbecue party. At the moment, Patrick is chatting with a Chinese woman called Yulan.

| YÙLÁN | Zhè shì nǐ dì yī cì lái Táiwān ma? |
| PATRICK | Bú shì. Wǒ jīhū měi nián dōu lái Táiwān. Qù nián, wǒ lái le liǎng cì. |

YÙLÁN	Shì ma? Shì lái chūchāi ma?
PATRICK	Bú shì. Dì yī cì, wǒmen lái cānjiā wǒ tàitai de mèimei de hūnlǐ. Dì èr cì, lái guò Chūn Jié.
YÙLÁN	Zhème shuō, nǐ tàitai shì Táiwānrén le?
PATRICK	Shì'a.
YÙLÁN	Nǐmen shì zěnme rènshi de?
PATRICK	Shuō lái huà cháng. Shí nián qián, tā qù Měiguó shàng dàxué. Wǒmen shì tóngxué. Yǒu yī tiān . . .
YÙLÁN	Zhēn làngmàn. Āiyō! Xiàyǔ le. Zánmen jìn qu tán ba.

YÙLÁN	这是你第一次来台湾吗？
PATRICK	不是。我几乎每年都来台湾。去年，我来了两次。
YÙLÁN	是吗？是来出差吗？
PATRICK	不是。第一次，我们来参加我太太的妹妹的婚礼。第二次，来过春节。
YÙLÁN	这么说，你太太是台湾人了？
PATRICK	是啊。
YÙLÁN	你们是怎么认识的？
PATRICK	说来话长。十年前，她去美国上大学。我们是同学。有一天 . . .
YÙLÁN	真浪漫。哎哟！下雨了。咱们进去谈吧。

(CD2; 44)

Vocabulary

dì yī cì	第一次	the first time
Táiwān	台湾	Taiwan
jīhū	几乎	almost
měi	每	every
qù nián	去年	last year
cānjiā	参加	to attend/to take part
hūnlǐ	婚礼	wedding
guò	过	to celebrate/to spend
Chūn Jié	春节	Chinese New Year [*lit.* 'spring festival']
shuōlái huà cháng	说来话长	it's a long story [*lit.* 'speak talk long']
qián	前	ago/before

yǒu yī tiān...	有一天...	one day... [*lit.* 'have one day']
làngmàn	浪漫	to be romantic/romantic
āiyō!	哎哟	whoops!
xiàyǔ	下雨	to rain
jìn qu	进去	to go in/to go inside
tán	谈	to talk/to chat

Notes on Dialogue 1

■ 1 Use of **dì... cì**

Simply add a number between **dì** and **cì** to form expressions such as **dì yī cì** (the first time/for the first time), **dì èr cì** (the second time/ for the second time), etc. This phrase is always placed before the verb it modifies or at the beginning of the sentence. For example:

> **Zhè shì wǒ *dì èr cì*** <u>qù</u> **Měiguó.**
> verb
>
> *Lit.* This is I   second time go to America.
> It will be *the second time* that I go to America.

> ***Dì yī cì,***   **wǒ bù zhīdào wǒ yīnggāi gàn shénme.**
> *Lit.* The first time, I   not know   I   should do what.
> *The first time,* I didn't know what I should do.

■ 2 Use of **cì**

If you want to say 'once', 'twice', 'three times', etc., add **cì** to the numeral. Thus we have **yī cì**, **liǎng cì**, **sān cì**, etc. These phrases must be placed after the verb. For example:

> **Měi ge xīngqī, wǒ <u>qí yī cì</u> <u>zìxíngchē</u>.**
> verbobject
> I ride my bike *once* every week.

If these phrases are used in the past tense, e.g. when **le** or **guo** is used, they can be placed either after **le** or **guo** or at the end of the sentence. For example:

> **Dàwèi qù *guo sān cì* Zhōngguó.** ⎫   David has been to China
> **Dàwèi qù *guo* Zhōngguó *sān cì*.** ⎭   *three times.*

In certain fixed verbal phrases such as **dǎ diànhuà**, you must put **yī cì** or **liǎng cì** after the verb or the particle **le**. For example:

Zuótiān wǒ gěi wǒ māma dǎ *le liǎng cì* diànhuà.
I phoned my mother *twice* yesterday.

To turn the above sentence into a question, use **jǐ**:

Zuótiān nǐ gěi nǐ māma dǎ le *jǐ* cì diànhuà?
How many times did you phone your mum yesterday?

■ 3 Use of **qù** in **qù nián**

Literally, **qù nián** means 'gone year'. **Qù nián** is a fixed expression for 'last year'. You cannot use **qù** with **yuè** (month) or **xīngqī** (week).

■ 4 More on verbs

As prepositions (e.g. 'at', 'in', 'on') are not extensively used in Chinese, one of the ways to articulate an idea expressed in English with a preposition is by using verbs. For example:

Wǒ xiǎng mǎi yī zhāng *qù* Běijīng de huǒchē piào.
Lit. I want buy one go Beijing train ticket.
I'd like to buy a train ticket *to* Beijing.

Dì èr cì, wǒmen *lái* *guò* Chūn Jié.
Lit. The second time, we come spend Spring Festival.
The second time, we came *for* the Spring Festival.

■ 5 **le** indicating a guess

If you want to ask a question requiring a yes or no answer and at the same time indicate that it is your guess, put **le** at the end of a sentence instead of **ma** and use the rising tone. Phrases such as **nàme** (so/in that case), **zhème shuō** (in that case), etc. are often used in this context. For example:

Nàme, nǐ bù xiǎng qù *le*? (↗)
So, you don't wish to go?

Zhème shuō, nǐ jiù shì Wáng jīnglǐ *le*? (↗)
In that case, you must be Mr Wang the manager?

■ 6 Use of **měi**

When **měi** (every) is used before a noun which requires a measure word, the measure word must be inserted after **měi** and before the noun. For example:

měi ge measure word	rén	*every* person/everyone
měi jiān measure word	fángjiān	*every* room
měi ge measure word	xīngqī	*every* week

As measure words are not used before **tiān** (day), **nián** (year), **jiā** (family), **fēnzhōng** (minute), etc., you can simply put **měi** before them on its own. For example:

měi tiān   *every* day   **měi nián**   *every* year

If you want to say 'every morning/evening' in Chinese, you must say 'every day morning/evening'. For example:

měi tiān   *every* morning   **měi tiān**   *every* evening
zǎoshang   **wǎnshang**

■ 7 More on the emphatic word **dōu**

In Lesson 8, we learnt the use of **dōu** with **suóyǒude** (all). **Dōu** is also frequently used with **měi** (every). Simply put **dōu** before the verb but after the phrase with **měi**. For example:

Wǒ *měi* **ge yuè** *dōu* **huí jiā kàn wǒ fùmǔ.**
Every month, I go home to see my parents.

Tā *měi* **fēnzhōng** *dōu* **zài xiǎng shàng dàxué.**
He is thinking about going to university *every* minute.

Note that **zài** in the above sentence indicates the continuous state of the verb **xiǎng** (to think).

■ 8 More on the verb **lái**

You must use **lái guo** (have been to) if you are currently in the place about which you are speaking. For example:

(The speaker is currently at her home:)
Xiǎo Lǐ *lái* guo wǒ jiā sān cì.
Xiao Li *has been* to my home three times.

(The speaker is currently in Taiwan:)
Wǒ *lái* guo liǎng cì Táiwān.
I've been here to Taiwan twice.

If you are in one place and talk about some other place you have been to, use the verb **qù**:

Wǒ *qù* guo sān cì Shànghǎi.
I've been to Shanghai three times.

■ 9 More on the omission of **de**

The sentence sounds awkward if there are more than two occurrences of **de** – try to omit those which can be omitted. For example, the **de** in **wǒde** can be omitted from **wǒ*de* tàitai *de* mèimei *de* hūnlǐ**. So we have **wǒ tàitai de mèimei de hūnlǐ** (my wife's younger sister's wedding).

■ 10 Use of **qián**

The word **qián** (ago/before) is always placed after a time expression, a verbal clause or a sentence. For example:

Tā shì <u>liǎng nián</u> *qián* lái Yīngguó de.
duration of time
It was two years *ago* that he came to Britain.

<u>Shàng dàxué</u> *qián*, Liú Xiǎohóng shì dǎoyóu.
verbal clause
Before going to university, Liu Xiaohong was a tourist guide.

<u>Wǒ lái Yīngguó</u> *qián* méi chī guo xī cān.
sentence
I hadn't had western food *before* I came to Britain.

<u>Qù Běijīng Dàxué</u> *qián*, xiān chácha dìtú.
verbal clause
Check the map *before* going to Beijing University.

■ 11 **le** used to indicate a change of state

When **le** is used in sentences that describe a present event, it indicates that a new situation has appeared. It also implies that something is happening gradually which was not the case previously. It is usually put after a predicative adjective or at the end of a sentence. It can be translated by the 'to be + doing' pattern. For example:

| **Wǒ lǎo *le*.** | I'm getting old. | (i.e. *I was not old before*) |
| **Xiàyǔ *le*.** | It's raining. | (i.e. *previously it was not*) |

■ 12 **jìn qu** versus **jìn lai**

Literally, **jìn qu** means 'enter go' and **jìn lai** means 'enter come'. If you are outside a house and wanting to go in, use **jìn qu** (to go in/to go into). If you are inside a house and asking someone else to come in, use **jìn lai** (to come in/to come inside). Here again, **qù** and **lái** are directional words, as we saw in Note 16 of Lesson 8, and they usually become toneless. For example:

Xiàyǔ le. Zánmen *jìn qu* tán, hǎo ma?
It's raining. Shall we *go inside* to talk?

Wàimian hěn lěng. Nǐmen wèishénme bú *jìn lai*?
It's cold outside. Why don't you *come in*?

You can negate **jìn qu** or **jìn lai** with **bù**. When **bù** is placed before **jìn qu** or **jìn lai**, it means 'do not go in' or 'do not come in'. When **bù** is placed in between **jìn** and **qù** or **lái**, it means 'cannot go in' or 'cannot come in', in which case **qù** and **lái** keep their tones as **bù** becomes a neutral tone in actual speech. For example:

Xiǎo Lǐ jìn *bu* qù tāde bàngōngshì.
Xiao Li *cannot go into* his office.

Wǒ bù zhīdào tā wèishénme jìn *bu* lái.
We don't know why she cannot come in.

Exercises

Exercise 1

Insert **le** in each sentence below in an appropriate position. Then translate the sentences into English:

(a) Zuótiān wǒ bàba gěi wǒ dǎ diànhuà.
(b) Nǐ kàn. Xiàxuě.
(c) Rúguǒ tā míngtiān hái bú dào, wǒ jiù zǒu.
(d) Sān tiān qián, tā chí dào bàn ge xiǎoshí.
(e) Wǒ bù xiǎng qù Tiān Tán. Wǒ lèi.
(f) Zhème shuō, nǐ shì Wáng Lǎoshī?

Exercise 2

Fill in the blanks below with **dì èr cì** or **liǎng cì**:

(a) Zhè shì Zhēnní _____ lái Táiwān.
(b) Wǒ chī guo _____ Běijīng kǎo yā.
(c) Wǒ _____ wàng le dài yàoshi.
(d) Zhè ge xīngqī, zánmen lǎobǎn de mìshū chí dào le _____.
(e) Dì yī cì, shì lái Běijīng lǚyóu, _____, shì lái gōngzuò.

Exercise 3

Fill in the blanks with **lái** or **qù** as either the verb or the directional word:

(a) Míngtiān, wǒ dài nǐ _____ guàng shāngdiàn.
(b) Zhèr hěn lěng. Zánmen jìn _____ tán, hǎo ma?
(c) (*On the phone and at home*) Nǐ kěyi ràng Xiǎo Lǐ dài nǐ _____ wǒ jiā.
(d) Zāogāo, wǒ méi dài yàoshi. Jìn bu _____ wǒde bàngōngshì.
(e) (*Xiǎo Lán knocks at Lao Wang's door. Lao Wang opens the door:*)

Xiǎo Lán: Wǒ yǒu yī jiàn shì xiǎng tóng nǐ shānglian. Nǐ yǒu kòng ma?
Lǎo Wáng: Yǒu kòng. Qǐng jìn _____ tán.

Exercise 4

Translate the following into Chinese:

(a) I go to work at eight o'clock every morning.
(b) Everybody likes him.
(c) I got to know her two years ago.
(d) She went to Hong Kong twice last year.
(e) I telephone my parents every two weeks.
(f) She is going to her parents' for the Chinese New Year.

Dialogue 2

Nǐ zuì xǐhuān nǎ ge dìfang?   你最喜欢哪个地方？
Which place do you like most? (CD2; 47)

John has just come back from a tour in China. He is in Boston today to meet his American Chinese friend Chen Ailin. At the moment, he is knocking at Ailin's door.

AÌLÍN   Nǐ hǎo, Yuēhàn. Jiàndào nǐ, zhēn gāoxìng. Kuài jìn lai. Zuò,
        zuò.
JOHN   Hǎo de. Nǐ hǎo ma, Aìlín?
AÌLÍN   Bú cuò. Xièxie. Nǐ xiǎng hē diǎnr shénme?
JOHN   Zhōngguó chá, xièxie.
AÌLÍN   (whilst making the tea) Shuōqǐ Zhōngguó, nǐde Zhōngguó
        zhī xíng zěnme yàng?
JOHN   Hěn chénggōng.
AÌLÍN   Nǐ qù le nǎ jǐ ge chéngshì?
JOHN   Běijīng, Shànghǎi, Xī'ān, Guìlín hé Guǎngzhōu.
AÌLÍN   Nǐ zuì xǐhuān nǎ ge dìfang?
JOHN   Zhè ge wèntí hěn nán huídá. Wǒ hěn xǐhuān Guìlín. Nàlǐ
        fēngjǐng hěn měi, dāngdìrén yě hěn yǒuhǎo, tóng tāmen
        tánhuà hěn yǒu yìsi.
AÌLÍN   Wǒ méi qù guo Guìlín. Xià cì yīdìng qù. Nǐ juéde
        Guǎngzhōu zěnme yàng?
JOHN   Hái xíng, jiù shì rén tài duō, yě tài rè.
AÌLÍN   Wǒ yě bú tài xǐhuān Guǎngzhōu. Qù Cháng Chéng le ma?
JOHN   Nà hái yòng shuō! Wǒ pāi le xǔduō zhàopiān . . .

AÌLÍN	你好，约翰。见到你，真高兴。快进来。坐、坐。
JOHN	你好，爱琳。你好吗，
AÌLÍN	不错，谢谢。你想喝点儿什么？
JOHN	中国茶，谢谢。
AÌLÍN	说起中国，你的中国之行怎么样？
JOHN	很成功。
AÌLÍN	你去了哪几个城市？
JOHN	北京、上海、西安、桂林和广州。
AÌLÍN	你最喜欢哪个地方？
JOHN	这个问题很难回答。我很喜欢桂林。那里风景很美，当地人也很友好，同他们谈话很有意思。
AÌLÍN	我没去过桂林。下次一定去。你觉得广州怎么样？
JOHN	还行，就是人太多，也太热。
AÌLÍN	我也不太喜欢广州。去长城了吗？
JOHN	那还用说！我拍了许多照片...

(CD2; 46)

B Vocabulary

chá	茶	tea
shuōqǐ	说起	talking about
zhī xíng	之行	the trip to ... [*lit*. 'of trip']
chénggōng	成功	to be successful
chéngshì	城市	city
huídá	回答	to answer
fēngjǐng	风景	scenery
měi	美	to be beautiful/beautiful
dāngdìrén	当地人	the locals
tánhuà	谈话	to talk
yǒuhǎo	友好	to be friendly
xià cì	下次	next time
hái xíng	还行	it's all right
jiù shì ...	就是...	it's just that ...
Cháng Chéng	长城	The Great Wall [*lit*. 'long city wall']
nà hái yòng shuō	那还用说	it goes without saying; of course
pāi	拍	to take/to shoot
zhàopiàn	照片	photograph

Notes on Dialogue 2

■ 13 Lack of **qǐng** in many expressions

In Chinese, the word **qǐng** (please), as has been mentioned before, is seldom used among friends or on informal occasions. The omission of **qǐng** does not suggest any lack of politeness or warmth in expressions such as **kuài jìn lai, zuò**, etc. These expressions are often repeated to make the guest feel that he/she is very welcome. For example:

> (At the dinner table, the hostess says:)
> *Chī, chī.* Bié   kèqi.

Lit.   Eat, eat. Don't be polite.
Help yourself. Don't be polite.

> (Inviting your guest to come in:)
> *Jìn lai,   jìn lai.*

Lit.   Come in, come in.
Come in, please.

> (Offering your guest some tea:)
> *Hē   chá, hē   chá.*

Lit.   Drink tea, drink tea.
Do have some tea.

■ 14 Use of **zuò**

In English, phrases such as *to call in, to come around, to go to see,* etc. are used to talk about informal visits. In Chinese, the literal translation of similar expressions is 'to go someone's home sit sit' or 'sit for a while'. For example:

Wǒ kěyǐ dào nǐ jiā *zuòzuo* ma?
Could I *come around* to see you?

Zuówǎn, Guāngmèn lái *zuò* le yīhuìr.
Guangmen *called in* for a while last night.

■ 15 Use of retroflex ending **r**

The sound **r**, pronounced with the tongue rolled backward a bit, is often added to phrases such as **yīdiǎn, yǒu yīdiǎn, yīhuì** (a while), etc. In such cases, **yī** is usually omitted. For example:

Nǐ xiǎng hē diǎnr shénme?   What would you like to drink?

Wǒ yǒu diǎnr è.   I'm a bit hungry.

Děng huìr.   Wait for a second.

Note that when **r** is added to **diǎn**, the nasal **n** sound gets dropped off.

■ 16 Use of **. . . zhī xíng**

Although this is very much a written expression, it is often used in colloquial speech to refer to a particular trip. Simply put the place name before **zhī xíng**. For example:

Tīngshuō nǐde Zhōngguó zhī xíng hěn chénggōng.
I've heard that your *trip to* China was very successful.

■ 17 Use of **nǎ jǐ . . .**

Literally, **nǎ jǐ** + a measure word means 'which several'. It can be used to ask about either places or people when the questioner assumes that only a few places or people will be named in the reply. For example:

Nǐ qù guo Yīngguó nǎ jǐ ge chéngshì?
Which cities in Britain have you been to?

Nǐ zài nǎ jǐ jiā gōngsī gōngzuò guo?
For which companies have you worked?

■ 18 More on the 'topic structure'

The topic or theme of a sentence is often placed at the beginning of that sentence. In English, for example, you can say *It is difficult to answer this question*; but in Chinese, you must say 'This question is difficult to answer' or 'Answering this question is difficult'. For example:

    Tāde Yīngwén hěn nán   **dǒng.**
    Topic
Lit.   His English   very be difficult understand.
    It's very difficult to understand *his English*.

Zài Zhōngguó, _mǎi huǒchē piào_   hěn   nán.
                                Topic

Lit. In China,   buy train   tickets very be difficult.
Getting train tickets in China is very difficult.

■ 19 **Nǐ juéde . . . zěnme yàng?**

This question can be translated as 'What do you think of . . .?'. For example:

Nǐ juéde Zhāng Hóng zěnme yàng?
What do you think of Zhang Hong?

Nǐ juéde Měiguó zěnme yàng?
What do you think of America?

■ 20 **rén tài duō**

The complete sentence should be **Guǎngzhōu de rén tài duō** (_lit._ 'Guangzhou's people too many'). The reason that **Guǎngzhōu de** is omitted is that it can be elicited from the context. Whenever you wish to say 'There are too many . . . in . . .', use the pattern something + **tài duō**. For example:

Běijīng de zìxíngchē _tài duō_.
There are too many bikes _in_ Beijing.

A: **Táiwān zěnme yàng?**
    How is/was Taiwan?

B: **Hěn yǒu yìsi. Dànshì, rén _tài duō_.**
    Very interesting. But _too many_ people.

■ 21 Negative sentences with **yě**

In English, 'also' is used in positive sentences whilst 'either' is used in negative sentences; in Chinese, the adverb **yě** (also) is used in both sentence types. When the sentence with **yě** is negated, the negation word **bù**, **méiyǒu** or **méi** is placed after **yě**. Let us compare **yě** used in both positive and negative sentences:

Wǒmen _yě_ xiǎng qù cānjiā Xīn Hǎi de hūnlǐ.
We would like to attend Xin Hai's wedding _too_.

Tā yě *bù* xǐhuān Zhōngguó fàn.
She doesn't like Chinese food *either*.

Lǎo Lǐ zuótiān méi lái. Xiǎo Wáng yě *méi* lái.
Lao Li didn't come yesterday and Xiao Wang didn't come *either*.

Exercises

Exercise 5

What do you say on the following occasions:

(a) A friend of yours knocks at your door and you invite him in.
(b) Your neighbour comes around for a chat, and you invite her to sit down.
(c) Your friends have come to see you. You ask them what they would like to drink.
(d) You tell your mother that you are going round to Lao Li's.
(e) You are hosting a dinner party, and you ask your guests to help themselves.

Exercise 6

You ask your Chinese friend what she thinks of:

(a) America
(b) summer in Hong Kong
(c) the Beijing Hotel
(d) the locals
(e) David's Chinese

Exercise 7

Negate the following sentences with **bù** or (**méiyǒu**):

(a) Wǒ yě xǐhuān Zhōngguó fàn.
(b) Tā māma yě qù cānjiā Àilín de hūnlǐ le.
(c) Tā yě zhīdào yóuyǒng chí jǐ diǎn kāimén.
(d) Xiǎo Zhāng yě chí dào le.

Exercise 8

Translate the following into Chinese:

(a) It is very interesting to talk to the locals.
(b) Which cities did you go to?
(c) How was your trip to Taiwan?
(d) There are too many people in Guangzhou. It's very noisy and very hot in the summer.

Exercise 9

Pair work – one person asks questions based on Dialogue 2 and the other one answers them. For example:

A: Yuēhàn de zhōngguó zhī xíng zěnme yàng?
B: Hěn chénggōng.

Characters

Let us first recognize the following place names:

台 湾
tái   wǎn

西 安
xī   ān

桂 林
guì   lín

长 城
cháng chéng

Literally, 台湾 means 'high and flat harbour', 西安 means 'west peace', 桂林 means 'bay tree forest', and 长城 is a 'long city wall'.

Exercise 10

(1) Fill in the gaps using appropriate words/phrases from the vocabulary lists for both dialogues.

From Dialogue 1 Vocabulary:

(a) 我下个月去西安 _____ 我妹妹的婚礼。
Wǒ xià ge yuè qù Xī'an _____ wǒ mèimei de hūnlǐ.

(b) 你打算在哪儿 _____ 春节？
Nǐ dǎsuàn zài nǎr _____ Chūn Jié?

(c) 三年 _____，我在台湾工作。
Sān nián _____ wǒ zài Táiwān gōngzuò.

From Dialogue 2 Vocabulary:

(d) 我不会 _____ 这个问题。
Wǒ bú huì _____ zhè ge wèntí.

(e) 桂林人怎么样？他们 _____ 吗？
Guìlínrén zěnme yàng? Tāmen _____ ma?

(2) Read the character text in the Reading/listening comprehension and circle the characters that you recognize.

Reading/listening comprehension

(CD2; 48)

Read the following passage in pinyin or characters or both (if you have access to the audio material, listen first) and then answer the questions which follow in Chinese.

Vocabulary

相处	**xiāng chǔ**	to get along
度	**dù**	to spend
蜜月	**mìyuè**	honeymoon

Shufang tells her friend about her husband Dayong and her wedding.

Wǒ hé Dàyǒng shì dàxué tóngxué. Wǒmen shì qù nián jiéhūn de. Dàyǒng de fùmǔ zhù zài Táiwān. Tāmen cóng Táiwān lái cānjiā le wǒmen de hūnlǐ. Nà shì wǒ fùmǔ hé Dàyǒng de fùmǔ dì yī cì jiànmiàn. Tāmen xiāng chǔ de hěn hǎo. Wǒmen hái qǐng le hěnduō péngyou cānjiā wǒmende hūnlǐ. Hūnlǐ hòu, wǒ hé Dàyǒng qù Guìlín dù le liǎng ge xīngqī mìyuè.

我和大勇是大学同学。我们是去年结婚的。大勇的父母住在台湾。
他们从台湾来参加了我们的婚礼。那是我父母和大勇的父母第一次
见面。他们相处得很好。我们还请了很多朋友参加我们的婚礼。
婚礼后，我和大勇去桂林度了两个星期的蜜月。

QUESTIONS

(1) Dàyǒng de fùmǔ zhù zài shénme dìfang?

(2) Dàyǒng de fùmǔ cānjiā Shūfāng hé Dàyǒng de hūnlǐ le ma?

(3) Shūfāng de fùmǔ hé Dàyǒng de fùmǔ shì dì èr cì jiànmiàn ma?

(4) Shūfāng hé Dàyǒng qù shénme dìfang dù mìyuè le? Qù le duō
     jiǔ?

Lesson Fifteen

Gěi Zhōngguó péngyou
xiě xìn 给中国朋友写信

Writing a letter to a Chinese friend

By the end of this lesson, you will be able to:

- write a simple letter
- use the correct format to write names and addresses on an envelope
- express a continuous action in the past
- express more sophisticated sentences such as 'When I was in China, I . . .'

Text

Wǒ bǎozhèng 我保证 I promise

Elena and Liu Xiaomei are close friends. They met when Elena was studying Chinese at a university in Beijing. Although Elena is back in Italy, they write to each other very often. Below is a letter from Elena to Xiaomei.

TO: People's Republic of China

Yóubiān: 100081
Zhōngguó Běijīng Dōng Zhí Mén Wài Dàjiē 22 Hào 16
Dòng 1 Hào

Liú Xiǎoméi Shōu

Crosa Maccarina, Milan, Italy

Qīn'àide Xiǎoméi:

Nǐ hǎo!

Nǐde láixìn shōudào le. Wǒ zhēn gāoxìng nǐ xǐhuān nǐde xīn gōngzuò.

Wǒ yīqiē hái hǎo, jiùshi gōngzuò tài máng. Shàng ge xīngqī, wǒ yīzhí zài Lúndūn kāi huì. Huílái hòu, máng zhe xiě yī fèn bàogào. Měi tiān zǎoshang liù diǎn bàn qǐ chuáng, wǎnshang shí'èr diǎn cái shuìjiào. Wǒ bìxū zài xīngqīwǔ zhīqián xiě wán zhè fèn bàogào.

Yīnwéi wǒde diànnǎo huài le, wǒ hǎo jiǔ méi gěi nǐ fā diànzǐ yóujiàn le. Děng zhè ge zhōumò wǒ xiūxí de shíhóu, yīdìng ràng rén lái xiūxiu, ránhòu gěi nǐ fā yī fēng chángcháng de yóujiàn. Wǒ bǎozhèng.

Hǎo yǒu,

Àilì'nà

2008, 8, 30

TO: P. R. China

邮编：100081
中国北京东直门外大街22号16栋1号

刘 小 梅　　收

Crosa Maccarina, Milan, Italy

亲爱的小梅：

你好！

你的来信收到了。我真高兴你喜欢你的新工作。

我一切还好，就是工作太忙。上个星期，我一直在伦敦开会。回来后，忙着写一份报告。每天早上六点半起床，晚上十二点才睡觉。我必须在星期五之前写完这份报告。

因为我的电脑坏了，我好久没给你发电子邮件了。等这个周末我休息的时候，一定让人来修修，然后给你发一封长长的邮件。我保证。

    好友，

                           爱丽娜

                          2008, 8, 30

B Vocabulary

yóu biān	邮编	post code
Dōng Zhí Mén Wài	东直门外	[street name]
dàjiē	大街	avenue
dòng	栋	block
hào	号	number
shōu	收	to be received by . . . /to
qīn'àide	亲爱的	dear
Xiǎoméi/Àilì'nà	小梅/爱丽娜	[given name]
xìn	信	letter
láixìn	来信	letter [*lit.* 'come letter', see Note 3]
shōu dào	收到	to receive
yīqiē	一切	everything
yī zhí	一直	all that time
Lúndūn	伦敦	London

kāi huì	开会	to attend a meeting/conference
hòu	后	after/in/ . . . later
zhe	œʃ	[grammar word, see Note 8]
fèn	份	[measure word for documents]
bàogào	报告	report
qǐ chuáng	起床	to get up
cái	才	[emphatic word, see Note 9]
shuìjiào	睡觉	to sleep/sleep
bìxū	必须	must
zài . . . zhīqián	在 . . . 之前	before . . . /by . . .
diànnǎo	电脑	computer
fā	发	to send
diànzi yóujiàn	电子邮件	email
. . . de shíhòu	. . . 的时候	when/while
zhōumò	周末	weekend
xiūxí	休息	to be off work; to rest
fēng	封	[measure word for letters]
cháng de	长的	long
bǎozhèng	保证	to promise
hǎo yǒu	好友	good friend

Notes on text

■ 1 Writing a letter

When writing a letter or postcard to a Chinese person, there is usually no need to write 'Dear' (**qīn'àide**) in front of the person's name. You simply use the form of address that is usually used (e.g. **Xiǎo Liú**, **Liú Xiǎoméi**, or **Xiǎoméi**). The term **qīn'àide** (dear) is reserved for close family and friends. A colon (:), instead of a comma, is used after the person's name. The greeting expression **Nǐ hǎo** is usually used to begin a letter and appears in the second line. You can start the main part of the letter either on the same line after **Nǐ hǎo** if space is a problem, or on the next line. The closing phrase usually takes up a separate line. The commonly used closing phrases are **Duō bǎozhòng** (Take care), **Zhù hǎo** (Best wishes), **Zhù shēntǐ jiànkāng** (Wishing you good health), **Hǎo yǒu** (Good friend), etc. After the closing phrase, you sign your name and then date the letter underneath your signature. Note that you do not need to put your address in a personal letter (as opposed to a business letter).

■ 2 Writing an envelope

When writing a name and address on an envelope in Chinese, you first write the recipient's address in one line at the top of the envelope (use a second line if it is a long address); then write the recipient's name in the centre of the envelope and finally put the sender's address at the bottom of the envelope towards the right-hand corner. The word **shōu** is usually put after the recipient's name and it means 'to be received by . . .'. For example:

Recipient's address: XXXXXXXXXXXXXXXXXXXXXXXXX

　　　　　Recipient's name: XXX　　　Shōu

　　　　　Sender's address: XXXXXXXXXXXX

In writing the address (**dìzhǐ**), the largest unit comes first. So you put the country first (if you write from abroad) followed by the city, then the street name (or name of an organization), and finally the flat number. Note that the recipient's postcode is placed before the address but the sender's postcode goes after the address. For example, if you write to Mr Wang Lisheng, whose address is 26 Dongdan Ave., Beijing, postcode 816001 and your address is Flat 6, Block 10, Xi'an Foreign Languages College, postcode 716001, the envelope should look like this:

816001 Běijīng Dōngdān Dàjiē 26 Hào

　　　　　Wáng Lìshēng　　　Shōu

　　　　　Xī'ān Wàiguóyǔ Xuéyuàn 10 Dòng 6 Hào
　　　　　Yóubiān:716001

If you send a letter from abroad, all you need to do is to put 'To: People's Republic of China' in English or in the language that is spoken wherever you are at the top of the envelope (see the envelope in the Text).

■ 3 Difference between **xìn**, **láixìn** and **qùxìn**

The word **xìn** means 'letter'. Literally, **láixìn** means 'come letter' and **qùxìn** means 'go letter'. **Láixìn** refers to the letter you have received; and **qùxìn** refers to the letter you have written to someone. The measure word for letters is **fēng**. For example:

> **Zhèr yǒu nǐde yī fēng** *xìn*.
> *Lit.* Here have your   one letter.
> Here is a *letter* for you.

> **Xièxie nǐde** *láixìn*.
> Thank you for your *letter*.

> **Wǒde** *qùxìn* **nǐ shōu dào le ma?**
> *or* **Nǐ shōu dào wǒde** *qùxìn* **le ma?**
> Have you received my *letter*?

Whilst **láixìn** and **qùxìn** are very different, **xìn** can always replace **láixìn** or **qùxìn**.

■ 4 **Wǒ yīqiè hái hǎo**

This is a very common expression used in writing personal letters to mean 'Everything is all right with me'. You can also turn it into a question. For example:

> **Nǐ yīqiè hái hǎo ma?**
> Is everything all right with you?

■ 5 Use of **jiù shì**

When a general positive statement is followed by another sentence beginning with **jiù shì**, a mild criticism is expected because **jiù shì** in this context can be broadly translated as 'it's just that . . .'. For example:

Xiāng Gǎng hěn yǒu yìsi, *jiù shì* xiàtiān tài rè.
Hong Kong is very interesting. *It's just that* it's too hot in the
   summer.

Nà ge yóuyǒng chí hěn hǎo, *jiù shì* yǒu diǎnr yuǎn.
That swimming pool is very good *except that* it's a bit far away.

■ 6 Use of **yīzhí**

When you want to emphasize the continuation of an event, use **yīzhí**
in front of **zài** to mean 'all the time'. For example:

Zuótiān wǎnshang, wǒ *yīzhí zài* xiě xìn.
I was writing letters all night last night.

However, if you want to say 'He was attending a conference in
Taiwan last month', you must say **Tā shàng ge yuè *yīzhí zài* Táiwān
kāi huì.** Since **zài** is used in **zài Táiwān** to mean 'in Taiwan', the
continuous indicator **zài** must not be used. Thus you cannot say **Tā
shàng ge yuè yīzhí *zài* Táiwān *zài* kāi huì.**

■ 7 Use of **hòu**

In English, *after* or *in* is placed before a phrase or a sentence (e.g.
In three days' time . . . , *After* he came back . . .) and *later* is placed
after a phrase or a sentence (e.g. *A week later* . . .). But in Chinese,
hòu (after/in/ . . . later) always occurs at the end of a phrase or a
sentence. For example:

Cóng Bālí huílai *hòu*, wǒ shēntǐ bú tài hǎo.
I haven't been very well *since* I came back from Paris.

Sān tiān *hòu*, wǒ gěi nǐ dǎ diànhuà.
I'll telephone you *in* three days' time.

Yī ge xīngqī *hòu*, Xiǎo Fāng jiàndào le tāde mèimei.
Xiao Fang met her younger sister a week *later*.

■ 8 Grammar word **zhe**

Zhe is placed between the predicative adjective **máng** (to be busy)
and a verb to mean 'to be busy doing something'. For example:

Wǒ máng *zhe* zhǎo gōngzuò.   I'm busy looking for a job.
Tā máng *zhe* xué Zhōngwén.   She is busy learning Chinese.

■ 9 Emphatic word **cái**

Cái is an adverb used to indicate that something happens too late (e.g. 'start, end, etc. too late'). Sometimes, it can be broadly translated as 'only' or 'just', but other times, it can be translated as '. . . until . . .' For example:

Nǐ zěnme cái qǐ chúang?
How come you *just* got up?

Wǒ māma měi tiān wǎnshang shí'èr diǎn cái shuìjiào.
Every night, my mother doesn't go to bed *until* 12 o'clock.
(For the speaker, 12 o'clock is very late.)

Dàwèi zuótiān cái zǒu.
David *only* left yesterday.

The sentence **Dàwèi zuótiān cái zǒu** implies that he planned to leave earlier or the speaker wanted him to leave earlier. Another thing to notice is that the past particle **le** cannot be used with **cái** if the event described happened in the definite past.

■ 10 Use of **zài . . . zhī qián**

The phrase **zài . . . zhī qián** means 'before . . .' or 'by . . .', which emphasizes that something must be done by a certain date/day. That certain date/day is always placed between **zài** and **zhī qián**. For example:

Zài nǐ qù Zhōngguó zhī qián, kěyi gěi wó dǎ ge diànhuà ma?
Could you give me a ring *before* you go to China?

Tā bìxū zài xīngqīwǔ zhī qián xiě wán zhè běn shū.
She must finish writing this book *by* Friday.

■ 11 Use of **. . . de shíhou**

The expression **. . . de shíhou** (when/while) is placed at the end of the first half of a phrase or sentence. It can be used to describe present, past or future events. For example:

Shàng dàxúe de shíhou, wǒ hěn xǐhuān yóuyǒng.
I liked swimming very much *when* I was at university.

Bù gāoxìng *de shíhou*, yǒuxiē rén xǐhuān guàng shāngdiàn.
Some people like to go shopping *when* they are unhappy.

When . . . **de shíhou** is used to describe a future event, the verb **děng** (to wait) is usually put at the very beginning of a phrase or sentence. For example:

Děng zhè ge zhōumò wǒ yǒu kòng *de shíhou*, yīdìng gěi nǐ xiě fēng cháng xìn.
I'll definitely write you a long letter *when* I have time this weekend.

■ 12 Use of **gěi** + somebody + do something

We have seen this pattern used in Lessons 8 and 13 (**gěi lǎobǎn dǎ diànhuà**, telephone the boss). In this lesson, the pattern is used twice:

    Gěi Zhōngguó péngyou xiě   xìn.
Lit. to Chinese   friend   write letter
    Writing a letter to a Chinese friend.

    gěi nǐ fa   yī fēng chángcháng de diànzǐ yóujiàn
Lit. to you send one   long   email
    send a long email to you

Exercises

Exercise 1

Write a short letter to your family or friend.

Exercise 2

Write the following information on an envelope:

Recipient's name: Li Lin; recipient's address: No. 3, Block 46, 6 Chang An Avenue, Xi'an, postcode 710061, P.R. China. You are the sender and are currently in another country (make up your own address).

Exercise 3

Fill in the blanks with **xìn, láixìn** or **qùxìn**:

(a) (*Telling someone*) Zuótiān, wǒ shōu dào le sān fēng _____.
(b) (*Writing to someone*) Wǒ zhēn gāoxìng shōu dào le nǐde_____.
(c) (*Telling someone*) Wǒde nán péngyou bù xǐhuān xiě_____.
(d) (*Writing to someone*) Wǒde _____ nǐ shōu dào le ma?

Exercise 4

Match the words in the left column with those in the right column (there are several possible combinations):

(a) qù   1 tiān (*day*)
(b) shàng ge   2 nián (*year*)
(c) míng   3 xīngqī (*week*)
(d) xià ge   4 yuè (*month*)
(e) zuó

Exercise 5

Translate the following sentences into Chinese:

(a) Your home is beautiful but it is not easy to find.
(b) I was at home writing letters all night last night.
(c) I like writing letters to good friends.
(d) What's your email address?
(e) I went to the market after work.
(f) Our boss is busy making phone calls.
(g) I only received my parents' letter yesterday.
(h) I often cycled when I was in China.
(i) He will definitely return you that book by next Monday.

Exercise 6

Use **gěi** + somebody + do something with the following verbs to make up sentences:

(1) xiě xìn   (2) fā diànzǐ yóujiàn
(3) mǎi lǐwù   (4) dǎ diànhuà
(5) mǎi huǒchē piào

Exercise 7

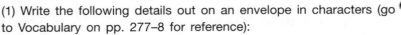

(1) Write the following details out on an envelope in characters (go to Vocabulary on pp. 277–8 for reference):

Recipient: Wu Yue
Address: No. 1, Block 6, 103 East Avenue, Beijing
Postcode: 100081

(2) Group all the characters that you have learnt so far into the following categories. Write down as many as you can remember:

(a) characters that have to do with speaking/mouth
(b) characters that have to do with money
(c) characters that have to do with food
(d) characters that have to do with water
(e) characters that have to do with hands
(f) characters that have to do with mind and heart
(g) characters that have to do with people

(3) Read the character version of the postcard in the Reading comprehension section on page 286 and write a postcard in characters to a Chinese friend of yours.

Reading comprehension

Read the postcard and then answer the questions in English.

Vocabulary

dào shíhòu	到时候	around that time/then
huí xìn	回信	to reply (a letter)
zhù hǎo	祝好	best wishes [*lit.* 'wish well']
xì	系	department
xìn xiāng	信箱	post box

Xiǎo Yuè:

Nǐ hǎo! Hǎo jiǔ méiyǒu shōu dào nǐde xìn le. Nǐ yīqiè hái hǎo ma? Wǒ xià ge yuè bā hào zuǒyòu yào qù Guǎngzhōu kāi huì. Rúguó nǐ dào shíhou yǒu kòng dehuà, wǒ hěn xiǎng jiànjian nǐ. Qǐng huí xìn gàosu wó nǐde diànhuà hàomǎ.

Zhù hǎo

Zhāng Xīn

2008. 6. 18

Yóubiān: 100081

Běijīng Běijīng Dàxué

Yīngwén Xì 10 Hào Xìnxiāng

Wáng Xiǎo Yuè Shōu

Guǎngzhōu Dōng Ān Mén

1 Hào

Yóubiān: 510450

小月：

你好！好久没有收到你的信了。你一切还好吗？我下个月八号左右去广州开会。如果你到时候有空的话，我很想见见你。请回信告诉我你的电话号码。

祝好

张新

2008. 6. 18

邮编：100081

北京北京大学英文系10号信箱

王 小 月　收

广州东安门1号

邮编：510450

QUESTIONS

(1) Who is the recipient of this postcard?

(2) What is the recipient's address?

(3) Where does the recipient work (based on the recipient's address)?

(4) Where does Zhang Xin live?

(5) Why is Zhang Xin going to Guangzhou?

(6) When is Zhang Xin going to Guangzhou?

(7) Does Zhang Xin know Xiao Yue's telephone number?

Grammar summary

This is not an exhaustive summary of Chinese grammar. It is just a summary of the main grammatical concepts which have been introduced in this book.

Word order

It is easier to talk about word order with the help of some grammatical terms. Let us first define the following terms:

Subject – the topic of a sentence. Nouns, noun phrases, verbal phrases can all function as the subject in Chinese.

Verb – a doing word.

Object – a noun or its equivalent acted upon by (a) a verb whose meaning is incomplete unless followed by something (e.g. in 'I play table-tennis', 'table-tennis' is the object of the verb 'play'); or (b) a preposition (e.g. in 'I'm not against him', 'him' is the object of the preposition 'against').

Prepositional phrase – a preposition followed by a noun or equivalent such as place names, etc. (e.g. 'in London').

Word order in Chinese is quite fixed. The common patterns are:

subject + verb + object
Wǒ mǎi dōngxi.   I buy things.

subject + time + verb + object
Wǒ *liù diǎn* qù mǎi dōngxi.   I'm going shopping *at six o'clock*.
Tā *qù nián* lái de Yīngguó.   She came to Britain *last year*.

subject + prepositional phrase + verb + object
Wǒ zài Běijīng jiàndào le tā.   I saw him *in Beijing*.

object + subject + verb (to emphasize the object)
Xìn wǒ xiě le.   I did write *the letter*.

Topic structure

In English, the topic or theme of a sentence can be put at the end of the sentence by using the *It is . . . to . . .* pattern (e.g. in *It is very interesting to talk to him*, *to talk to him* is the topic). In Chinese, since the 'It is . . . to . . .' pattern is not used, the topic always occurs at the beginning of a sentence:

Nǐ jiā hěn nán zhǎo.   It is difficult to find *your house*.
Qí zìxíngchē hěn yǒu yìsi.   It is very interesting *to cycle*.

Nouns

Nouns are the same regardless of number:

Wǒ yǒu yī ge *mèimei*.   I have one younger *sister*.
Wǒ yóu liǎng ge *mèimei*.   I have two younger *sisters*.

Articles

Definite (in English, 'the') and indefinite (in English, 'a' or 'an') articles do not exist in Chinese. Whether something is specific or general can be inferred from the context:

Tā hái méi huán gěi wǒ *shū*.   She still hasn't returned *the book* to me.

Definite or indefinite reference may be indicated by demonstratives or 'numerals + measure word' phrases: **zhè běn shū** (this book), **yī běn shū** (a book/one book).

Adjectives

1 Descriptive adjectives

These are always placed before nouns. **De** is usually inserted between the adjective and the noun (a) if the adjective is modified by an adverb; and (b) if a two-syllable adjective is used to modify a noun:

hǎo zhǔyi	good idea
hěn hǎo de zhǔyi	very good idea
xióngwěi de guǎngchǎng	the magnificent square

2 Predicative adjectives

Some adjectives are both descriptive and predicative. Predicative adjectives occur after a noun or a pronoun, for example, **lǎo** in **Tā lǎo** (He *is old*). Remember that the verb **shì** (to be) is not used when adjectives function in a predicative position, and these predicative adjectives are usually modified by adverbs such as **hěn** (very), **tǐng** (rather), **tài** (too), etc. For example:

Tā   tǐng   lǎo.
Lit. He/she rather be old.
She is rather old.

Tāmen hěn máng.
Lit. They   very busy.
They are very busy.

Measure words

Measure words are a distinctive feature of the Chinese language. A measure word is usually used between (a) a numeral and a noun; and (b) a demonstrative adjective (i.e. **zhè** (this) or **nà** (that)) and a noun. The most common measure word is **gè** (often pronounced with a neutral tone):

Wǒ yǒu sān ge dìdi.	I have three younger brothers.
Zhè ge rén hěn qíguài.	This person is very strange.

Different measure words are used with different nouns. Below are some commonly used measure words:

Pinyin	Character	Category	Nouns (e.g.)
bǎ	把	objects with a handle	toothbrush, knife, umbrella, chair
bāo	包	parcel, packet	cigarettes, noodles
bēi	杯	cup, glass	tea, orange juice
běn	本	volume	book, dictionary
bù	部	volume	film, encyclopedia
fèn	份	material, food	newspaper, report, food [a portion of]
fēng	封	letter	letter
gè (ge)	个	people, things which do not fall into other categories; substitute measure word	girl, man
jiā	家	organization	company, factory
jiān	间	space	room
jiàn	件	piece	jumper, luggage, matter
jù	句	phrase	remarks, comments
kē	棵	plants, trees	tree, spring onion
kuài	块	square piece	soap, field
liàng	辆	things with wheels	bike, bus, taxi
píng	瓶	bottles, jars	beer, jam
qún	群	crowd	people, cattle
tái	台	machine	television, washing-machine
tào	套	set	flat, furniture
tiáo	条	long and winding	fish, river, tie, scarf
tóu	头	big animals	pig, elephant
wèi	位	people (polite)	teacher, leader
zhāng	张	flat	paper, map, ticket, blanket
zhāng	章	book	chapter
zhī	只	small animals	chicken, cat
zuò	座	solid things, architecture	mountain, bridge

Currency words, unit words and nouns such as **tiān** (day), **nián** (year), etc. do not require measure words:

bā *yuán*   eight *yuan*   **sì** *jīn*   two *kilos*
liǎng *tiān*   two *days*   **wǔ** *nián*   five *years*

Pronouns

1 Personal pronouns

wǒ	I, me
nǐ	you (singular)
nín	you (polite form)
tā	he/she/, him/her
wǒmen	we, us
nǐmen	you (plural)
tāmen	they, them

These personal pronouns can be used in both subject and object positions:

Wǒ xiǎng wǒde māma.	*I* miss my mother.
Wǒde māma xiǎng wǒ.	My mother misses *me*.

There is another pronoun, also pronounced 'ta' (but written differently in character), to refer to non-animated objects.

Ta is seldom used to mean 'it' as a subject. It occasionally occurs in the object position:

Mōmo tā.   Touch *it*.

Most of the time, any reference to 'it' can be inferred from the context:

Wǒ xǐhuān Zhōngguó fàn.   I like Chinese food. *It's very tasty.*
Hěn hǎochī.

Similarly, **tāmen** is rarely used to refer to things.

2 Possessive adjectives and possessive pronouns

Possessive adjective and possessive pronoun	Possessive adjective (in front of nouns)	Possessive pronoun (at the end of the sentence)
wǒde	my	mine
nǐde	your	yours
tāde	his/her	his/hers
wǒmende	our	ours
nǐmende	your	yours
tāmende	their	theirs

To form possessive adjectives and possessive pronouns, simply add **de** to personal pronouns **wǒ, nǐ, tā, wǒmen, nǐmen, tāmen**:

Wǒde shū diū le.	*My* book is missing.
Zhè běn shū shì wǒde.	This book is *mine*.

3 Demonstrative pronouns

zhè	this
nà	that
zhèxiē	these
nàxiē	those

Zhè or **nà** never occurs in object positions. **Zhè** is used in many cases where 'it' is used in English:

Zhè hěn yǒu yìsi.	*It* is very interesting.

When a measure word is added to **zhè** and **nà**, we get demonstrative adjectives:

Nà ge rén hěn gāo.	*That person* is very tall.
Zhè liàng zìxíngchē huài le.	*This bike* is broken.

Numbers

1 Cardinal numbers

0–99:

0–9		10–19		20–29	
líng	zero	shí	ten	èrshí	twenty
yī	one	shíyī	eleven	èrshíyī	twenty-one
èr (liǎng)	two	shí'èr	twelve	èrshí'èr	twenty-two
sān	three	shísān	thirteen	èrshísān	twenty-three
sì	four	shísì	fourteen	èrshísì	twenty-four
wǔ	five	shíwǔ	fifteen	èrshíwǔ	twenty-five
liù	six	shíliù	sixteen	èrshíliù	twenty-six
qī	seven	shíqī	seventeen	èrshíqī	twenty-seven
bā	eight	shíbā	eighteen	èrshíbā	twenty-eight
jiǔ	nine	shíjiǔ	nineteen	èrshíjiǔ	twenty-nine

The numbers 30, 40, etc. up to 90 are formed by adding **shí** (ten) to **sān** (three), **sì** (four), etc. Thus we have **sānshí** (thirty), **sìshí** (forty), etc. to **jiǔshí** (ninety). The numbers 31–9, 41–9 etc., use the same principle as 21–9 above. An apostrophe (') is used to mark the break between two syllables whenever there is ambiguity in pronunciation. Thus we have *shí'èr* (twelve) instead of *shíèr*.

100–10,000
The same pattern continues with **bǎi** (hundred), **qiān** (thousand) and **wàn** (ten thousand):

yī bǎi èrshí	one hundred and twenty
wǔ qiān líng liùshí	five thousand and sixty

2 Ordinal numbers

Simply add **dì** to cardinal numbers:

dì yī	first
dì shíyī	eleventh
dì èrshí'èr	twenty-second

Verbs

Chinese verbs remain the same regardless of first-, second-, or third-person pronouns, singular or plural:

wǒ *shì*   I *am*
tā *shì*   he/she *is*
tāmen *shì*   they *are*

Verbs do not indicate tenses. Let us take the verb **qù** (to go), for example:

Wǒ míngtiān *qù* **Zhōngguó.**	I *am going* to China tomorrow.
Zuótiān, wǒ *qù* **kàn**	Yesterday, I *went* to see
péngyou le.	my friends.
Tā *qù* **túshūguǎn le.**	He *has gone* to the library.

The future and the past are indicated by the time phrases such as **míngtiān** (tomorrow), and **zuótiān** (yesterday) and some grammar words such as **le** (see Grammar words below).

Grammar words (particles)

1 **le** indicates that:

(a) an action happened in the past:

Wǒ zuótiān mǎi *le* yī liàng zìxíngchē.
I bought a bike yesterday.

(b) an action has happened and may still be happening:

Tā qù túshūguǎn *le*.   He has gone to the library.
                              (He has not come back yet.)

(c) there is a change of state (when used at the end of a sentence):

Xiàyǔ *le*.   It's raining. (It wasn't raining before.)
Wǒ lèi *le*.   I'm getting tired. (I wasn't tired before.)

2 **guo**, although also indicating a past event, puts emphasis on the aspect that something has been experienced:

Wǒ chī *guo* Zhōngguó fàn.   I have had Chinese food.
Tā qù *guo* Měiguó liǎng cì.   He has been to America twice.

3 **zài** or **zhèngzài** indicates the continuous state of a verb. It is placed before the verb:

Wǒ *zài* chī wǎnfàn.   I *am*/was hav*ing* supper.

Negation words

1 **bù** is used with most verbs and predicative adjectives:

Wǒ *bù* xǐhuān zhè ge chéngshì.   I *don't* like this city.
Tā *bù* máng.   He is *not* busy.

2 **méi** is used to negate the verb **yǒu** (to have):

Wǒ méi yǒu gēge.   I *do not* have brothers.

3 **méiyǒu** or **méi** is used to indicate that:

(a) something has not happened:

Wǒ *méiyǒu* (or *méi*) chī guo Zhōngguó fàn.
I haven't had Chinese food.

(b) something did not happen:

Tā zuótiān *méiyǒu* (or *méi*) lái shàng bān.
She did not come to work yesterday.

Questions

To form questions that require a 'yes' or 'no' answer, simply add the particle **ma** to the end of a sentence:

Nǐ shì Yīngguó rén.   →   **Nǐ shì Yīngguó rén *ma*?**
You are British.   Are you British?

Another way of forming a yes/no question is to repeat the verb with the negation word **bù** or **méi** as appropriate inserted in between:

Nǐ *chī bù chī* dàsuàn?   Do you eat garlic?
Nǐ *yǒu méi yóu* jiějie?   Do you have elder sisters?

When question words such as **shénme** (what), **shénme shíhou** (when), **nǎr** (where), etc. are used to ask questions, the sentence order is not changed. The question word occupies the position in the sentence where the information required should appear in the reply:

A: **Nǐ jiào shénme?**
What are you called?

B: **Wǒ jiào Lǐ Xīng.**
I am called *Li Xing.*

A: **Nǐ shénme shíhou qù Zhōngguó.**
When are you going to China?

B: **Wǒ míngtiān qù Zhōngguó.**
I'm going to China *tomorrow.*

Directional words

In English, words such as *in* and *out* are used to indicate the direction of a verb, for example *Please come in* and *I'd like to go out*. In Chinese, directional words such as **lái** (*lit.* 'come'), **qù** (*lit.* 'go'), etc. are used after a verb in these cases:

Qǐng jìn lai.
Please *come in*.

Wǒ xiǎng chū qu yīhuìr.
I'd like to *go out* for a while.

Adverbs

1 When adverbs describe adjectives, they are placed before adjectives:

Tā fēicháng piàoliang.   She is extremely good-looking.

2 When adverbs describe the manner of an action:

(a) they are placed before the verb in an imperative sentence (e.g. order, suggestion):

> **Kuài zǒu. Wǒmen yào chí dào le.**
> *Lit.* Quickly walk. We   will late arrive.
> Hurry up. We'll be late.

(b) they are placed after the verb and linked by **de** if the degree or result of an action is indicated:

> **Wǒ zuótiān wǎnshang shuì de hǎo.**   I slept well last night.

There are some other locations of adverbs. The above two have been covered in this book.

Many adverbs usually have the same form as adjectives.

Prepositions

Prepositions are not used as often as in English. The preposition **zài** (at/in/on) is not used in conjunction with time expressions in Chinese:

> **Wǒ měi tiān *qī diǎn* qǐchuáng.**
> I get up *at seven o'clock* every day.

> **Tā *xīngqīsān* yǒu Zhōngwén kè.**
> He has Chinese lessons *on Wednesdays.*

To indicate location, the prepositional phrase introduced by **zài** is normally placed before the verb:

> **Wǒ _zài_ Běijīng dāi le sì tiān.**
> preposition
> I stayed in Beijing for four days.

But with the verb **zhù**, the **zài** phrase can appear both before or after the verb:

> **Yuēhàn _zài Běijīng_ zhù.**   **Yuēhàn zhù _zài Běijīng_.**
> John lives *in Beijing.*

But if there is a duration phrase such as 'three months', the prepositional phrase must be placed before the verb:

> **Yuēhàn _zài Běijīng_ zhù le sān ge yuè.**
> John lived *in Beijing* for three months.

Key to the exercises and reading/listening comprehension questions

Lesson 1

Exercise 1

(a) (i) Zhāng jīnglǐ/Zhāng xiānsheng/Zhāng Gōngmín; (ii) Lín xiǎojie/ Lín Fāng/Xiǎo Lín; (iii) Xiǎo Gǒng/Qíbīn. (b) Nǐ hǎo, Wáng Lín. (c) Hěn gāoxìng jiàndào nǐ.

Exercise 2

(a) shì; (b) tā; (c) Shì de.

Exercise 3

(a) Nǐ shì Wáng xiānsheng ma? (b) Tā hěn gāoxìng jiàndào nǐ ma? (c) Tāmen lái Zhōngguó ma?

Exercise 4

(a) Wǒ yě hěn gāoxìng jiàndào nǐ. or Jiàndào nǐ, wǒ yě hěn gāoxìng. (b) Qǐng jiào wǒ Dàwèi. (c) Huānyíng nǐ lái Zhōngguó.

Exercise 5

(2) (a) 你好 hello; (b) 中国 China; (c) 中国人 Chinese person.

Exercise 6

(1) and (2) (a) Nǐ lèi ma? (Lèi *or* Bú lèi). (b) Nǐ gāoxìng ma? (Gāoxìng *or* Bù gāoxìng.) (c) Nǐ xiǎng hē kāfēi ma? (Xiǎng *or* Bù xiǎng.)

Exercise 7

(a) B: Nǐ hǎo. (b) B: Bú kèqi. (c) B: Shì de . . . (d) B: Bú shì . . . (e) B: Xiǎng, xièxie.

Exercise 8

(a) Lǎo Wáng *bù* xiǎng hē kāfēi. (b) Dàwèi *bù* hěn gāoxìng. (c) Dàwèi hěn *bù* gāoxìng. (d) Wǒ yīlù *bù* hěn shùnlì. (e) Wǒ yīlù hěn *bú* shùnlì. (f) Tā *bú* shì Shǐmìsī xiānsheng.

Exercise 9

(a) Hěn lèi. (b) Yǒu yīdiǎnr lèi. (c) Bú tài lèi.

Exercise 10

(a) wǒde, tāde; (b) Tāde; (c) wǒde, Dàwèi de.

Exercise 11

(2) (a) mouth; (b) heart; (c) person; (d) female.

Reading/listening comprehension questions

I (2) (a) gāoxìng; (b) kèqi; (c) huānyíng; (d) xiānsheng.

II (1) John. (2) No, he had a very rough trip. (3) She asks John if he would like a coffee. (4) He would very much like a coffee.

Lesson 2

Exercise 1

1(c) Germany; 2(h) Italy; 3(b) France; 4(a) Japan; 5(e) Hong Kong; 6(d) Australia; 7(f) New Zealand; 8(g) Singapore.

Exercise 2

(a) Yīngguórén; (b) Měiguórén; (c) Zhōngguórén; (d) Yìdàlìrén; (e) Táiwānrén; (f) Xiānggǎngrén; (g) Aǒdàlìyàrén; (h) Rìběnrén.

Exercise 3

(a) Yīngwén; (b) Yīngwén; (c) Zhōngwén; (d) Yìdàlìwén; (e) Zhōngwén; (f) Fǎwén; (g) Zhōngwén/Yīngwén/Guǎngdōnghuà (Cantonese); (h) Rìwén.

Exercise 4

(a) Nǐ jiào shénme? (b) Nǐ shì nǎli rén? (c) Nǐ huì shuō Yīngwén ma?

Exercise 5

(a) yīdiǎnr; (b) yǒu yīdiǎnr; (c) yǒu yīdiǎnr; (d) yīdiǎnr.

Exercise 6

(a) A: Nǐ shì nǎ guó rén? (b) A: Tā shì nǎli rén? (c) B: Nǎli, nǎli. (d) B: Bú huì.

Exercise 7

(a) Àimǐ shì nǎ guó rén? (b) Wǒ bú huì shuō Yīngwén. (c) Tā bú shì Rìběnrén. (d) Wǒ bù zhīdào tā jiào shénme.

Exercise 8

(3)
(a) from Beijing (*lit.* 'Beijing person')
(b) Chinese (*lit.* 'China person')

Exercise 9

For your reference only:
Àimǐ shì Měiguórén. Tā jīn nián èrshíyī suì le. Tā huì shuō yīdiǎnr Zhōngwén. Tā hěn gāoxìng rènshi Fāng Chūn. Fāng Chūn shì Zhōngguó Běijīngrén. Tā sānshí'èr suì. Tā kànshangqu hěn niánqīng. Tā yě hěn gāoxìng rènshi Àimǐ.

Exercise 10

(a) B: Nǎli, nǎli/Guòjiǎng. (b) B: Sānshí suì zuǒyòu. (c) B: Bú duì.

Exercise 11

(a) zhīdào; (b) rènshi/zhīdào; (c) zhīdào; (d) rènshi.

Exercise 12

(a) Tā jiào shénme? (b) Xiǎo Fāng shì nǎli rén? (c) Àimǐ jīn nián duō dà le?

Exercise 13

(a) Tā kànshangqu bù hěn gāoxìng. (b) Lǎo Wáng kànshangqu hěn niánqīng. (c) Nǐ kànshangqu yǒu yīdiǎnr lèi yǒu diǎnr lèi.

Exercise 14

(1)(a) 六; (b) 十八; (c) 二十三; (d) 四十五.

Reading/listening comprehension questions

I (1) Yes, he does. (2) Britain. (3) Yes, a little. (4) No, he does not. (5) Yes, she would very much like to.

II *Tones* (1) xièxie (fourth, neutral); (2) Yīngguórén (first, second, second); (3) shuō Zhōngwén (first, first, second); (4) tài hǎo le (fourth, third, neutral); (5) zàijiàn (fourth, fourth); (6) wó yě shì (second, third, fourth); (7) bú kèqi (second, fourth, neutral); (8) bú duì (second, fourth).

Lesson 3

Exercise 1

For your reference only:
(a) Hǎo jiǔ bú jiàn. Nǐ zěnme yàng?/Nǐ hǎo ma? Zhēn gāoxìng jiàndào nǐ. (b) Ràng wǒ jièshào yīxià. Xiǎo Lín, zhè shì wǒde hǎo péngyou, Àimǐ. Àimǐ, zhè shì wǒde Zhōngguó péngyou, Xiǎo Lín.

Exercise 2

(a) Yuēhàn SHÌ bú tài máng. (John is *not* very busy.) (b) Xiǎolán de gōngzuò SHÌ hěn máng. (Xiaolan *is* very busy with her work.) (c) Wáng Lín kànshangqu SHÌ hěn lǎo. (Wang Lin *does* look rather old.)

Exercise 3

(a) A: Nǐ zuótiān qù nǎr le?/Zuótiān nǐ qù le nǎr?
B: Qù Lúndūn le./Qù le Lúndūn.
(b) A: Nǐ xià ge xīngqī qù nǎr?/Xià ge xīngqī nǐ qù nǎr?
B: Zhōngguó./Qù Zhōngguó.
(c) A: Yánzhōng qù nǎr le?
B: Tā qù Měiguó le.

Exercise 4

(a) Ānnà qù le Měiguó./Ānnà qù Měiguó le. (Anna went to America./Anna has gone to America.) (b) Xiǎolán hē le yī bēi kāfēi. (Xiaolan had her coffee./Xiaolan has had her coffee.) (c) Yánzhōng zuótiān chūmén le. (Yanzhong went out yesterday.)

Exercise 5

(a) jiàndào; (b) jiànmiàn; (c) jiànmiàn; (d) jiàndào.

Exercise 6

(2) *For your reference only:*
忙 – your heart will suffer and perhaps die if you are too busy!
男 – men should work in the field!

(3)

亡 (semi-phonetic) for 忙

又 for 友

门 for 们

(4)

男 Gentlemen/Men

女 Ladies/Women

Exercise 7

(a) Rènshi. Tāmen shì hǎo péngyou. (b) Bú rènshi. (c) Méi jiéhūn. (d) Tā shì wǒmen gōngsī de fù jīnglǐ, yě shì Àimǐ de nán péngyou.

Exercise 8

(a) shíwǔ ge Měiguórén; (b) liǎng ge Zhōngguórén; (c) sān ge nánde; (d) bā bēi kāfēi; (e) sì ge hǎo péngyou.

Exercise 9

(a) Yǒu. (b) Méi yǒu. (c) Zhēn kěxī!

Exercise 10

(a) Yánzhōng qù nǎr le? (b) Shéi shì nǐmen gōngsī de fù jīnglǐ? (c) Xiǎolán shì nǎ guó rén? (d) Nǐ xià ge xīngqī qù nǎr?

Exercise 11

(a) Wǒ xià ge xīngqī *bú* qù Zhōngguó. (I'm not going to China next week.) (b) Zhēnní *méiyǒu* jiéhūn. (Jane hasn't got married.) (c) Xiǎo Fāng *méi* yǒu Yìdàlì kāfēi. (Xiao Fang hasn't got Italian coffee.) (d) Wáng Píng *bú* rènshi Měixīn. (Wang Ping does not know Meixin.) (e) Zuótiān wǒmen *méi* qù Lúndūn. (We didn't go to London yesterday.) (f) Wǒ *bù* xiǎng hē kāfēi. (I don't want to have coffee.) (g) Wǒ *bù* zhīdào tā yǒu nǚ péngyou le. (I didn't know he had a girlfriend.)

Exercise 12

(a) jiù; (b) SHÌ; (c) SHÌ; (d) jiù.

Exercise 13

(1) (a) i); (b) ii); (c) ii); (d) iii).

(2)
(a) 他，你
(b) 忙
(c) 没
(d) 好，她

Reading/listening comprehension questions

I (2)
(a) gōngsī
(b) búguò
(c) kěxī
(d) jiéhūn

II (1) true; (2) false; (3) false; (4) true; (5) false; (6) true; (7) false.

Lesson 4

Exercise 1

(a) shí diǎn èrshíwǔ (fēn); (b) liǎng diǎn bàn/liǎng diǎn sānshí (fēn); (c) shí'èr diǎn sān kè/shí'èr diǎn sìshíwǔ/yī diǎn chà shíwǔ/yī diǎn chà yī kè; (d) liù diǎn shí fēn; (e) sì diǎn yī kè/sì diǎn shíwǔ (fēn); (f) jiǔ diǎn wǔ fēn/jiǔ diǎn líng wǔ (fēn).

Exercise 2

(a) (4) jiǔ diǎn yī kè; (b) (6) sì diǎn chà wǔ fēn; (c) (5) liǎng diǎn sìshíwǔ; (d) (2) shíyī diǎn èrshí fēn; (e) (1) bā diǎn líng wǔ; (f) (3) shí'èr diǎn bàn.

Exercise 3

(a) Zǎoshang hǎo. (b) Xiànzài jǐ diǎn le? (c) Qǐng wèn, nǐ jiào shénme? (d) Bú kèqi/Bú xiè.

Exercise 4

(a) cóng . . . dào . . . (Breakfast is from seven to half past eight.)
(b) fēnzhōng (We have five minutes for coffee.) (c) Xiànzài . . . (It's
half past six now.) (d) yǐjing (She is already married.)

Exercise 5

(a) Cāntīng jǐ diǎn kāimén? (b) Nǐ zhīdao cāntīng jǐ diǎn kāimén ma?
(c) Dàwèi yǐjing sānshí suì le. (d) Qǐng kuài lái Yīngguó.

Exercise 6

(2)
(a) bù hǎo	(it's) not good
(b) wǒ xiǎng jiàn nǐ	I'd like to see you
(c) tā xiànzài máng	she is busy now
(d) zǎoshang hǎo	good morning

Exercise 7

(a) Dùibuqǐ. (b) Qǐng wèn, yóuyǒng chí jǐ diǎn kāimén?
(c) Dùibuqǐ.

Exercise 8

For your reference only:
(a) Wǒ qī diǎn èrshí chī zǎofàn. (b) Wǒ shí'èr diǎn bàn zuǒyòu chī
wǔfàn. (c) Wǒ bā diǎn chī wǎnfàn. (d) Wǒ sān diǎn zuǒyòu
yóuyǒng. etc.

Exercise 9

(a) Dàlián yǒu èrshí ge dà fàndiàn. (b) Wǒmen(de) fàndiàn yǒu liǎng
ge cāntīng. (c) Zhè ge gōngsī yǒu Zhōngguórén ma? (d) Zhè ge
fàndiàn méi yǒu yóuyǒng chí.

Exercise 10

(a) Tā shì bù shì Yīngguórén? (Is he/she British?) (b) Nǐ zuìjìn máng
bù máng? (Have you been busy recently?) (c) Zhāng Bīn yǒu méi
yǒu nǚ péngyou? (Does Zhang Bin have a girl-friend?) (d) Nǐ xiǎng
bù xiǎng qù Zhōngguó? (Do you want to go to China?)

Exercise 11

(a) Duìbuqǐ. (b) Xiànzài jǐ diǎn le? (c) Cāntīng jǐ diǎn kāimén?
(d) Huí jiàn.

Exercise 12

(a) Shí'èr diǎn bàn chī wǔfàn, xíng bù xíng?/xíng ma?/hǎo ma?/hǎo
bù hǎo?/zěnme yàng? (b) Xiàwǔ sì diǎn qù yóuyǒng, hǎo ma?/hǎo
bù hǎo?/xíng bù xíng?/xíng ma?/zěnme yàng? (c) Jiào nǐ 'Xiǎo Lǐ',
xíng ma?/xíng bù xíng?

Exercise 13

(2) breakfast
(3) lunch
(4) (a) (ii); (b) (iii); (c) (i).

Reading/listening comprehension questions

I (1) (b) bù hěn máng; (2) (a) yóuyǒng; (3) (c) chī wǔfàn; (4) (b) shí'èr
diǎn sānshí; (5) (a) shí'èr diǎn yī kè; (6) (b) sān diǎn.

II *Tones* (1) huí jiàn (second, fourth); (2) cāntīng (first, first); (3)
duìbuqǐ (fourth, neutral, third); (4) dàde (fourth, neutral); (5) bù máng
(fourth, second) (6) bú lèi (second, fourth).

Lesson 5

Exercise 1

(1) jiějie = (b) elder sister; (2) dìdi = (d) younger brother; (3) gēge =
(a) elder brother; (4) yéye = (e) grandfather; (5) mèimei = (c) younger
sister; (6) ā'yí = (h) aunt; (7) nǎinai = (f) grandmother; (8) shūshu =
(g) uncle.

Exercise 2

(a) Wǒ māma zài hē kāfēi. (My mum is having coffee.) (b) Yīngméi
zài chī zǎofàn ma? (Is Yingmei having her breakfast?) (c) Tā bú zài
yóuyǒng. (He/she isn't swimming.) (d) Nǐ bàba zài gōngzuò ma? (Is
your father working?)

Exercise 3

(a) shàng/qù; (b) shàng; (c) qù/shàng; (d) shàng.

Exercise 4

(a) Jié(hūn) le. (b) Xiùwén. (c) Zhōngguórén. (d) Yǒu. (e) Nǚ'ér jiào Měifāng. Érzi jiào Dàyǒng. (f) Bú shì. Tā shì dà xuésheng. (g) Měifāng de zhàngfu.

Exercise 5

(a) Tāmen yóu liǎng ge háizi, yī ge nǚ'ér, yī ge érzi. (b) Liǎng ge háizi dōu yǒu Zhōngwén míngzi. (c) Wǒmen dōu tuìxiū le. (d) Tāmen bù gōngzuò le. (e) Wǒ dìdi hái méi shàng xiǎo xué. (f) Shàng xué hěn yǒu yìsi. (g) Nǐ xué shénme zhuānyè? (h) Qǐng gěi wǒ jiǎngjiang nǐ zhàngfu. (i) Gāi wǒ shuō Zhōngwén le.

Exercise 6

(2) (a) 情 in 情况; (b) 讲 in 讲讲; (c) 漂 in 漂亮; (d) 退 in 退休; (e) 意思; (f) 理 in 心理学; (g) 休 in 退休.

Exercise 7

(a) He/she does not live in Beijing. (b) Are your parents still working? (c) Ma Lan is having her breakfast. (d) Wang Lin works at the Beijing Hotel.

Exercise 8

(a) Lǎo Wáng yóu jǐ ge háizi? (b) Nǐ zài Běijīng Fàndiàn zhù le jǐ tiān? (c) Tā hē le jǐ bēi kāfēi? (d) Lǐ Píng yǒu jǐ ge gēge?

Exercise 9

(a) Nǐ yǒu shíjiān qù yóuyǒng ma? (b) Duìbuqǐ, wǒ méi yǒu shíjiān. (c) Nǐ gàn shénme gōngzuò? (d) Qǐng wèn nǐ fùmǔ hǎo.

Exercise 10

(a) [no measure word needed]; (b) ge; (c) jiā/ge; (d) ge; (e) bēi.

Exercise 11

(a) Wǒ hěn xǐhuan wǒde gōngzuò. (b) Wǒ xiǎng qù kàn wǒ fùmǔ. (c) Tā huì lái kàn wǒ ma? (d) Fāng Shū zài Běijīng Lǚyóu Jú gōngzuò. (e) Nǐ zhù zài nǎr?

Exercise 12

(2) (b)(e) 北京; (g)(d) 广州; (h)(f) 深圳; (c)(a) 上海.

Reading/listening comprehension questions

I (1) Gu Liang is a translator/interpreter. (2) Yes, he finds it interesting. (3) Yang Ning has got married. (4) Yang Ning's wife is a primary-school teacher. (5) Gu Liang is going to meet Yang Ning's wife tomorrow night at Yang Ning's home.

II (1) jiéhūn; (2) lǚyóu; (3) shíjiān; (4) guǎnlǐ (Note the first third tone is changed to the second tone in the recording.); (5) dàxué.

Lesson 6

Exercise 1

(a) Jīntiān shì xīngqītiān./Jīntiān shì xīngqīrì. (b) Jīntiān shì wǔyuè yī hào. (c) Wǒ èr hào qù Zhōngguó. (d) Wǒ māma xīngqīwǔ lái Táiwān.

Exercise 2

(a) sān tiān [no measure word] (Xiao Fang stayed in Shenzhen for three days.) (b) sān ge yuè (I've got three months.) (c) liǎng ge xīngqī/liǎng xīngqī (My husband wants to travel in China for two weeks.) (d) sì nián [no measure word] (My younger brother worked in Xi'an for four years.) (e) wǔ ge gēge (Wang Dongping has five elder brothers.) (f) bāyuè [no measure word] (Paul wants to go to Taiwan in August.)

Exercise 3

(a) Liú Hóng zài Guǎngzhōu zhù le jǐ nián? (b) Míngtiān shì xīngqīsì. (c) Dàwèi xué le jǐ ge yuè Zhōngwén? (d) Wǒ xiǎng jīnnián sānyuè qù Zhōngguó. (e) Xià ge xīngqīwǔ shì jǐ hào? (f) Wǒ zhàngfu (*or* àiren) yǒu liǎng ge dìdi hē yī ge jiějie.

Exercise 4

(a) wǒ zuì hǎo de péngyou; (b) tèbié da de yóuyǒng chí/fēicháng dà de yóuyǒng chí; (c) xiǎo cāntīng/xiǎo fàndiàn; (d) nà ge niánqīng piàoliang de dà xuésheng; (e) zuì lǎo de nán rén.

Exercise 5

(a) Mǐkè dǎsuàn *shénme shíhou* qù Zhōngguó? (When is Mick going to China?) (b) Zhāng Jūn zài Táiwān gōngzuò le *duō jiǔ*? (For how long did Zhang Jun work in Taiwan?) (c) Lǎo Lǐ de nǚ'ér *shénme shíhou* shàng xué? (When is Lao Li's daughter starting school?) (d) Nǐ xiǎng zài Shànghǎi dāi jǐ tiān? (For how many days do you want to stay in Shanghai?)

Exercise 6

(a) zuǒyòu; (b) Dàyuē; (c) zuǒyòu; (d) dàyuē.

Exercise 7

(a) Nǐ xiǎng shí'èr diǎn háishì yī diǎn chī wǔfàn? (b) Nǐ cháng yóuyǒng ma?/Nǐ chángcháng yóuyǒng ma? (c) Nǐ zěnme bù gāoxìng?/Nǐ wèishénme bù gāoxìng? (d) Jìrán nǐ bú è, wǒ jiù xiān chī. (e) Nǐ zài Běijīng zhù jǐ tiān? (f) Nǐ xué le duō jiǔ Zhōngwén?

Exercise 8

(1)
(a) Zhāng Péng 张朋
(b) Wāng Jīng 王京
(c) Lǐ Hǎi 李海
(d) Wú Yùe 吴月

(2) (a) 期 in 星期, 明 in 明天; (b) 号, 和, 啊 in 是啊, 加; (c) 热, 打 in 打算; (d) 们 in 它们, 什 in 什么时候; (e) 怎 in 怎么.

Reading/listening comprehension questions

I (1) Xià ge xīngqīsān. (2) Bú shì. (3) Tā qù gōngzuò jiā kàn péngyou. (4) Liǎng ge xīngqī zuǒyòu. (5) Hěn rè. (6) Bú zài Měiguó.

II *Tones* (1) yīyuè (first, fourth); (2) sān ge yuè (first, neutral, fourth); (3) tèbié dà de fángjiān (fourth, second, fourth, neutral, second, first); (4) xīngqī'èr (first, first, fourth); (5) fēicháng lěng (first, second, third); (6) dǎsuàn (third, fourth).

Lesson 7

Exercise 1

(a) Qǐng wèn, cèsuǒ zài nǎr? (b) Qǐng wèn, fùjìn yǒu chāoshì ma? (c) Qǐng wèn, shí lù chē zài nǎr? (d) Qǐng wèn, qù huǒchē zhàn zěnme zǒu? (e) Qǐng wèn, qù Běijīng Fàndiàn zuò jǐ lù chē?

Exercise 2

(a) Lǎo Zhāng zài Āimǐ de zuǒ biān. (b) Āimǐ zài Lǎo Zhāng de yòu biān/Annà de zuǒ biān. (c) Ānnà zài Xiǎo Fāng de zuǒ biān/Āimǐ de yòu biān.

Exercise 3

I (a) Cèsuǒ zài gōngyòng diànhuà de zuǒ biān. (b) Gōngyòng diànhuà zài cèsuǒ de yòu biān./Gōngyòng diànhuà zài cāntīng de zuǒ biān. (c) Cāntīng zài gōngyòng diànhuà de yòu biān. (d) Diàntī zài cèsuǒ de zuǒbiān/Diàntī zài cèsuǒ de duìbiàn.

II (a) Dì èr ge hónglǜ dēng wǎng zuǒ guǎi, dào dì yī ge lùkǒu, zài wǎng yòu guǎi. (b) Dì èr ge hónglǜ dēng wǎng yòu guǎi.

Exercise 4

(a) Tā bú jìde wǒde míngzi. (He doesn't remember my name.) (b) Nǐ bú yòng gěi wǒ mǎi lǐwù. (You don't need to buy me any presents.) (c) Fùjìn méi yǒu chāoshì. (There's no department store nearby.)

(d) Wǒ méi kàn jiàn huǒchē zhàn. (I didn't see the railway station.)
(e) Wǒ kàn bú jiàn hónglǜ dēng. (I can't see the traffic lights.)

Exercise 5

(1) Nàr yǒu yī ge fàndiàn. (2) Tā huì shuō Zhōngwén. (3) Wǒ bù néng gàosu nǐ tāde qíngkuàng. (4) Dì yī ge lùkǒu wǎng yòu guǎi. Shíwǔ fēnzhōng jiù dào le. (5) (Wǒ) qù huǒchē zhàn zuò jǐ lù chē?

Exercise 6

(a) Qǐng wèn, qí zìxíngchē qù Zhōngguó Yínháng xūyào duō jiǔ? (b) Qǐng wèn, zǒulù qù huǒchē zhàn xūyào duō jiǔ? (c) Qǐng wèn, zuò chē qù Tiān'ānmén xūyào duō jiǔ?

Exercise 8

(a) Wǒ bú xìn (or bù xiāngxìn) nǐ méi yǒu zìxíngchē. (b) Xià ge xīng-qīliù wǒ yào qù Shànghǎi. (c) Dàwèi méi zhǎo dào Zhōngguó Yínháng. (d) Nǐ zuìhǎo chá yīxià dìtú. (e) Qí zìxíngchē dào wǒde dàxué yào yī ge duō xiǎoshí. (f) Zhè shì yī ge hǎo zhǔyi.

Exercise 9

(1) (a) (ii); (b) (iv); (c) (iii); (d) (vii); (e) (v); (f) (i); (g) (vi); (h) (viii).

(2) *For your reference only:*
山东，广东，南京，济南，西安，广西，山西，北京，河北，湖北．

Reading/listening comprehension questions

(1) (c); (2) (b); (3) (c); (4) (b); (5) (c).

Lesson 8

Exercise 1

(a) Píngguǒ bā kuài qī máo wǔ yī jīn. (b) Bōluó jiǔ kuài yī jīn. (c) Xiāngjiāo shísì kuài liù máo wǔ yī jīn. (d) Cǎoméi shí kuài yī máo yī jīn. (e) Lízi qī kuài líng wǔ yī jīn. (f) Shíwǔ kuài yī máo jiǔ yī jīn.

Exercise 2

(a) yào; (b) xiǎng/yào; (c) yào; (d) xiǎng/yào.

Exercise 3

(a) Wǒ xiǎng mǎi yīxiē Hǎinán Dǎo xiāngjiāo. (b) Tā bú yào cǎoméi. (c) Wǒ mǎi le liǎng jīn píngguǒ. (d) Nǐ hái yào biéde ma? (e) Wǒ bú zhīdào zhè ge duō shǎo qián. (f) A: Gěi nǐ wǔ kuài. B: Zhǎo nǐ liǎng máo wǔ.

Exercise 4

(a) Wǒ xiǎng mǎi yī tiáo zhēn sī lǐngdài./Wǒ yào . . . (b) Wǒ xiǎng mǎi liǎng jīn xiāngjiāo./Wǒ yào . . . (c) Wǒ xiǎng mǎi liǎng tiáo wéijīn./Wǒ yào . . . (d) Wǒ xiǎng mǎi yī jīn píngguǒ./Wǒ yào . . . (e) Wǒ xiǎng mǎi yī zhāng Běijīng dìtú./Wǒ yào . . . (f) Wǒ xiǎng mǎi liǎng zhāng míngxìnpiàn./Wǒ yào . . .

Exercise 5

(a) Nǐ kěyi dài wǒ qù bǎihuò shāngdiàn ma? (b) Nǐ kěyi dài wǒ qù yínháng ma? (c) Nǐ kěyi dài wǒ qù yóu jú ma? (d) Nǐ kěyi dài wǒ qù yóuyǒng chí ma?

Exercise 6

(a) Tài guì le. Wǒ bú yào. (b) Wǒ yào le. (c) Xiǎojie, yǒu lìzhī ma? (d) Nǐ tài hǎo le. Duō xiè.

Exercise 7

(a) gěi tāde nǚ péngyou (He bought a pure silk scarf for his girl-friend.) (b) mǎi yīxiē dōngxi (I should go to the department store and do some shopping.) (c) suǒyǒude yínháng dōu (All the banks are open on Sundays.) (d) jǐ bēi (Xiao Wang has had several cups of coffee.) (e) dài wǒ māma lái (My elder brother will bring my mother over to see us.)

Exercise 9

(1)
(a) fifteen yuan
(b) three yuan and seven mao
(c) sixty-eight yuan and one jiao
(d) twenty-five kuai

(2) *For your reference only:*

买 The top stroke looks like a hat and the bottom is the character for head, so you've just bought yourself a hat.

卖 The character over 买 is number ten, so you've got ten extra things, so you'll have to sell them!

要 You want a woman who is in the West/Western women are wanted!

(3)
(a) wǒ yào mǎi dōngxī. I want to buy things.
(b) wǒmen bú mài zhǎofàn. We do not sell breakfast.

(4)
女

Reading/listening comprehension questions

(1) yī jiàn shuìyī; (2) liǎng bǎi bāshí wǔ yuán; (3) hěn hào, yě bú guì; (4) jǐ tiáo zhuōbù.

Lesson 9

Exercise 1

(a) Zhōngguó bǐ Měiguó dà./Měiguó bǐ Zhōngguó xiǎo. (b) Bōluó bǐ píngguǒ guì. (c) Yuēhàn bǐ Wáng Lín gāo. (d) Zhè ge yóuyǒng chí bǐ nà ge yóuyǒng chí dà. (e) Āimǐ bǐ Línlin dà./Línlin bǐ Āimǐ niánqīng./Línlin bǐ Āimǐ xiǎo.

Exercise 2

For your reference only:
(a) Wǒ zuì xǐhuan lán yánsè. (I like the blue colour most.) (b) Wǒ bǐjiào xǐhuan Zhōngguó fàn. (I quite like Chinese food.) (c) Zhōngwén bǐ Fǎwén nán. (Chinese is more difficult than French.) (d) Shì de. (Yes, it is.)

Exercise 3

(a) with 4 lán tiān (blue sky); (b) with 1 or 3 lǜ píngguǒ; lǜ chá; (c) with 2 huáng xiāngjiāo; (d) with 1 or 3 hóng píngguǒ; hóng chá (black tea).

Exercise 4

(a) Nǐ kěyi jiè gěi wǒ liǎng ge píngguǒ ma? (b) Tā bù xǐhuan jiè gěi péngyou qián. (c) Tā shénme shíhou huán gěi wǒ qián?/Tā shénme shíhou huán wǒ qián? (d) Wǒ wàng le dài qiánbāo. (e) Xièxie nǐ dài lái yīxiē Zhōngguó chá. (f) Tā dài máoyī le ma? (g) Liú Hóng kànshangqu bǐ Xiǎo Fāng niánqīng./Liú Hóng bǐ Xiǎo Fāng kànshangqu niánqing.

Exercise 5

(a) borrow; (b) lend; (c) borrow; (d) lend.

Exercise 6

(a) shàng; (b) guàng; (c) qù; (d) shàng.

Exercise 7

(a) Duìbuqǐ. Wǒ chí dào le. (b) Méi wèntí. (c) Zhōngwén zěnme shuō 'good bargain'? (d) Wǒ míngtiān yīdìng huán gěi nǐ qián.

Exercise 8

(a) Zhè tiáo lǐngdài mōshangqu hěn shūfu. (This tie feels very nice.) (b) Wǒ guàng le guàng shāngdiàn. (I had a look around in the shops.) (c) Tāng Bīn jiè gěi le wǒ èrshí kuài qián. (Tang Bin lent me twenty yuan.) (d) Tā jīntiān zǎoshang chí dào le èrshí fēnzhōng. (She was twenty minutes late this morning.)

Exercise 9

(a) gòu; (b) zúgòu de; (c) A: gòu; B: gòu; (d) zúgòu de.

Exercise 10

(a) Tā méi yǒu shénme hǎo péngyou. (b) Míngtiān wǒ bú shàng bān. Wǒ kěyi chōu kòng qù yóuyǒng. (c) Wǒ cāi tā wǔshí duō suì. (d) Duìbuqǐ. Shēn lán sè de máoyī mài guāng le. Hēi sè xíng ma? (e) Zhēn hésuàn. Hái yǒu ma? (f) Wǒ de bàba māma (fùmǔ) shēntǐ bú cuò.

Exercise 11

(1) 绿　给　钱

(2) (a) 定 in 一定, 宜 in 便宜; (b) 听; (c) 忘, 急; (d) 摸 in 摸上去; 抽 in 抽空.

(3) (a) 她没有钱　　　She has no money.
(b) 我想买绿电话　　I'd like to buy a green telephone.

Reading/listening comprehension questions

(1) (b); (2) (c); (3) (a); (4) (b); (5) (a); (6) (b); (7) (a).

Lesson 10

Exercise 1

(a) Wǒ yào yī bēi chénzi zhī. (b) Wǒ yào yī píng píjiǔ. (c) Wǒ yào liǎng bēi bái pútao jiǔ. (d) Wǒ yào yīxiē Zhōngguó chá.

Exercise 3

(a) Qǐng zuò. (b) Wǒ xiǎng kànkan càidān./Wǒ xiǎng kàn yīxià càidān./Wǒ kěyi kàn yīxià càidān ma? (c) Qǐng gēn wǒ lái. (d) Wǒ è sǐ le. (e) Qǐng shāo děng./Děng yīxià./Děngdeng.

Exercise 4

(a) Xiǎohuá qù guo Zhōngguó ma? (b) Dàwèi zuó tiān qù Lúndūn le. (c) Tā méiyǒu chī guo Zhōngguó fàn. (d) A: Nǐ chī zǎofàn le ma? B: Hái méi chī.

Exercise 5

(a) Wǒ chī bǎo le./Wǒ bǎo le. (b) Wǒ zài yào yīxiē bǐng./Wǒ hái xiǎng yào yīxiē bǐng. (c) Qǐng dì gěi wǒ jiàng. (d) Duō chī yīxiē. (e) Duìbuqǐ, wǒ zài yào yī píng píjiǔ.

Exercise 6

(a) Rúguǒ nǐ yǒu shíjiān dehuà, zánmen qù chī kǎo yā, hǎo ma? (b) Nǐ děi lái kàn wǒmen. (c) Jīntiān zǎoshang wǒ shàng bān chí dào le èrshí fēnzhōng. (d) Rúguǒ nǐ chī bǎo le, zánmen jiù mǎidān ba. (e) Xiǎo Zhāng bù xiǎng qǐng Lǎo Wáng.

Exercise 7

(a) Yóuyǒng chí jīntiān zǎoshang kāi de hěn zǎo. (b) Qǐng zǎo yīdiǎnr lái./Qǐng zǎo yīxiē lái. (c) Jīntiān zǎoshang wǒ lái de hěn chí. (d) Yuēhàn shuō de hěn kuài.

Exercise 8

(a) Nǐ shuō de bú duì. (b) Wǒ mèimei lái de bù hěn zǎo. (c) Yīngguó de xiàtiān bù hěn rè. (d) Tāde fùmǔ tuìxiū de bù hěn zǎo. (e) Xiǎohuá bù gāoxìng.

Exercise 9

(1) 菜 in 菜单; 烤 in 烤鸭.
(2) 味 in 味精; 啤 in 啤酒; 吗 in 是吗; 饿 in 饿死了, 饼, 饱.
(3) (a) v); (b) iv); (c) ii); (d) i); (e) iii).

Reading/listening comprehension questions

(1) false; (2) true; (3) true; (4) true; (5) false; (6) true.

Lesson 11

Exercise 1

(a) Wǒ mǎi sān zhāng qù Tiān'ānmén de piào. (I'll buy three tickets for Tian'anmen.) (b) Nà ge gāng dào de nánhái shì Lǎo Liú de érzi.

(The boy who has just arrived is Lao Liù's son.) (c) Wáng jīnglǐ bù xǐhuan nàxiē chángcháng chí dào de rén. (Manager Wang doesn't like those who are always late.)

Exercise 2

(a) tiáo; (b) zhāng; (c) zhàn; (d) píng.

Exercise 3

(a) Zāogāo! Wǒ zuò cuò chē le. (b) Zāogāo! Wǒ diǎn cuò cài le. (c) Zāogāo! Wǒ jiào cuò tāde míngzi le. (d) Zāogāo! Wǒ mǎi cuò kāfēi le.

Exercise 4

(a) Bié jí. (b) Bié zuò chūzūchē. (c) Bié gàosu Lǎo Wáng wǒ duō dà le. (d) Bié shuō Yīngwén. (e) Bié jiè gěi Liú Hóng nǐde zìxíngchē.

Exercise 5

(a) Xià yī zhàn shì Běijīng Dàxué. (b) Wǒ bù zhīdào nǐ xià liǎng ge xīngqī yào chūmén. (c) Nǐ xūyào xià yī zhàn xià chē. Huàn yī hào xiàn. (d) Nà biān dū chē dū de lìhai. (e) Qù Tiān Tán yīnggāi zài nǎ yī zhān xiàchē? (f) Qǐng dài wǒ qù Běijīng kǎo Yā Diàn.

Exercise 7

(a) Wǒ xiǎng mǎi liǎng zhāng qù Běijīng de piào. (b) Wǒ xiǎng mǎi yī zhāng sānyuè bā hāo qù Shànghǎi de piào. (c) Wǒ xiǎng mǎi sān zhāng qù Guìlín de yìngwò. (d) Wǒ xiǎng mǎi liǎng zhāng èrshíliù cì lièchē de piào.

Exercise 8

(a)   Qīngdǎo píjiǔ bǐ Běijīng píjiǔ guì liù máo.
      Běijīng píjiǔ bǐ Qīngdǎo píjiǔ piányi liù máo.
      Běijīng píjiǔ méiyǒu Qīngdǎo píjiǔ guì.
(b)   Xiǎoméi bǐ Dàwèi dà yī suì.
      Dàwèi bǐ Xiǎoméi xiǎo yī suì.
      Dàwèi méi Xiǎoméi dà.

(c) Lǎo Wáng juéde Zhōngguó fàn bǐ xīcān hǎochī.
      Lǎo Wáng juéde xīcān méi Zhōngguó fàn hǎochī.
(d) Běijīng de xiàtiān bǐ Lúndūn de xiàtiān rè.
      Lúndūn de xiàtiān méi Běijīng de xiàtiān rè.

Exercise 9

(a) Huǒchē dì èr tiān shísān diǎn líng wǔ fēn dào Guìlín. (b) Wǒ xīngqīwǔ zǒu, jiù shì sānyuè èrshíwǔ hào. (c) Zhè cì chē lièchē jǐ diǎn dào Běijīng? (d) Liùshíqī cì chē lièchē jǐ diǎn fāchē?

Exercise 10

(1) 土

(2) (a) 去 I would like to buy a ticket to Beijing.
      (b) 坐 Which line (shall I) take to get to the railway station?
      (c) 去 Where should I get off for Tian Tan?
      (d) 懂 I do not understand what you are saying.

Reading/listening comprehension questions

I   (1) Jiǔ diǎn wǔshí; (2) T-wǔshíliù; (3) Guìlín; (4) Shēngzhèn; (5) Bú qù.

II (1) true; (2) false; (3) false; (4) true.

Lesson 12

Exercise 1

(a) (iv); (b) (v); (c) (iii); (d) (i); (e) (ii).

Exercise 2

(a) Wǒ yào yī jiān biāozhǔn jiān, zhù sān tiān. (b) Wǒ yào yī jiān yǒu liǎng zhāng chuáng de fángjiān. (c) Wǒ yào liǎng jiān biāozhǔn jiān, zhù yī tiān.

Exercise 3

(a) Nǐmen yǒu kòng fángjiān ma? (b) Wǒde fángjiān méi yǒu diànhuà. (c) Nǐde fángjiān zài wǔ céng. (d) Zuǒ biān dì sān liàng zìxíngchē shì wǒde.

Exercise 5

(a) diàndēng; (b) chǔlǐ; (c) fàndiàn.

Exercise 6

(a) 3 xiū diàndēng; (b) 1 chǔlǐ zhè jiàn shì; (c) 5 yǒu kòng fángjiān; (d) 2 mǎi lǐwù; (e) 6 kàn péngyou; (f) 4 děng gōnggòng qìchē.

Exercise 7

(a) Wǒde fángjiān li yǒu ge diàndēng huài le./Wǒde fángjiān li de diàndēng huài le. (b) Gébì fángjiān hěn chǎo./Gébì de rén hěn chǎo. (c) Wǒde fángjiān hěn lěng.

Exercise 8

(a) Zhēn bàoqiàn. (b) Lǎoshí shuō . . . (c) Nǐ shuì de hǎo ma? (d) Kàn qíngkuàng. (e) Sīfāng ràng wǒ gàosu nǐ tā xià ge xīngqīsì zǒu. (f) Wǒde qiánbāo li méi yǒu qián. (g) A: Hái yǒu biéde wèntí ma? B: Zànshí méi yǒu.

Exercise 9

For your reference only:
(a) Zuótiān wǒde fángjiān hěn lěng. (b) Zuówǎn, wǒ bù xiǎng chūmén. (c) Zuówǎn, gé bì hěn chǎo. (d) Wǒde fángjiān méi yǒu yùpén. (e) Wǒ bù zhīdào wǒ fángjiān li de kōngtiáo huài le.

Exercise 10

(1) (a) 是 shì; (b) 是 shì, 事 shì; (c) 事 shì.
(2) (a) 房间 fángjiān; (b) 空 kòng; (c) 入住 rù zhù; (d) 坏了 huài le; (e) 修 xiū; (f) 问题 wèntí.

Reading comprehension questions

The odd words or phrases are in italics and the words or phrases that replace them are in the parentheses. If a word/phrase needs crossing out, it is indicated in the parentheses.

A   Nǐ hǎo!
B   *Xièxie.* (Nǐ hǎo!) Nǐmen yǒu kōng fángjiān ma?
A   Yào kàn qíngkuàng. Nǐ yào biāozhǔn jiān háishì *píjiǔ* (shāngwù jiān)?
B   Yào biāozhǔn jiān. Biāozhǔn jiān yǒu wèishēngjiān ma?
A   Yǒu. Nǐ dǎsuàn zhù jǐ tiān?
B   Liǎng *ge* tiān. (cross out 'ge')
A   Ràng *nǐ* (wǒ) chácha. Gānghǎo yǒu yī jiān biāozhǔn jiān.
B   Duō shǎo qián yī *jīn* (tiān)?
A   Sān bǎi yuán. Xíng ma?
B   Xíng. Wǒ yào le.

A   你好！
B   *谢谢*！（你好！）你们有空房间吗？
A   要看情况。你要标准间还是*啤酒*（商务间）？
B   要标准间。标准间有卫生间吗？
A   有。你打算住几天？
B   两个天。(cross out 个)
A   让*你*（我）查查。刚好有一间标准间。
B   多少钱一斤（天）？
A   三百元。行吗？
B   行。我要了。

Lesson 13

Exercise 1

(a) A: Qǐng zhǎo yīxià Lǐ Bīn./Qǐng wèn, Lǐ Bīn zài ma? (b) B: Shì de. Nǐ zhǎo shéi? (c) A: Qǐng wèn, Zhēnní zài ma?/Qǐng zhǎo yīxià Zhēnní. (d) A: Qǐng wèn, nǐ shì shéi?/Qǐng wèn, nǐ shì nǎli?

Exercise 2

(a) Sīfāng shì zhù zài Xīnjiāpō *de* Zhōngguórén. (b) Línlin shì xué Zhōngwén *de* dà xuéshēng. (c) Wǒde Zhōngwén lǎoshí shì cóng Zhōngguó dàlù lái *de* Zhōngguórén.

Exercise 3

(a) Dàwèi shì shénme shíhou zǒu de? (b) Jīntiān zǎoshang, wǒ shì qí zìxíngchē lái shàng bān de. (c) Shénme shíhou dōu xíng. Nǐ juédìng. (d) Tā shénme shíhou dōu bù xǐhuan zuò gōnggòng qìchē. (e) Nǐ kěyi néng lái jiē wǒ ma? (f) Wǒmen jǐ diǎn zài shénme dìfang jiànmiàn? (g) Wǒ zài Běijīng Dàxué shàng xué shí, wǒ fùmǔ qù Zhōngguó lǚyóu le sān ge yuè.

Exercise 4

(a) Nǐ zuótiān jǐ diǎn xià bān de?/Nǐ zuótiān shì jǐ diǎn xià bān de? (b) Nǐ zuótiān shì zěnme qù shàng bàn de?/Nǐ zuótiān zěnme qù shàng bān de? (c) Nǐ mèimei shì zuótiān wǎngshang lái de ma? (d) Nǐ mèimei shì shénme shíhou kāishǐ xué Yīngwén de?

Exercise 5

For your reference only:
(a) Zhōngwén bù hǎo xué. (It's not easy to learn Chinese.) (b) Shànghǎi huǒchē zhàn bù hǎo zhǎo. (It's not easy to find Shanghai railway station.) (c) Guǎngdōnghuà bù hǎo dǒng. (It's not easy to understand Canton dialect.)

Exercise 6

(a) Wǒ jiějie shì dǎoyóu. (b) Wǒmen jīnglǐ de bàngōngshì zài èr céng. (c) [cannot omit]; (d) Tā fùmǔde jiā hěn piàoliang. (e) [cannot omit].

Exercise 7

(a) gěi; (b) gěi; (c) tóng; (d) gěi; (e) tóng.

Exercise 8

(a) Nǐ chí wán wǎnfàn le ma? (Have you finished with your supper?) (b) Tā yòng wán diànhuà le. (She has finished with the phone.) (c) Tā diǎn wán cài le. (He has finished ordering the dishes.) (d) Xiǎo Lǐ xiū wán diàndēng le. (Xiao Li has finished repairing the light.)

Exercise 9

(a) Zài Yīngguó, dǎ diànhuà hěn guì. (b) Nǐde shǒu jī hàomǎ shì duō shǎo? (c) Zuówǎn, nǐ bàba gěi nǐ dǎ diànhuà le. (d) Nǐ jiā yǒu diànhuà ma?

Exercise 10

(a) Zhēnní wàng le gěi lǎobǎn dǎ diànhuà. (Jane forgot to phone the boss.) (b) Nǐ kěyi gàosu wǒ nǐde diànhuà hàomǎ ma? (Could you tell me your telephone number?) (c) Tā jīntiān bù zài bàngōngshì. (She is not in the office today.)

Exercise 11

(1) (a) Zhang Wen is calling Xiao Li.
     (b) He has gone to the bank.
     (c) About six o'clock.

(2) 激 in 激动   港 in 香港

Reading/listening comprehension questions

(1) Bú zài. (2) Tāde māma. (3) Míngtiān wǎnshang liù diǎn shí fēn dào Shànghǎi. (4) T-Shíliù cì chē. (5) Xiǎng.

Lesson 14

Exercise 1

(a) Zuótiān wǒ bàba gěi wǒ dǎ diànhuà le. (My father phoned me yesterday.) (b) Nǐ kàn. Xiàxuě le. (Look, it's snowing.) (c) Rúguǒ tā míngtiān hái bú dào, wǒ jiù zǒu le. (If he does not arrive tomorrow, I'm leaving.) (d) Sān tiān qián, tā chí dào le bàn ge xiǎoshí. (Three days ago, he was half an hour late.) (e) Wǒ bù xiǎng qù Tiān Tán. Wǒ lèi le. (I don't want to go to the Temple of Heaven. I'm getting tired.) (f) Zhème shuō, nǐ shì Wáng Lǎoshī le? (In that case, you are Teacher Wang, aren't you?)

Exercise 2

(a) dì èr cì; (b) liǎng cì; (c) liǎng cì; (d) liǎng cì; (e) dì èr cì.

Exercise 3

(a) qù; (b) qu; (c) lái; (d) qù; (e) lai.

Exercise 4

(a) Měitiān zǎoshang, wǒ bā diǎn qù shàng bān. (b) Měi ge rén dōu xǐhuān tā. (c) Liǎng nián qián, wǒ rènshi le tā. (d) Qù nián, tā qù le Xiāng Gǎng liǎng cì. (e) Méi liǎng ge xīngqī, wǒ gěi wǒ fùmǔ dǎ yī cì diànhuà. (f) Tā yào qù tā fùmǔ jiā guò Chūn Jié.

Exercise 5

(a) Qǐng jìn, qǐng jìn./Kuài jìn lai. (b) Zuò, zuò. (c) Nǐmen xiǎng hē shénme? (d) Wǒ qù Lǎo Lǐ jiā zuòzuo. (e) Chī, chī. Bié kèqi.

Exercise 6

(a) Nǐ juéde Měiguó zěnme yàng? (b) Xiāng Gǎng de xiàtiān zěnme yàng? (c) Běijīng fàndiàn zěnme yàng? (d) Dāngdì rén zěnme yàng? (e) Dàwèi de Zhōngwén zěnme yàng?

Exercise 7

(a) Wǒ yě bù xǐhuan Zhōngguó fàn. (b) Tā māma yě mèi(yǒu) qù cānjiā Àilín de hūnlǐ. (c) Tā yě bù zhīdào yóuyǒng chí jǐ diǎn kāimén. (d) Xiǎo Zhāng yě méi(yǒu) chí dào.

Exercise 8

(a) Tóng dāngdì rén tánhuà hěn yǒu yìsi. (b) Nǐ qù le ná jǐ ge chéngshì? (c) Nǐde Táiwān zhī xíng zěnme yàng? (d) Guǎngzhōu de rén tài duō. Hěn chǎo, xiàtiān hěn rè.

Exercise 10

(a) 参加 cānjiā; (b) 过 guò; (c) 前 qián; (d) 回答 huídá; (e) 友好 yóuhǎo.

Reading/listening comprehension questions

(1) Táiwān. (2) Cānjiā le. (3) Bú shì, shì dì yī cì. (4) Guìlín. Tāmen qù le liǎng ge xīngqī.

Lesson 15

Exercise 1

Check your letter with a Chinese speaker if you can find one. Otherwise, go back to the book and check the letter yourself by going through the vocabulary and the language points.

Exercise 2

TO: People's Republic of China

Yóubiān: 710061
Xī'ān Cháng Ān Jiē 6 Hào 46 Dòng 3 Hào

Lǐ Lín Shōu

126 SE, 42 Place, Bellevue, WA 98006, USA

Exercise 3

(a) xìn/láixìn; (b) láixìn/xìn; (c) xìn; (d) qùxìn/xìn.

Exercise 4

(a) *with* 2 qù nián; (b) *with* 3 or 4 shàng ge xīngqī/shàng ge yuè; (c) *with* 1 or 2 míngtiān/míng nián; (d) *with* 3 or 4 xià ge xīngqī/xià ge yuè; (e) *with* 1 zuótiān.

Exercise 5

(a) Nǐde jiā hěn piàoliang, jiù shì bù hǎo zhǎo. (b) Zuówǎn wǒ yīzhí zài jiā xiě xìn. (c) Wǒ xǐhuān gěi hǎo péngyou xiě xìn. (d) Nǐde diànzǐ yóujiàn dìzhǐ shì shénme? (e) Xià bān hòu, wǒ qù le shìchǎng. (f) Wǒmende láobǎn máng zhe dǎ diànhuà. (g) Wǒ zuótiān cái shōu dào wǒ fùmǔ de xìn. (h) Zài Zhōngguó de shíhou, wǒ chángcháng qí zìxíngchē. (i) Tā yīdìng huì zài xià ge xīngqīyī zhī qián huán gěi nǐ nà běn shū de.

Exercise 7

(1)

邮编: 100081
北京东大街103号6栋1号
　　吴月　收

(2) *For your reference only:*
(a)　说，讲，喝，吃，问
(b)　钱，银
(c)　饭，饿，饺(子), 饼
(d)　(香)港，(台)湾，(上)海
(e)　打，摸
(f)　想，忘，急
(g)　他，你

Reading comprehension questions

(1) Wang Xiaoyue. (2) Post Box 10, English Department, Beijing University, Beijing, Postcode: 100081. (3) English Department of Beijing University in Beijing. (4) Guangzhou. (5) To attend a conference. (6) Around 8 July. (7) No, he does not.

Chinese–English glossary

This glossary includes all the words that have been introduced in this book and a small number of some commonly useful words and expressions which have not been introduced in this book. For nationalities and numbers, please see Note 7 and Note 12 of Lesson 2.

a	啊	[auxiliary word]
āi	唉	[exclamation word]
ài	爱	to love
āiyō	唉哟	whoops!
ba	吧	[auxiliary word]
bā	八	eight
bàba	爸爸	father/dad
bǎi	百	hundred
bái mǐfàn	白米饭	boiled rice
bǎifēnzhī	百分之	per cent
bǎihuò shāngdiàn	百货商店	department store
bàn	半	half
bàngōngshì	办公室	office
bànyè	半夜	midnight
bǎo	饱	to be full
bàogào	报告	report
bāoguǒ	包裹	parcel
bǎozhèng	保证	to promise
bàozhǐ	报纸	newspaper
bāozi	包子	steamed bun with filling
bāyuè	八月	August
bēi	杯	cup; glass
Běijīngrén	北京人	Beijing person/people
běn	本	[measure word for books]
běnlái	本来	originally
bǐ	比	to be compared with
biàn	便	then
biān	边	side

bié	别	do not
biéde	别的	anything else/other
bǐjiào	比较	quite/rather/relatively
bǐjìběn	笔记本	notebook
bīn guǎn	宾馆	guest room
bīng	冰	ice
bìng le	病了	to be ill
bīngjīlíng	冰激凌	ice-cream
bù	不	no/not
bú cuò	不错	quite good/quite well
cān chē	餐车	dining car
cháng/chángcháng	常/常常	often
cān'guǎn	餐馆	restaurant
chāoshì	超市	supermarket
chū chāi	出差	to be on a business trip
chúshī	厨师	chef
cídiǎn	词典	dictionary
dǎ bù tōng	打不通	cannot get through (telephone)
dǎ dī	打的	to take a taxi [colloquial]
dǎ diànhuà	打电话	to make telephone calls/to telephone
dà xuéshēng	大学生	university student
dàde	大的	the large one/the big one
dài	带	to include/to have
dài (lái)	带(来)	to bring
dài (qù)	带(去)	to take
dài/dāi	呆/待	to stay
dàjiē	大街	avenue
dānwèi	单位	organization (work unit)
dāng	当	to become
dāngdìrén	当地人	the locals
dāngrán	当然	of course
dānrén	单人	single
dànshì	但是	but
dào	到	to arrive/to get there; until/up to
dǎoyóu	导游	tourist guide
dǎsuàn	打算	to plan
dàtáng	大堂	lobby
dàxiā	大虾	king prawn
dàxué	大学	university
dàyuē	大约	approximate/about/around
de	的	[grammar word]

děi	得	to have to/must
... de shíhòu	... 的时候	when/while
dì	递	to pass
dì èr tiān	第二天	the following day
dì yī	第一	first
dì yī cì	第一次	the first time/for the first time
diàn	店	restaurant/snack-bar/shop
diǎn	点	o'clock
diǎn cài	点菜	to order (food)
diànchē	电车	tram/streetcar
diàndēng	电灯	light bulb
diànhuà	电话	telephone
diànnǎo	电脑	computer
diǎnr	点儿	a little/some
diàntī	电梯	lift/elevator
diànzi yóujiàn	电子邮件	email
dìtiě	地铁	tube/underground/subway
dìtú	地图	map
diū le	丢了	to have lost
dìzhǐ	地址	address
dòng	栋	block (of building)
dǒng	懂	to understand
dōng	东	east
dōngtiān	冬天	winter
dòngwùyuán	动物园	the zoo
dōngxi	东西	things
dōngzhímén wài	东直门外	[street name]
dōu	都	both; all [emphatic word]
dòufu	豆腐	tofu
dǔ chē	堵车	traffic jam (lit. 'blocked car')
duì	对	to be correct
duì le	对了	right/by the way
duìbuqǐ	对不起	sorry; excuse me; pardon
duō	多	more, over, more than
duō jiǔ	多久	how long
duō shǎo	多少	how much/how many
duō shǎo qián	多少钱	how much is it?
duō xiè	多谢	many thanks
dùzi téng	肚子疼	stomach-ache
è	饿	to be hungry/hungry
è sǐ le	饿死了	starving
érzi	儿子	son

fā	发	to send (email, fax)
fā shāo	发烧	to have a temperature/fever
fāchē	发车	to depart/departure
fǎn	反	opposite
fàndiàn	饭店	hotel
fángjiān	房间	room
fāngxiàng	方向	direction
fántǐ zì	繁体字	complex characters
fēicháng/tèbié	非常/特别	extremely/very
fēijī	飞机	aeroplane
fèn	份	[measure word]
fēn	分	minute; [currency word]
fēng	封	[measure word for letters]
fēngjǐng	风景	scenery
fēnjī	分机	extension
fēnzhōng	分钟	minute
fù	副	deputy/vice
fùjìn	附近	nearby/close by
fùmǔ	父母	parents
fúwù	服务	service
fúzhuāng	服装	clothing
gāi . . . le	该 . . . 了	It is (somebody's) turn to . . .
gàn	干	to do
gǎnmào	感冒	flu
gāng	刚	just
gānghǎo	刚好	to happen to/by chance/ just as well
gàosu	告诉	to tell
gāoxìng	高兴	to be pleased/glad/happy
gè/ge	个	[measure word]
gè zhǒng	各种	various kinds
gébì	隔壁	next door
gēge	哥哥	elder brother
gěi	给	for/to/to be for/to be to
gěi nǐ	给你	here you are
gēn	跟	to follow
gōngchéng shī	工程师	engineer
gōngsī	公司	company
gōngyòng	公用	public
gōngzuò	工作	work/to work
gòu	够	to be enough
guàng	逛	to look around

guǎnlǐ	管理	management/to manage
guānmén	关门	to be closed to/to close
guānxì	关系	connection
guì	贵	to be expensive
guo	过	[grammar word]
guó	国	country
guò	过	to celebrate/to spend
guòjiǎng	过奖	I'm flattered
hái	还	still/also
hái hǎo	还好	to be all right
hǎinán dǎo	海南岛	Hainan Island
háishì	还是	or [question word]
hǎixiān	海鲜	seafood
háizi	孩子	children
hàn zì	汉字	Chinese characters
hào	号	date; number
hǎo	好	good/fine/well; to be good/ to be well/to be fine
hǎo	好	very
hǎo ba	好吧	all right/fine
hǎo yǒu	好友	good friend
hǎo zhǔyì	好主意	good idea
hǎochī	好吃	tasty/delicious
háohuá tàofáng	豪华套房	deluxe suite
hǎokàn	好看	to be nice/to be good-looking
hàomǎ	号码	number
hé	和	and
hē	喝	to drink
hěn	很	very; very much
hěnduō	很多	many/much/a lot
hésuàn	合算	good bargain
hónglǜ dēng	红绿灯	traffic light
hòu	后	after/in . . . later
hòuchē shì	候车室	waiting room (at the station)
huá qiáo	华侨	overseas Chinese
huài le	坏了	to have broken/does not work
huán	还	to return
huàn	换	to change
huáng	黄	yellow
huānyíng	欢迎	to welcome
huì	会	can/to be able to
huì . . . de	会 . . . 的	will

huí jiàn	回见	see you later
huídá	回答	to answer
huílai	回来	to return/come back
hùliánwǎng	互联网	internet
hūnlǐ	婚礼	wedding
huǒchē piào	火车票	train ticket
huǒchē zhàn	火车站	railway station
hùshi	护士	nurse
hùzhào	护照	passport
jí	急	hurry/to be urgent/urgent
jì	寄	to post
jǐ	几	several; how many?
jī	鸡	chicken
jī dīng	鸡丁	diced chicken
jí shì	急事	urgent matter
jiā	家	home; family [measure word]
jiā	加	plus
jiàn	件	[measure word for clothes and matters]
jiān	间	[measure word for rooms]
jiàndào	见到	to meet
jiàng	酱	sauce
jiǎng	讲	to tell
jiànmiàn	见面	to meet
jiǎntǐ zì	简体字	simplified characters
jiào	叫	to call/to be called
jiàoxǐng fúwù	叫醒服务	wake-up call
jīchǎng	机场	airport
jìde	记得	to remember
jīdòng	激动	to be excited/exciting
jiè	借	to lend
jiē	接	to collect/to meet (somebody)
jiéhūn	结婚	to be married
jièshào	介绍	to introduce
jīhū	几乎	almost
jìjié	季节	season
jīn	斤	half a kilo
jīn nián	今年	this year
jìn qù/lái	进去/来	to go in/to come in
jīng jù	京剧	Peking Opera
jǐngchá	警察	police; policeman/policewoman
jīnglǐ	经理	manager

jīntiān	今天	today
jīntiān wǎnshang	今天晚上	this evening/tonight
jìrán . . . jiù . . .	既然 . . . 就 . . .	as . . . then
jiù	就	[emphatic word]
jiǔ	久	long
jiù . . . le	就 . . . 了	[emphatic structure]
jiù shì . . .	就是 . . .	the only thing is . . . ; that is . . .
jiǔbā	酒吧	bar
jiǔdiàn	酒店	hotel (luxurious)
jìzhě	记者	journalist
jú	局	bureau/office
juéde	觉得	to think/to feel
juédìng	决定	to decide/decision
kāfēi	咖啡	coffee
kāi	开	to be open/to open; to leave
kāi huì	开会	to attend a meeting/to attend a conference
kāi mén	开门	to be open/to open
kāi shuǐ	开水	boiled water
kàn	看	to see/to visit/to watch/to read
kàn de jiàn	看得见	to be able to see/can see
kàn yīshēng/kàn dàfu	看医生/看大夫	to see a doctor
kànshangqu	看上去	to look/to seem
kǎo	烤	to roast
kè	刻	quarter
kèfáng fúwù	客房服务	room service
kèhù	客户	client
késòu	咳嗽	cough
kěxī	可惜	pity that . . .
kěyǐ	可以	could/can/may
kòng	空	vacant/available; free
kǒngpà	恐怕	I'm afraid . . .
kōngtiáo	空调	air-conditioning
kuài	快	soon/quickly/to be fast/ to be quick; nearly; hurry up
kuài	块	[currency word]
kuàijì	会计	accountant
kuàizi	筷子	chopsticks
lā dùzi	拉肚子	to have diarrhoea
lái	来	to come/to come to; to arrive
láixìn	来信	letter
làjiāo	辣椒	chilli

làngmàn	浪漫	to be romantic/romantic
lǎo	老	to be old/old
lǎobǎn	老板	boss
lǎoshi shuō	老实说	frankly speaking/to be honest
le	了	[grammar word]
lèi	累	to be tired
lěng	冷	to be cold/cold
lǐ	里	inside/in
liàng	辆	[measure word for vehicle]
liǎng	两	two; unit of weight
liáng shuǐ	凉水	cold water
lièchē	列车	train
lièchēyuán	列车员	train attendant
lìhai	厉害	serious
lǐngdài	领带	tie
línshí	临时	last minute/temporary
línyù	淋浴	shower
lǐwù	礼物	presents/gifts
lìzhī	荔枝	lychee
lù	路	route/road
lǜ	绿	green
lǚdiàn	旅店	hotel (mid-range)
lǚguǎn	旅馆	hotel (mid-range)
lùkǒu	路口	crossroads
Lúndūn	伦敦	London
lǚyóu	旅游	tourism/to travel
ma	吗	[question word]
mài	卖	to sell
mǎi	买	to buy
mǎi dān	买单	to settle the bill/bill (please)
mǎi dōngxi	买东西	go shopping/do shopping
mài guāng le	卖光了	to be sold out
māma	妈妈	mother/mum
màn	慢	slow; slowly
máng	忙	to be busy/busy
máo	毛	[currency word]
máoyī	毛衣	sweater/jumper
màoyì	贸易	trading/trade
měi	美	to be beautiful/beautiful
měi	每	every
méi guānxi	没关系	It doesn't matter./It's all right./It's ok.

méi shénme	没什么	nothing
méi wèntí	没问题	no problem
méiyǒu	没有	not
miàntiáo	面条	noodles
míng nián	明年	next year
míngtiān	明天	tomorrow
míngxìnpiàn	明信片	postcard
míngzi	名字	name
mínǐ bā	迷你吧	mini-bar
mìshū	秘书	secretary
mōshangqu	摸上去	it feels . . .
nà	那	that [demonstrative pronoun]
nǎ	哪	which
nà hái yòng shuō	那还用说	it goes without saying; of course
nǎ yī wèi	哪一位	Who is it speaking?
nàge	那个	that [pronoun]
nǎlǐ	哪里	whereabouts; not at all
nàme	那么	in that case
nán	男	male; men's
nán	难	to be difficult/difficult
nánde	男的	the man
nǎr	哪儿	where
néng	能	can/could
nǐ	你	you
nǐ hǎo	你好	how do you do?/hello
nǐ juédìng	你决定	You decide.
nǐ kàn	你看	Have a look.
nǐ tài duì le	你太对了	You are so right.
nǐ zuìhǎo	你最好	you'd better
nián	年	year
niánqīng	年轻	to be young/young
nǐde	你的	your/yours
nǐmende	你们的	your/yours [plural]
nín	您	you [polite form]
nín ne	您呢	What about you?/And you?
niúròu	牛肉	beef
nǚ	女	female
nǚ'ér	女儿	daughter
nǚde	女的	woman
pāi	拍	to take/to shoot
péngyou	朋友	friend
piányi	便宜	to be cheap/cheap/inexpensive

piào	票	ticket
piāoliang	漂亮	to be beautiful/beautiful
píjiǔ	啤酒	beer
píng	瓶	[measure word]
píngguǒ	苹果	apple
qí	骑	to ride
qǐ chuáng	起床	to get up
qǐ fēi	起飞	to take off
qián	前	ago/before
qián	钱	money
qián tái	前台	reception
qiánbāo	钱包	wallet/purse
qiánmiàn	前面	ahead
qiānzhèng	签证	visa
qǐchuáng	起床	to get up
qīn'àide	亲爱的	dear
qǐng	请	to invite/take someone out; please
qīngchǔ	清楚	to be clear/clearly
qíngkuàng	情况	situation/present condition
qíshí	其实	in fact
qítā	其它	other
qiūtiān	秋天	autumn
qīyuè	七月	July
qù	去	to go
qù nián	去年	last year
ràng	让	to let/to allow
ràng rén	让人	to send for somebody
rè	热	to be hot/hot
rén	人	person/people
rènshi	认识	to know (somebody)/to get to know sb.
róngyì	容易	easy
ruǎnwò	软卧	soft-sleeper
rúguǒ	如果	if
shàng	上	to go to/attend
shàng bān	上班	to go to work/be at work
shàng ge	上个	last
shàng kè	上课	to attend class
shāngdiàn	商店	shop
shāngliang	商量	to discuss/to consult
shāngwù jiān	商务间	executive room
shāo děng	稍等	it won't be long

shéi/shuí	谁	who
shēn	深	dark/deep/to be dark/to be deep
shēngqì	生气	to be angry/to be cross
shénme	什么	what; any/anything
shénme dìfang	什么地方	whereabouts/what place
shénme shíhòu	什么时候	when; any time/whenever
shēntǐ	身体	health
shì	是	be (am, is, are)
shì	事	thing/matter
shì de	是的	yes
shì ma	是吗	Is that so?
shì'a	是啊	yes
shícài	什菜	seasonal vegetables
shìchǎng	市场	market
shífēn	十分	extremely
shíjiān	时间	time
shíyuè	十月	October
shōu	收	to be received by . . . /to receive
shōu dào	收到	to receive
shǒujī	手机	mobile
shòupiào chù	售票处	ticket office
shū	书	book
shū huà	书画	calligraphy and painting
shuài	帅	to be smart/smart
shuāngrén	双人	double
shūdiàn	书店	bookshop
shūfu	舒服	comfortable/to be comfortable
shuì jiào	睡觉	to go to bed/to sleep
shuǐguǒ	水果	fruit
shùnlì	顺利	to be smooth/nice
shuō	说	to speak/to say
shuō lái huà cháng	说来话长	it's a long story
shuōqǐ	说起	to mention/to talk
sīchóu	丝绸	silk
suānlà	酸辣	hot and sour
suì	岁	years old
suǒyǒude	所有的	all
tā	他	he/she/it
tài bàng le	太棒了	Superb!
tài hǎo le	太好了	wonderful
tài . . . le	太 . . . 了	extremely/very much/too
tàitai	太太	wife/Mrs

tāmen	它们	they/them [inanimate objects]
tāmen	他们	they/them
tán	谈	to talk/to chat
tāng	汤	soup
tángcù	糖醋	sweet and sour
tánhuà	谈话	to talk
tào	套	set (of stamps)
táozi	桃子	peach
tèbié	特别	extremely
tiān	天	very
Tiān Tán	天坛	Temple of Heaven
tiáo	条	[measure word]
tīng	听	to listen to
tīng hǎo	听好	to listen carefully
tīngshuō	听说	to have heard
tóng	同	with/and
tóngxué	同学	classmate; pupil, student
tóuténg	头疼	headache
tuì fáng	退房	to check out (of hotel)
tuìxiū	退休	to be retired/retired
wài xiàn	外线	external line
wàiguórén	外国人	foreigner
wán	完	[the completion of an action]
wàng	忘	to forget
wǎng . . . guǎi	往 . . . 拐	to turn
wǎnshang	晚上	evening
wèi	位	[measure word]
wèi	喂	hello [only used on the telephone]
wéijīn	围巾	scarf
wèishēngjiān	卫生间	bathroom, toilet
wèishénme	为什么	why
wèn	问	to ask
wèntí	问题	problem
wǒ	我	I/me
wǒ xiǎng	我想	I think
wǒmen	我们	we
wǒmende	我们的	our/ours
wǔfàn	午饭	lunch
wúxiàn liánjiē	无线连接	wireless connection
xià bān	下班	to finish work
xià chē	下车	to get off
xià cì	下次	next time

xià kè	下课	to finish class
xià yī zhàn	下一站	next stop
xià ge	下个	next
xiàn	线	line [used at the underground station]
xiān	先	first of all
xiànchāo jī	现钞机	cash machine, ATM
xiǎng	想	would like to/to want to; to think
xiāngjiāo	香蕉	banana
xiāngxìn	相信	to believe
xiānsheng	先生	Mr/husband
xiànzài	现在	now
xiǎo	小	little/small/young
xiǎo bīngxiāng	小冰箱	small fridge
xiǎo lóng	小笼	small steamer
xiǎohái	小孩	small children
xiǎojiě	小姐	Miss
xiǎoshí	小时	hour
xiàtiān	夏天	summer
xiàwǔ	下午	afternoon
xiàxuě	下雪	to snow
xiàyǔ	下雨	to rain/raining
xiě	写	to write
xièxie	谢谢	thank you
xǐhuān	喜欢	to like
xìn	信	letter
xīn	新	new/to be new
xíng	行	to be OK/can do/will do
xíng ma	行吗	Is it OK?
xínglǐ	行李	baggage
xīngqī	星期	week
xīngqī'èr	星期二	Tuesday
xīngqītiān	星期天	Sunday
xīnxiān	新鲜	fresh
xǐshǒu chí	洗手池	sink
xǐshoujiān	洗手间	toilet, washroom
xiū	修	to repair/fix
xiūxi	休息	to rest/to take time off work
xué	学	to learn/to study
xūyào	需要	to need/take
yā	鸭	duck
yánsè	颜色	colour

yǎnyuán	演员	actor/actress
yào	要	to want; to be going to
yāo	幺	one
yào kàn qíngkuàng	要看情况	It depends.
yàoshi	钥匙	key
yáténg	牙疼	toothache
yě	也	also/too
yěxǔ	也许	perhaps
yī bēi	一杯	one cup/one glass
yī xiǎo pán	一小盘	a small plate
yīdiǎnr	一点儿	a little bit
yīdìng	一定	definitely/must
yīgòng	一共	altogether
yǐjing	已经	already
yīlù	一路	journey/trip
yīng hàn	英汉	English-Chinese
yīng'ér chuáng	婴儿床	cot
yīnggāi	应该	should/ought to
yīngguó	英国	Britain
yìngwò	硬卧	hard-sleeper
yínháng	银行	bank
yǐnliào	饮料	beverage, drinks
yīnyuèjiā	音乐家	musician
yīqiè	一切	everything
yīshēng	医生	doctor
yīxià	一下	one second
yīxiē	一些	some
yīyàng	一样	to be the same/same
yīyuè	一月	January
yīzhí	一直	all the time
yòng	用	to use
yǒu	有	to have/have got
yǒu (yī)diǎnr	有(一)点儿	a little bit
yǒu kòng	有空	to have time/to be free
yǒu rén	有人	anybody/somebody
yǒu yī tiān	有一天	one day . . .
yǒu yìsi	有意思	to be interesting
yóubiān	邮编	postcode
yǒuhǎo	友好	to be friendly/friendly
yóujú	邮局	post office
yóupiào	邮票	stamp (for letters)
yóuyǒng	游泳	to swim

yóuyǒng chí	游泳池	swimming pool
yú	鱼	fish
yuè	月	month
yùndǒu	熨斗	iron
yùpén	浴盆	bath
zài	在	[continuous particle]
zài	在	to be at/to be in/at/in/on
zài	再	once again
zài ... zhī qián	在 ... 之前	before ... /by
zàijiàn	再见	goodbye
zánmen	咱们	we [colloquial term]
zànshí	暂时	at the moment/temporarily
zǎo	早	early
zǎocān	早餐	breakfast [formal]
zǎofàn	早饭	breakfast
zāogāo	遭糕	Oh, no!
zǎoshang	早上	morning
zázhì	杂志	magazine
zěnme	怎么	how; why
zěnme huí shì	怎么回事	What's the matter?
zěnme yàng	怎么样	How are you?/How are things?
zěnme zǒu	怎么走	How do I get there?/How do I get to ...?
zhá	炸	to deep fry
zhāng	张	[measure word]; [surname]
zhàngfu	丈夫	husband
zhàntái	站台	platform
zhǎo	找	to look for
zhǎo dào	找到	to find something (successfully)
zhàopiàn	照片	photograph
zhe	œf	[grammar word]
zhè	这	this
zhè cì	这次	this time
zhè ge zhōumò	这个周末	this weekend
zhè jiàn shì	这件事	this matter
zhème	这么	so
zhème shuō	这么说	in that case
zhēn	真	really
zhēn bàoqiàn	真抱歉	many apologies
zhēn kěxī	真可惜	What a shame!
zhēn qiǎo	真巧	What a coincidence!; what good luck

zhēn sī	真丝	pure silk
zhēnde	真的	really
zhèxiē	这些	these
. . . zhī xíng	. . . 之行	the trip to . . .
zhīdào	知道	to know/to be aware of
zhǐyǒu	只有	only
zhǒng	种	kind
Zhōngguó	中国	China
Zhōngwén	中文	Chinese [as a language]
zhōngxīn	中心	centre
zhōng xué	中学	secondary/middle school
zhòngyào	重要	important
zhōngyú	终于	finally/in the end/at last
zhōumò	周末	weekend
zhù	住	to live
zhuàngguān	壮观	magnificent
zhuānyè	专业	subject/major
zhuōzi	桌子	table
zhǔyì	主意	idea
zìxíngchē	自行车	bicycle
zǒu	走	to leave; to walk
zúgòude	足够的	enough
zuì	最	most
zuìhǎo	最好	best
zuìhòu	最后	the last
zuìjìn	最近	recently
zuò	坐	to sit/to sit down; to take (e.g. bus)
zuǒ	左	left
zuòjiā	作家	writer
zuótiān	昨天	yesterday
zuǒyòu	左右	about/approximate

English–Chinese glossary

able to see, to be	**kàn de jiàn**	apple	**píngguǒ**
about, approximate	**zuǒ yòu**	approximately/	**dàyuē**
address	**dìzhǐ**	about/around	
afraid: I'm afraid . . .	**kǒngpà**	arrive	**dào/lái**
after/in/ . . . later	**hòu**	as . . . then	**jìrán** . . .
afternoon	**xiàwǔ**		**jiù** . . .
ago/before	**qián**	ask (question)	**wèn**
ahead	**qiánmian**	ask (sb. to do sth.)	**ràng**
all	**suǒyǒude** . . .	at/be at/be in	**zài**
	dōu/dōu	at last/finally	**zhōngyú**
all right	**hái hǎo/**	at the moment/	**zànshí**
	hǎo ba	temporarily	
all right: is it all	**hǎo bù hǎo?/**	attend/take part	**cānjiā**
right?/is it OK?	**xíng ma?**	attend (a meeting/	**kāi huì**
all right: it's all	**méi guānxi**	conference)	
right/it doesn't		August	**bāyuè**
matter/it's OK		autumn	**qiūtiān**
all the time	**yīzhí**	avenue	**dàjiē**
almost	**jīhū**	away/to go	**chūmén**
already	**yǐjing**	away (v.)	
also, too	**yě**	banana	**xiāngjiāo**
altogether	**yīgòng**	bank (financial) (n.)	**yínháng**
American	**Měiguórén**	bar	**jiǔbā**
and	**hé**	bargain, good	**hésuàn**
angry/cross	**shēngqì**	bathroom	**wèishēng jiān**
(pred. adj.)		to be (am, is, are)	**shì**
answer	**huídá**	beautiful (adj.)/	**měi/piàoliang**
any/anything	**shénme**	to be beautiful	
any time/whenever	**shénme**	(pred. adj.)	
	shíhou	to become (v.)	**dāng**
anybody/somebody	**yǒu rén**	beef	**niúròu**
anything else	**biéde**	beer	**píjiǔ**
apology: many	**zhēn bàoqiàn**	before . . . /by . . .	**zài** . . .
apologies			**zhī qián**

Beijing person/ people	**Běijīngrén**	check in (hotel) (v.) chicken/diced	**rù zhù** **jī/jī dīng**
believe (v.)	**xiāngxìn**	chicken	
bicycle (n.)	**zìxíngchē**	children	**háizi**
big, large (adj.)/	**dà**	China	**Zhōngguó**
to be big, large		Chinese (as a	**Zhōngwén**
(pred. adj.)		language)	
block	**dòng**	Chinese New Year	**chūnjié**
boiled rice	**bái mǐ fàn**	city	**chéngshì**
book (n.)	**shū**	classmate	**tóngxué**
bookshop	**shūdiàn**	clear/clearly	**qīngchǔ**
to borrow	**jiè**	close/to be	**guānmén**
boss	**lǎobǎn**	closed (v.)	
breakfast	**zǎofàn**	coffee	**kāfēi**
to bring/take	**dài**	cold (adj.)/to be	**lěng**
Britain	**Yīngguó**	cold (pred. adj.)	
British	**Yīngguórén**	collect/meet	**jiē**
broken down,	**huài le**	(somebody) (v.)	
to be/does		colour (n.)	**yánsè**
not work (v.)		come/come to (v.)	**lái**
brother, elder	**gēge**	come from . . .	**cóng . . . lái**
brother, younger	**dìdi**	to be comfortable	**shūfu**
bureau/office	**jú**	(pred. adj.)	
bus	**gōnggòng**	company	**gōngsī**
	qìchē/chē	compared with	**bǐ**
to be busy	**máng**	computer	**diànnao**
(pred. adj.)		contain (v.)	**hán**
but	**dànshì**	country	**guó**
buy (v.)	**mǎi**	crossroads	**lùkǒu**
call/called (v.)	**jiào**	dark (colour)	**shēng**
can/be able to	**huì**	date (n.)	**hào**
can/could (ability)	**néng**	daughter	**nǚ'ér**
can/could/may	**kěyi**	day	**tiān**
(permission)		dear	**qīn'àide**
car	**chē**	decide (v.)/	**juédìng;**
case: in that case	**nà: zhème**	decision (n.);	**Nǐ juédìng.**
	shuō nàme	You decide.	
celebrate/spend (v.)	**guò**	deep fry (v.)	**zhá**
change (v.)	**huàn**	definitely	**yīdìng**
to be cheap	**piányi**	depart (v.)	**fāchē**
(pred. adj.)		department store	**bǎihuò**
check (v.)	**chá**		**shāngdiàn**

depend: it depends	yào kàn qíngkuàng	fact: in fact	qíshí
deputy/vice	fù	family	jiā
difficult, to be (pred. adj.)	nán	fast	kuài
		father/dad	bàba
dining room (public)	cāntīng	feel: it feels (with hands) . . .	mōshangqu . . .
discuss/consult (v.)	shāngliang	female	nǚ
do (v.)	gàn	find (v.)	zhǎo
do not	bié	find, not easy to	bù hǎo zhǎo
do/does/are/is . . . or . . . ?	háishi	fine, to be (pred. adj.)	hǎo
double room	shuāngrén fángjiān	finish (work)	xià bān
drink (v.)	hē	first	dì yī
duck (n.)	yā	first of all	xiān
early/to be early (adj./adv./ pred.adj.)	zǎo	first time/for the first time	dì yī cì
		fish (n.)	yú
east	dōng	flatter (v.): I'm flattered	guò jiǎng
eat (v.)	chī		
eight	bā	floor/layer	céng
enough	zúgòu de	follow	gēn
enough, to be (pred. adj.)	gòu	following day	dì èr tiān
		forget	wàng
evening; this evening/tonight	wǎnshang; jīntiān wǎnshang	found, to have	zhǎo dào
		frankly speaking/ to be honest	lǎoshí shuō
every	měi	free, to be	yǒu kòng/yǒu shíjiān
everything	yīqiè		
to be excited/ exciting	jīdòng	fresh	xīnxiān
		friend; good friend	péngyou; hǎo yǒu
excuse me/I'm sorry	duìbùqǐ		
expensive, to be (pred. adj.)	guì	friendly from . . . to . . .	yǒuhǎo cóng . . . dào . . .
extension	fēnjī	fruit	shuíguǒ
extremely		full	bǎo
extremely/very	fēicháng/ tèbié/ shífēn/ tài . . . le	get off	xià chē
		get up	qǐchuáng
		give (v.)	gěi
		give (change in shops) (v.)	zhǎo

glad, to be (pred. adj.)	gāoxìng	how are you?/how are things?	zěnme yàng?
go/go to (v.)	qù	how do I get there?/how do I get to . . .?	Zěnme zǒu?
go into (v.)	jìn qu		
go shopping	mǎi dōngxi		
go to (school)	shàng	how do you do?/ hello	nǐ hǎo
go to work	shàng bān		
good (adj.)/to be good (pred. adj.)	hǎo	how long	duō jiǔ
		how many?	jǐ/duō shǎo
good-looking, to be (pred. adj.)	hǎokàn	how much?	duō shǎo
		how much is it?	duō shǎo qián?
goodbye	zàijiàn		
Great Wall	Cháng Chéng	however/but	búguò
green	lǜ	hundred	bǎi
guess (v.)	cāi	hungry, to be (pred. adj.)	è
Hainan Island	Hǎinán Dǎo		
half	bàn	hurry up (adv.)	kuài
half a kilo	yī jīn	husband	zhàngfu/ xiānsheng/ àiren
happen to	gānghǎo		
happy, to be (pred. adj.)	gāoxìng		
		I/me	wǒ
hard-sleeper (on a train)	yìngwò	idea, good	hǎo zhǔyi
		ideally	zuìhǎo
have/has (v.)	yǒu	if	rúguǒ
have (to include) (v.)	dài	incorrect	bú duì
have to/must	děi	inside	lǐ
he/him	tā	interesting, to be (pred. adj.)	yǒu yìsi
health	shēntǐ		
hear (v.)	tīng	internet	hùliángwǎng
hear clearly, did not	méi tīng qīng	introduce	jièshào
heard, have	tīngshuō	January	yīyuè
hello (only used on the telephone)	wéi	journey/trip	yīlù
		July	qīyuè
here you are	géi nǐ	just/just a second	gāng/shāo děng
home	jiā		
hot (adj.)/to be hot (pred. adj.)	rè	key (n.)	yàoshi
		kind (sort)	zhǒng
hot and sour	suānlà	king prawn	dà xiā
hotel	fàndiàn	know (somebody)	rènshi
hour	xiǎoshí	know/be aware of	zhīdào
how	zěnme	large one/big one	dà de

last (previous)	shàng ge	married	jiēhūn
last (not first)	zuìhòu	matter (this)	zhè jiàn shì
last minute/	línshí	meet	jiànmiàn/
temporary			jiàndào
late	chí	mention/talk	shuōqǐ
learn/study (v.)	xué	menu	càidān
leave (v.)	zǒu	minute (telling the	fēn
left (adj.)	zuǒ	time)	
lend	jiè	minute (duration of	fēnzhōng
let/allow	ràng	time)	
letter (mail)	xìn	Miss	xiǎojie
lift (n.)	diàntī	mobile phone	shǒu jī
light bulb	diàn dēng	money	qián
like (v.)	xǐhuān	month	yuè
listen carefully	tīng hǎo	more	duō
listen to	tīng	more than/over	duō
a little/some	diǎnr	morning	zǎoshang
a little bit	yīdiǎnr/yǒu	most	zuì
	(yī)diǎnr	mother/mum	māma
little, small (adj.)/to	xiǎo	Mr	xiānsheng
be little, to be		Mrs	tàitai
small (pred. adj.)		must	bìxū/děi
live (v.)	zhù	name	míngzi
local	dāngdì	near by/close by	fùjìn
London	Lúndūn	nearly	kuài
long (adj.)	jiǔ	need (v.)	xūyào
long (adj.)/to be	cháng	need, do not	bú yòng
long (pred. adj.)		new (adj.)/to be	xīn
look around	guàng	new (pred. adj.)	
look for	zhǎo	next	xià ge
look/seem	kànshangqu	next door	gébì
look, have a	nǐ kàn	next stop	xià yī zhàn
to love	ài	next time	xià cì
lunch	wǔfàn	next year	míng nián
lychee	lìzhī	nice (adj.)/to be	hǎo/hǎokàn
male	nán	nice (pred. adj.)	
man	nánde	no	bú shì
management	guǎnlǐ	noisy	chǎo
manager	jīnglǐ	noodles	miàntiáo
many/much	hěnduō	not	bù/méi/
map	dìtú		méiyǒu
market	shìchǎng	not bad	bú cuò

not really/not at all	nǎlǐ	postcode	yóubiān
nothing	méi shénme	presents	lǐwù
now	xiànzài	primary school	xiǎo xué
number	hàomǎ/cì/hào	problem; no	wèntí; méi
o'clock	diǎn	problem	wèntí
October	shíyuè	promise (v.)	bǎozhèng
office	bàngōngshì	public (adj.)	gōngyòng
often/always/	cháng	quarter	kè
frequently		a quarter of a kilo	bàn jīn
OK	hǎo de/xíng	quite/rather/	bǐjiào
old (adj.)/to be old	lǎo/dà	relatively	
(pred. adj.)		quite good/quite	bú cuò
once	yīcì	well	
once again	zài	railway station	huǒchē zhàn
one	yī yāo	rain/raining	xiàyǔ
one cup	yī bēi	really	zhēn
one day . . .	yǒu yī tiān	really?/is that so?	shì ma?/zhēn
	. . .		de?
only	zhǐyǒu	receive	shōu dào
the only thing	jiù shì . . .	received by . . . /	shōu
is . . .		receive	
open (something)	kāi	recently	zuìjìn
open (v.)/to be open	kāimén	remember	jìde
(pred. adj.)		repair (v.)	xiū
orange juice	chéngzi zhī	report (n.)	bàogào
order (food) (v.)	diǎn cài	require/need	xūyào
other	qítā/biéde	rest/take time off	xiūxi
our/ours	wǒmende	work	
pancake	bǐng	restaurant	cān'guǎn
parents	fúmǔ	retired (adj.)/to be	tuìxiū
pass (v.)	dì	retired (pred. adj.)	
peach	táozi	return (v.)	huílai
perhaps	yěxǔ	return (give back)	huán
person/people	rén	ride (v.)	qí
photograph	zhàopiān	right: You are so	Nǐ tài duì le.
pity that . . .	kěxī	right.	
plan (v.)	dǎsuàn	roast duck	kǎo yā
please	qǐng	romantic (adj.)	làngmàn
pleased, to be	gāoxìng	room	fángjiān
(pred. adj.)		route/road	lù
plus	jiā	same	yīyàng
post office	yóujú	sauce	jiàng

scarf	wéijīn	sold out	mài guāng le
scenery	fēngjǐng	some	yīxiē
seafood	hǎixiān	son	érzi
season	jìjié	soon/quickly	kuài
seasonal vegetables	shícài	sorry: I'm sorry/ excuse me	duìbuqǐ
secondary/middle school	zhōng xué	soup	tāng
		speak/say (v.)	shuō
secretary	mìshū	spring (season) (n.)	chūntiān
see/visit/watch/read	kàn	starving	è sǐ le
see to/handle	chǔlǐ	stay (v.)	dāi
see you again/see you later	huíjiàn	steamed bun with filling	bāozi
sell	mài	still/also	hái
send for someone	ràng rén	stir-fry (v.)	chǎo
seven	qī	strawberry	cǎoméi
several	jǐ	subject/major (academic)	zhuānyè
she/her	tā		
shop	shāngdiàn	successful (adj.)/ success (n.)	chénggōng
should/ought to	yīnggāi		
side (n.)	biān	summer	xiàtiān
silk; pure silk	sīchóu; zhēn sī	Sunday	xīngqītiān
		Superb!	Tài bàng le!
single	dān	supermarket	chāoshì
sit/sit down	zuò	sweater/jumper	máoyī
situation/present condition	qíngkuàng	sweet and sour	tángcù
		swim (v.)	yóuyǒng
sleep (v.) (n.)	shuìjiào	swimming pool	yóuyǒng chí
slowly (adv.)/slow (adj.)	màn	take (sb. to somewhere) (v.)	dài . . . qù
small (adj.)/to be small (pred. adj.)	xiǎo	take (a picture)/ shoot	pāi
small children	xiǎohái	take (bus)	zuò/chéng
small one	xiǎo de	talk/chat (v.)	tánhuà/tán
small plate	yī xiǎo pán	talk (about)	shuōqǐ
smart (well dressed)	shuài	taste (v.)	cháng
smooth, to be (pred. adj.)	shùnlì	tasty, to be (pred. adj.)	hǎochī
snow (v.)	xiàxuě	taxi	chūzūchē
so	zhème	tea	chá
soft-sleeper (on a train)	ruǎnwò	telephone (n.)	diànhuà
		telephone (v.)	dǎ diànhuà

tell	gàosu	two	liǎng
tell/narrate	jiǎngjiang	understand	dǒng
Temple of Heaven	Tiān Tán	underground/	dìtiě
ten	shí	subway	
thank you	xièxie	university	dàxué
thanks: many	duō xiè	university	dà xuésheng
thanks		student	
that	nà/nà ge	until (up to)	dào
that is	jiù shì	urgent	jí
there	nàr	urgent matter	jí shì
these	zhèxiē	use	yòng
thing (an issue, a	shì	vacant	kòng
matter)		various/various	gè zhǒng
thing (an item/	dōngxi	kinds	
object)		very	hěn/hǎo
think/feel	juéde	very much	hěn
think: I think . . .	wó xiǎng . . .	walk (v.)	zǒu/zǒulù
this	zhè	wallet/purse	qiánbāo
ticket	piào	want (something)	yào
ticket office	shòupiào chù	way: by the way	duì le
tie (n.)	lǐngdài	we [colloquial]	zánmen
time; this time	shíjiān; zhè cì	we/us	wǒmen
time: have time/	yǒu kòng/	wear (v.)	chuān
make time	chōu kòng	wedding	hūnlǐ
tired, to be (pred.	lèi	week	xīngqī
adj.)		weekend; this	zhōumò; zhè
to/for (somebody)	gěi	weekend	ge zhōumò
today	jīntiān	welcome (v.); you	huānyíng; bú
tofu	dòufu	are welcome	kèqi
toilet	cèsuǒ	well, to be (pred.	hǎo
tomorrow	míngtiān	adj.)	
tourist guide	dǎoyóu	what	shénme
(person)		What good luck!	zhēn qiǎo
traffic light	hónglǜ dēng	What a shame!	Zhēn kěxī!
train	lièchē	What about you?/	Nín ne?/Nǐne?
train ticket	huǒchē piào	And you?	
tram/streetcar	diànchē	What's the matter?	Zěnme huí
travel (n.) (v.)	lǚyóu		shì?
(the) trip to	zhī xíng	when (question)	shénme
Tuesday	xīngqī'èr		shíhou
turn (v.)	wǎng . . .	when/while	. . . de shíhou
	guǎi	(statement)	

where/what place	**năr/shénme dìfang**	write	**xiě**
where exactly/ whereabouts	**náli**	wrong (to have done something wrong) (adv.)	**cuò**
which	**nă/něi**	year; this year/last year	**nián; jīn nián/ qù nián**
who	**shéi/shuí**		
Who is it speaking?	**Nă yī wèi?**	. . . years old	**suì**
		yellow	**huáng**
whoops!	**āiyō!**	yes	**shì de**
why	**wèishénme**	yesterday	**zuótiān**
wife	**tàitai/qīzi/ àiren**	you	**nĭ**
		you [polite form]	**nín**
will (v.)	**huì . . . de**	young (adj.)/to be young (pred. adj.)	**niánqīng**
winter	**dōngtiān**		
with	**tóng/hé**		
wonderful	**tài hăo le**	your/yours	**nĭde**
work (n.) (v.)	**gōngzuò**	your/yours [pl.]	**nĭmende**
would like/want (to do)	**xiăng**		

Appendix A
Useful signs

The characters introduced in the book are simplified. In this appendix, complex characters (traditional form) are placed alongside their simplified versions whenever they differ from them. This appendix consists of those character signs that are introduced in the Character section of each lesson and some other useful signs.

English	Simplified form	Complex form	Pinyin
airport	飞机场	飛機場	**fēijīchǎng**
America	美国	美國	**Měiguó**
bank	银行	銀行	**yínháng**
bar	酒吧		**jiǔba**
barber shop	理发店	理髮店	**lǐfǎ diàn**
Beijing	北京		**Běijīng**
bookshop	书店	書店	**shū diàn**
Britain	英国	英國	**Yīngguó**
bus stop	公共汽车站	公共汽車站	**gōnggòng qìchē zhàn**
chemist's	药店	藥店	**yào diàn**
China	中国	中國	**Zhōngguó**
cinema	电影院	電影院	**diàn yǐng yuàn**
clothes shop	服装店	服裝店	**fúzhuāng diàn**
cold drinks	冷饮	冷飲	**lěng yǐn**
dining hall/restaurant	餐厅	餐廳	**cāntīng**
entrance	进口	進口	**jìnkǒu**
entrance	入口		**rùkǒu**
exit/way out	出口		**chūkǒu**
Forbidden City	故宫	故宮	**Gù Gōng**
Great Wall	长城	長城	**Cháng Chéng**
Guangzhou	广州	廣州	**Guǎngzhōu**
Guilin	桂林		**Guìlín**
hairdresser	发廊	發廊	**fāláng**
Hong Kong	香港		**Xiāng Gǎng**
hospital	医院	醫院	**yīyuàn**
hotel	饭店	飯店	**fàndiàn**

information/enquiry	问询处	問詢處	**wènxún chǔ**
Ladies'	女		**nǚ**
left-luggage	行李寄存处	行李寄存處	**xínglǐ jìcún chǔ**
library	图书馆	圖書館	**túshūguǎn**
lift	电梯	電梯	**diàntī**
meat	肉		**ròu**
Men's	男		**nán**
menu	菜单	菜單	**càidān**
museum	博物馆	博物館	**bówùguǎn**
no photographs	请勿拍照	請勿拍照	**qǐng wù pāi zhào**
no smoking	请勿吸烟	請勿吸煙	**qǐng wù xīyān**
police station	警察局	警察局	**jǐngchá jú**
post office	邮局	郵局	**yóujú**
public phone	公用电话	公用電話	**gōngyòng diànhuà**
railway station	火车站	火車站	**huǒchē zhàn**
restaurant	餐馆	餐館	**cān'guǎn**
Shanghai	上海		**Shànghǎi**
Shenzhen [city]	深圳		**Shēn zhèn**
shop	商店		**shāngdiàn**
sterling pound	英镑	英鎊	**yīng bàng**
supermarket	超市		**chāoshì**
swimming pool	游泳池	游泳池	**yóuyǒng chí**
Taiwan	台湾	台灣	**Táiwān**
taxi	出租车	出租車	**chūzūchē**
Temple of Heaven	天坛	天壇	**Tiān Tán**
ticket office	售票处	售票處	**shòupiào chǔ**
toilet	厕所	廁所	**cèsuǒ**
toilet	洗手间	洗手間	**xǐshǒujiān**
toilet	卫生间	衛生間	**wèishēngjiān**
travel agency	旅行社		**lǚxíng shè**
underground/subway	地铁	地鐵	**dìtiě**
US dollars	美元		**měi yuán**
vegetable	蔬菜		**shūcài**
vegetarian restaurant	素菜馆	素菜館	**sùcài guǎn**
Xi'an	西安		**Xī'ān**

Appendix B

Table of combinations of the initials and finals in *Putonghua*

I† \ F†	a	o	e	er	ai	ei	ao	ou	an	en	ang	eng	ong	i	i*	ia	iao	ie	…
	a	o	e	er	ai	ei	ao	ou	an	en	ang	eng		yi		ya	yao	ye	y
b	ba	bo			bai	bei	bao		ban	ben	bang	beng		bi			biao	bie	
p	pa	po			pai	pei	pao	pou	pan	pen	pang	peng		pi			piao	pie	
m	ma	mo	me		mai	mei	mao	mou	man	men	mang	meng		mi			miao	mie	m
f	fa	fo				fei		fou	fan	fen	fang	feng							
d	da		de		dai	dei	dao	dou	dan	den	dang	deng	dong	di			diao	die	d
t	ta		te		tai		tao	tou	tan		tang	teng	tong	ti			tiao	tie	
n	na		ne		nai	nei	nao	nou	nan	nen	nang	neng	nong	ni			niao	nie	n
l	la		le		lai	lei	lao	lou	lan		lang	leng	long	li		lia	liao	lie	l
z	za		ze		zai	zei	zao	zou	zan	zen	zang	zeng	zong		zi				
c	ca		ce		cai		cao	cou	can	cen	cang	ceng	cong		ci				
s	sa		se		sai		sao	sou	san	sen	sang	seng	song		si				
zh	zha		zhe		zhai	zhei	zhao	zhou	zhan	zhen	zhang	zheng	zhong		zhi				
ch	cha		che		chai		chao	chou	chan	chen	chang	cheng	chong		chi				
sh	sha		she		shai	shei	shao	shou	shan	shen	shang	sheng			shi				
r			re				rao	rou	ran	ren	rang	reng	rong		ri				
j														ji		jia	jiao	jie	j
q														qi		qia	qiao	qie	
x														xi		xia	xiao	xie	x
g	ga		ge		gai	gei	gao	gou	gan	gen	gang	geng	gong						
k	ka		ke		kai	kei	kao	kou	kan	ken	kang	keng	kong						
h	ha		he		hai	hei	hao	hou	han	hen	hang	heng	hong						

† I stands for 'initial'; F stands for 'final'.

* See pp. 2–5 for pronunciation.

n	in	iang	ing	iong	u	ua	uo	uai	ui	uan	un	uang	ueng	ü	üe	üan	ün
an	yin	yang	ying	yong	wu	wa	wo	wai	wei	wan	wen	wang	weng	yu	yue	yuan	yun
an	bin		bing		bu												
an	pin		ping		pu												
ian	min		ming		mu												
					fu												
an			ding		du		duo		dui	duan	dun						
an			ting		tu		tuo		tui	tuan	tun						
an	nin	niang	ning		nu		nuo			nuan				nü	nüe		
an	lin	liang	ling		lu		luo			luan	lun			lü	lüe		
					zu		zuo		zui	zuan	zun						
					cu		cuo		cui	cuan	cun						
					su		suo		sui	suan	sun						
					zhu	zhua	zhuo	zhuai	zhui	zhuan	zhun	zhuang					
					chu	chua	chuo	chuai	chui	chuan	chun	chuang					
					shu	shua	shuo	shuai	shui	shuan	shun	shuang					
					ru	rua	ruo		rui	ruan	run						
an	jin	jiang	jing	jiong										ju	jue	juan	jun
an	qin	qiang	qing	qiong										qu	que	quan	qun
an	xin	xiang	xing	xiong										xu	xue	xuan	xun
					gu	gua	guo	guai	gui	guan	gun	guang					
					ku	kua	kuo	kuai	kui	kuan	kun	kuang					
					hu	hua	huo	huai	hui	huan	hun	huang					

Appendix C
Dialogues in characters for Lessons 1 to 3

1 初次见面

DIALOGUE 1　你好！

WÁNG LÍN	您是史密斯先生吗？
DAVID SMITH	是的，您是...？
WÁNG LÍN	你好，史密斯先生。我是王林。
DAVID SMITH	你好，王先生。很高兴见到你。
WÁNG LÍN	我也很高兴见到你。请叫我老王吧。
DAVID SMITH	好吧，老王。叫我大卫吧。
WÁNG LÍN	好的，大卫。欢迎你来中国。

DIALOGUE 2　你累吗？

LǍO WÁNG	你一路顺利吗？
DAVID	很顺利，谢谢。
LǍO WÁNG	你累吗?
DAVID	有一点儿累。
LǍO WÁNG	你想喝一杯咖啡吗？
DAVID	太想了。
...	
LǍO WÁNG	这是你的咖啡，大卫。
DAVID	谢谢。
LǍO WÁNG	不客气。

2 姓名，国籍和年龄

DIALOGUE 1 你叫什么？

FĀNG CHŪN	你会说中文吗？
AMY	会说一点儿。
FĀNG CHŪN	太好了。我叫方春，叫我小方吧。你叫什么？
AMY	我叫艾米。
FĀNG CHŪN	你是英国人吗？
AMY	不是。
FĀNG CHŪN	你是哪国人？
AMY	你猜。
FĀNG CHŪN	我不知道。
AMY	我是美国人。你是哪里人，小方？
FĀNG CHŪN	我是北京人。你的中文很好。
AMY	哪里，哪里。

DIALOGUE 2 你多大了？

AMY	小方，你今年多大了？
XIĂO FĀNG	我三十二岁了。
AMY	真的？你看上去二十五岁左右。
XIĂO FĀNG	过奖。你多大了？
AMY	我二十一。
XIĂO FĀNG	你真年轻。这么说，我应该是老方。
AMY	对不起，请慢一点儿说。
XIĂO FĀNG	我应该是老方。
AMY	不对，不对。你是'小方'。
...	
XIĂO FĀNG	认识你，我很高兴。
AMY	我也是，小方。
XIĂO FĀNG	再见，艾米。
AMY	再见，小方。

3 在公司的聚会上

DIALOGUE 1 怎么样？

AMY	小兰，好久不见，你怎么样？
XIĂOLÁN	我很好。你好吗，艾米？你看上去有点儿累。
AMY	我是很累。最近我的工作很忙。延中怎么样？
XIĂOLÁN	还好，谢谢。他昨天出门了。
AMY	去哪儿了？
XIĂOLÁN	美国。下个星期回来。你的男朋友来了吗？
AMY	来了。
...	
AMY	大卫，让我介绍一下。这是我的好朋友小兰。小兰，这是我的男朋友，大卫。
DAVID	你好，小兰。见到你我很高兴。
XIĂOLÁN	我也是，大卫。我们终于见面了。

DIALOGUE 2 他结婚了吗？

LÍN FĀNG	小兰，那两个人是谁？
XIĂOLÁN	男的叫大卫，是我们公司的副经理。
LÍN FĀNG	他真帅。你知道他结婚了吗？
XIĂOLÁN	没有结婚。不过，他有女朋友了。
LÍN FĀNG	唉！真可惜。
XIĂOLÁN	为什么？
LÍN FĀNG	没什么。那个女的是谁？
XIĂOLÁN	她就是大卫的女朋友。她叫艾米。

Appendix D
English translations of dialogues from Lesson 6 to Lesson 15

Please note that the translation of the dialogues below sometimes may not use the exact wording as the translations of words and phrases in the Vocabulary sections. This is because the dialogues have been translated into colloquial English.

Lesson 6

Dialogue 1: What day is it today?

T   Hello, pupils!
AP Hello, teacher!
T   What day is it today?
PA Today is Tuesday.
T   How many days are there in a week?
PB There are seven days in a week.
T   How many months are there in a year?
PC There are twelve months in a year.
T   What's tomorrow's date?
PD Tomorrow is 18th January 2008.
T   How many seasons are there in a year and what are they?
PE Four seasons, and they are spring, summer, autumn and winter.

Dialogue 2: When . . .?

M   Li Fang, is it cold in Beijing in the winter?
L   Extremely cold. It often snows.
M   How about the summer?
L   July and August are very hot.
M   What is the best season?
L   Autumn, around October. Why, are you planning to go to Beijing?

M   Yes
L   When?
M   As you've said that October is best, I'll go in October next year.
L   Are you going there to travel or to work?
M   Travel plus work.
L   How long are you going for, Mick?
M   Travelling for two weeks and working for three days.
    Altogether about three weeks.

Lesson 7

Dialogue 1: Where is . . .?

(a) *Inside a hotel*
YOU   Where is the toilet/bar/lift/public phone, please?
CHINESE   On the left of the dining-room.

(b) *In the street*
YOU   Is there a supermarket nearby?
CHINESE   Yes. Can you see the traffic lights ahead?
YOU   Yes, I can.
CHINESE   When you get to the traffic lights, turn right. I remember
          there is one there.

(c) *In the street*
YOU   Could you tell me which bus to take to go to the railway
          station?
CHINESE   No need to take the bus. It takes ten minutes to walk
          there.
YOU   How do I get there?
CHINESE   Turn east at the first junction.

Dialogue 2: Borrowing a bike

D   Can I borrow your bike?
L   Of course you can. Where are you going?
D   I am going to the Bank of China on Jianguo Road to change
    some money.
L   Do you know how to get there?
D   No. But I think I can find it.

L I don't believe you. You'd better check the map first.
D Good idea. How long does it take approximately to cycle there?
L About half an hour. If you pass by a post office, could you post a letter for me?
D No problem.

Lesson 8

Dialogue 1: How much is it?

S Hello. What would you like to buy?
A I'd like to buy some fruit.
S Have a look. We've got fresh strawberries, Hainan Island bananas and various kinds of apples.
A What are these?
S Lychees.
A How much are they per *jin*?
S Fifteen *kuai* and eight *mao*.
A I'll have one *jin* of lychees. How much are strawberries?
S Twelve *kuai* and five *mao* per *jin*.
A I'll have half a *jin* of strawberries. Do you have peaches?
S No, sorry. Anything else?
A No, thank you.
S Altogether twenty-two *kuai* and five *fen*.
A Here are thirty *kuai*.
S OK. Here is your change – eight *kuai* seven *mao* and five *fen*.
A Thanks.

Dialogue 2: It's too expensive

D Xiao Fan, are the shops closed on Sundays?
F No. All the shops, banks and post offices are open. Why, do you want to do some shopping?
D Yes. I'd like to buy several silk scarves for my wife, some presents for the kids and friends.
F That's not difficult. I can take you to a department store.
D You are so kind. Many thanks.
D Miss, how much is this silk tie?

S   Two hundred and fifty *yuan* for one.
D   It's too expensive.
S   Two hundred *yuan*, is that OK?
D   How about three hundred and fifty *yuan* for two?
S   All right, all right.
D   I'll take them.

Lesson 9

Dialogue 1: Which is better?

P   Xiao Liu, out of these two jumpers, which one do you think is better?
L   I think the green one is better than the yellow one. Green suits you quite well.
P   OK. I'll take your advice.

P   Oh, no! I forgot to bring my wallet. Xiao Liu, could you lend me some money?
L   No problem. How much do you need?
P   Three hundred *kuai*, is that OK?
L   Yes. Is it enough?
P   Yes, it is.
L   Here you are.
P   Thanks a lot. I'll definitely return the money tomorrow.
L   There's no hurry. Shall we go and have a look in the bookshop? I'd like to buy a couple of books.
P   OK.

Dialogue 2: It's a bargain

J   Sorry. I'm late.
Y   That's all right. I've just arrived.
J   I finished work early today and went to have a look around the clothes market.
Y   Is there any good stuff?
J   Yes, a lot. Shame I didn't have enough money with me.
     I bought er . . . how do you say 'jumper' in Chinese?
Y   *Maoyi.*

J   Right. I bought a jumper.
Y   Let me have a look. (. . . .) Really good. It feels very
    comfortable. How much was it?
J   Over eighty *kuai*.
Y   It's really cheap. A real bargain. I like this colour very much.
    Are there any more of those left?
J   Dark red is sold out. This was the last one. But there are
    many other nice colours.
Y   I'm not working tomorrow. I'll find some time to go and have a look.

Lesson 10

Dialogue 1: Ready to order?

W   Good evening! How many of you?
L   Three.
W   Follow me please.

W   Sit down, please. What would you like to drink first?
D   I'd like to have a *Qingdao* beer.
L   Same for me.
W   What would you like to drink, Miss?
J   A glass of orange juice.
W   OK. Please have a look at the menu.

W   Ready to order?
L   Yes. I'll do the ordering. One seafood soup, one diced chicken
    with seasonal vegetables and one . . .
D   A portion of steamed buns with various fillings too.
    How many are there per portion?
W   Six.
D   In that case, two portions please. I'm starving.
W   OK. It won't be long.
L   Another thing, please don't put MSG in our dishes.
W   Got it.

Dialogue 2: Have you ever had roast duck?

C   Have you ever had Beijing roast duck, Xiaohua?
X   No, I haven't.

C   Really? In that case, you must try it. Are you free tonight?

X   Yes, I am.

C   Then I'll take you out to have roast duck tonight. How does that sound?

X   Wonderful. Which restaurant are we going to?

C   The Beijing Roast Duck Restaurant.

X   You were so right. It's delicious.

C   I'm so pleased you like the roast duck. Have some more.

X   OK. Please pass me the sauce.

C   Are there enough pancakes?

X   Enough for me. I'm nearly full.

C   I'm already full. I eat faster than you do. In that case, I'll settle the bill.

X   OK, thanks.

C   Waiter, can we have the bill please?

Lesson 11

Dialogue 1: Please take me to . . .

J   Please take me to the Temple of Heaven.

TD   Sorry, I'm not going to the Temple of Heaven.

J   Why?

TD   There is a traffic jam up there. You can take the subway.

J   Where's the subway station?

TD   I'll take you there.

J   Thank you.

J   I'd like to buy a ticket to the Temple of Heaven. Which line should I take please?

TA   Take No. 2 Line first, towards the direction of Pingguoyuan. Get off at Dongdan and change to No. 5 Line.

J   Thank you.

J   Excuse me, which stop should I get off at for the Temple of Heaven?

P   You took the wrong train. This is going in the opposite direction.

J   Oh, no!

P   Don't worry. It happens that I'm getting off at the next stop. Follow me please.

J   Thank you so much.

Dialogue 2: Buying train tickets

C   Is this the ticket office?

T   Yes, it is.

C   I'd like to get a train ticket to Guilin.

T   When are you leaving?

C   Next Wednesday, that is 4th June.

T   Which number train do you plan to take?

C   I'm not sure. Ideally, I'd like to take the train that leaves at around six o'clock in the evening.

T   How about T-81? It departs at nineteen forty-five.

C   When does it arrive at Guilin?

T   It arrives at sixteen twenty the following day.

C   Good timing. I'll get a ticket for this train.

T   Would you like a hard-sleeper or soft-sleeper?

C   I don't understand.

T   A hard-sleeper is fifty yuan cheaper than a soft-sleeper, but not as comfortable.

C   I'll have one hard-sleeper.

Lesson 12

Dialogue 1: Any rooms available?

J   Do you have any rooms available please?

R   It depends. What kind of room do you want?

J   A room with two beds.

R   Oh, that's a standard room. Which day do you want to check in and for how many days do you want to stay?

J   I'd like to check in today, and stay for three days.

R   Let me check. . . . What luck! There is one room available.

J   How much is it per night?

R   Five hundred and thirty yuan.

J   Does it include breakfast?
R   Yes, it does.
J   I'll take it.

R   Here is the key to your room. Your room is on the second
    floor.

Dialogue 2: The light is not working

D   Good morning. Did you sleep well last night?
J   To be honest, I didn't sleep well.
D   What's the matter?
J   Last night the room next door was very noisy all the time until
    2am in the morning.
D   Many apologies. I'll see to this matter.
J   Thanks. Oh, by the way, a light in my room is not working.
D   Really? I'll definitely send for someone to fix it. Any other
    problems?
J   Not for the moment. See you later.

Lesson 13

Dialogue 1: Hello

A   Hello, could you get Li Bin for me please?
L   I am Li Bin. Who is speaking?
A   It's Alan, your classmate when you attended university in the
    UK.
L   Really? When did you get here? How come I didn't know
    anything about it?
A   I came last Thursday. It was a last-minute decision.
L   I'm so excited. When are you coming to see me?
A   Any time. You decide.
L   How about tonight? I'm going on a business trip to
    Hong Kong tomorrow.
A   Of course tonight is fine. Whereabouts do you live?
L   It's not easy to find my home. I'll come to collect you.
A   Wonderful!

Dialogue 2: Mobile phone numbers

J Yongmei, have you finished with the phone?

Y Yes, I have.

J I have to give our boss a call.

Y He is not in the office today. He may have gone to the airport to collect that important client.

J Is that so? Do you have his new mobile number?

Y No. You could give his secretary a call and ask her for it.

J Good idea.

S Extension 268. Who is speaking please?

J It's John. I've an urgent matter to discuss with Manager Fang. I've heard he is not in the office today. What's his mobile number?

S Just a second, please. Listen carefully. The number is 13887462183.

J 13887462183.

S Correct.

Lesson 14

Dialogue 1: It's raining

Y Is this your first time in Taiwan?

P No. I come to Taiwan almost every year. Last year, I was here twice.

Y Really? Was it for business?

P No. The first time, we came for my wife's younger sister's wedding. And the second time, it was for the Spring Festival.

Y In that case, your wife must be Taiwanese, is that so?

P Yes, she is.

Y How did you get to know each other?

P It's a long story. Ten years ago, she went to the States for her university education and we were classmates. One day . . .

Y Very romantic. Whoops! It's raining. Let's go inside to talk.

Dialogue 2: Which place do you like most?

A Hi, John. So nice to see you. Come on in. Please take a seat.

J Hello. Are you well, Ailin?

A   Quite well, thank you. What would you like to drink?

J   Chinese tea, please.

A   Talking of China, how was your trip to China?

J   Very successful.

A   Which cities did you go to?

J   Beijing, Shanghai, Xi'an, Guilin and Guangzhou.

A   Which place did you like most?

J   It's a very difficult question to answer. I liked Guilin very much. The scenery there is beautiful. The locals are very friendly. It's very interesting to talk to them.

A   I haven't been to Guilin yet. I'll definitely go there next time. What do you think of Guangzhou?

J   It's all right. It's just that there are too many people there, and it is also too hot.

A   I don't like Guangzhou that much either. Did you go to the Great Wall?

J   Of course! I took a lot of photos . . .

Lesson 15

Text: I promise

Dear Xiaomei:

Hi!

I've received your letter. I'm so pleased that you like your new job. Everything is fine with me, except that I'm too busy. Last week, I had meetings in London. I've been busy writing up the report since I returned. I've been up at six thirty every morning and can't go to bed until twelve at night. I've got to finish this report by Friday. Due to my computer breaking down, I haven't emailed you for a long time. When I have some time off this weekend, I will definitely get someone to fix it and then write you a long email. I promise.

Your good friend,
Elena

30.8.2008

Index to grammar and cultural notes